Places

A Travel Companion for Music and Art Lovers

Robert Craft

Places

A Travel Companion for Music and Art Lovers

Thames & Hudson

For Alexander

First published in hardcover in the United States of
America in 2000 by Thames & Hudson Inc.
500 Fifth Avenue, New York, New York 10110

Library of Congress Catalog Card Number 99-66974
ISBN 0-500-01990-8

Printed and bound in Slovenia by Mladinska Knjiga

Contents

Acknowledgments

I wish to thank Stanley Baron, my editor at Thames & Hudson, for suggestions that enhanced the shape of the book. I also thank the editor of The New Republic for permission to reprint the notes on Korea, the editor of The Times Literary Supplement for permission to reprint the pages on Florida, and the editors of The New York Review of Books for permission to reprint the entries on Nepal, the USSR, Las Vegas, and excerpts from those on Venice, Bayreuth, and Thailand. For many suggestions and improvements, as well as for deciphering and typing the text, my gratitude to Olivia Pittet is boundless. I owe a debt to my sister Phyllis Crawford for proofreading the manuscript, and my wife, Alva, deserves a Purple Heart and various other medals for enduring with me the experiences related after 1989.

Preface

And see all sights from pole to pole,
And glance, and nod, and bustle by...
Matthew Arnold

Though possessed by wanderlust at an early age, I did not begin to travel until 1948, when I met Igor Stravinsky. After a concert in New York in which I shared the podium with him, he invited me to Red Rocks, Colorado, where he would be conducting in July, and then to visit him in Hollywood. When I turned up in Denver, he persuaded me to detour to Mexico on my way westward, which I did, by bus and train, under the influence of his fascination with the country. I soon understood that Mexico and the Russia in which he grew up were remarkably similar, both being societies of the very rich and very poor, landowners and muzhiks, and both dominated by the Church. Stravinsky had been deeply moved by the peon families who approached the Shrine of the Virgin at Guadalupe on their knees. I had a diametrically different reaction, more in sympathy with Joyce's "In the name of the former and of the latter and of their holocaust. Allmen." After a week in Mexico I continued by airplane to the rendezvous that redirected my life.

The Stravinskys, who had led nomadic lives as a result of the Russian Revolution, were keener and hardier travelers than I would ever be. While still a child he had voyaged down the Volga to his uncle's estate near Poltava, and throughout his mature years in Europe and America he was never in one place for long. My first journeys with the Stravinskys were in their automobile. We crossed the continent seven times in 1950-53, Mrs. Stravinsky and I alternating as drivers, her husband, seated next to her, maps spread on his lap, navigating. They were indefatigable, always wanting to go a little farther. We drove from Los Angeles to Las Cruces, New Mexico, in a single day, and at another time the 700 desolate miles from El Paso to Del Rio,

7

Texas, where, in preference to sleeping in the car, we stayed in what proved to be a bordello. On a return journey from New York we braved a dirt road through the Dakota Badlands and a totally deserted one in eastern Oregon on which we surprised an eagle. We also visited the National Parks, virtually empty in those days, and some of the ghost towns, including spooky Virginia City, Nevada. In a recurring picture of the Stravinskys I see them crossing a desperate Western landscape, craving caviar and comfortable accommodations with bathroom facilities, desires never satisfied, yet pushing on.

My later peregrinations with the Stravinskys, in Europe, Japan, South America, Africa, the South Pacific, and Down Under, were, in effect, protracted concert tours. The journeys recounted in this book are post-Stravinsky, and, except for a few performances of his music, and visits to his grave, are personal odysseys, not concerned with him. Though the place names are familiar to everyone—indeed, overrun with tourists and over-described—most of the actual sites visited are not.

R. C.
January 2000

Italy

The Mezzogiorno

My love for southern Italy began in music, sixteenth- and early seventeenth-century Neapolitan polyphonic music, of which Don Carlo Gesualdo, the Prince of Venosa, was the greatest composer. In the early 1950s I transcribed a great many of his 150 or so surviving madrigals and in 1954 began to record them, eventually taping several long-playing discs. By the end of the decade Stravinsky had "re-composed" three of the madrigals for orchestra and composed the missing parts of three of the sacred motets. Naples was my first city in Europe, and I remember it more vividly from my three weeks there in the summer of 1951 than I do any other city except Venice. In 1956, when our Greece-bound steamer stopped in Naples for twelve hours, the Stravinskys and I drove to the town of Gesualdo to see the Prince's castle and, in the adjoining church, the famous profile painting of him kneeling next to his uncle, S. Carlo Borromeo. The several hours on narrow, coiling roads were made worthwhile by visits to Vanvitelli's church at Grottominarda and the stunning Baroque Convento di Loreto at Montevergine. Three years later Stravinsky and I returned to Gesualdo, via Benevento, with a photographer for Columbia Records, Robert Bright, who took colored pictures of the painting. Thirty-three years later, Alva and I drove from Rome, primarily to see the Prince's castle at Venosa in Basilicata, but this was only one among many indelible experiences in our discovery of Magna Graecia.

May 9, 1992. We leave Rome by the Porta S. Sebastiano and follow the Appian Way past Castel Gandolfo and Albano to Ariccia, where in the autumn of 38 B.C. Horatius Flaccus spent his first night en route to Bari in the mule train of Maecenas. Though we intend to follow the poet's path in his diary, *Journey to Brundisium,* this becomes impossible after Terracina and Capua. Besides, we cannot find Sinuessa, the most important of the "stopovers," since that is where Horace and Virgil met, and where Virgil joined the procession to Brindisi, from whence triremes carried Maecenas to an embassy in Athens. Neither poet was famous yet, and Horace scarcely knew Maecenas, who would soon become his greatest friend and give to him that celebrated Sabine farm.

After Terracina we visit Tiberius's banqueting cave at Sperlonga (*spelunca*). When I was here with Stravinsky in 1959, the coast was deserted, the only access to the cave a narrow, uneven path. Now it abuts a crowded beach, a whole city has been excavated in front of it, and the contents of its temples and houses—floors paved with small, thin bricks, walls made of blocks of tufa placed in herringbone pattern—moved to a new roadside museum. Since 1959, too, more than 7,000 fragments of marble statuary have been recovered from the grotto and pieced together by the German archeologist Bernard Andreae and his team. In 511, Abbot Fortunato and 200 monks, affronted by the pagan nudity of Tiberius's statues, smashed them to smithereens. Of the restorations, the most impressive is a towering depiction of the Scylla episode in the *Odyssey*, a copy of the Rhodean monument. This mythical creature, a beautiful young woman from head to waist, and a pair of scaly fishtails and pack of ravening hounds below, drags six of Ulysses's sailors to their deaths as the stern of his ship is rowed past her. The stone, said to weigh 80 tons, was quarried at Afyon in Turkey and brought to Sperlonga from Ephesus. Henceforth, Suetonius's portrait of Tiberius as a sex maniac should be mitigated to include an art-lover and classicist.

Formia, a little farther along, abode of the Laestrygones, is now a harbor for hydrofoils. At Scauri, the balconies of the *meridionale* first appear.

Near the Augustan colosseum in Santa Maria di Capua Vetere excavations are in progress on the supposed site of Hannibal's bivouac during his unsuccessful siege of the city after Rome recaptured it from him following Cannae. Livy's description of one of the encounters marvelously evokes the charivari of ancient warfare:

> The fight began with the usual wild battle-cry...the shouts of men, the neighing of horses, the clash of arms...and, from the non-

combatants on the city wall, the clattering of brazen pans such as is heard in the silence of the night during an eclipse of the moon.

The colosseum, second in size only to the one in Rome, but considerably older—the more famous one having been constructed on the site of Nero's palace—is unrestored, and the jagged, irregular ruins sprout weeds and plants in the style of eighteenth-century engravings. Still, the past is more alive in the emptiness here than in the arena in the teeming capital. Only two of the eighty tallest arches are standing, and only single columns or small clusters of them are upright on the surrounding grounds, but some of the four-storied bleachers are intact, and the underground galleries and cages are virtually undamaged. Fragments of statues, a frieze of lions pouncing on cattle, and pavement mosaics of Nereids and Tritons have been moved from the arena to the protection of a shed, but the important artifacts are in a museum.

Perhaps because we explore the premises alone, undisturbed by guards or guides, the place seems haunted, echoing with the cries of *venatores*, laquearians, the roars of animals, the shouts of spectators. Suddenly a "bride" in billowing white and a "groom" in cutaway coat appear with a photographer in tow, who poses the couple against the most striking back grounds, presumably for a fashion or travel magazine. These unlikely visitants depart for the next assignment so quickly that the memory of the scene soon fades from surreal to unreal. Why is this by no means remote amphitheater, the scene of Spartacus's revolt, so neglected?—which is not to advocate its replication in a Florida theme park. Augustus must have had it built late in life, or so one deduces, fancifully, simply because he died in the nearby Campanian town of Nola.

The Cathedral of San Prisco is said to be built over a temple to Priapus. Its tiny tomb-chapel of the Lusitanian Princess, Saint Matrona, has early sixth-century ceiling mosaics of flowers and birds, and, in one lunette, of Christ holding a book and flanked by the Greek letters Alpha and Omega and, in another, of a bull and an eagle, the Evangelist's symbols.

Naples has changed more since 1959 than any other Italian city. Its principal landmark then, Vesuvius, is now invisible in polluted air, superseded by oil refineries and dinosaur-like derricks, while the bay view extends only to the closest-to-shore tankers. The "Zi Teresa" restaurant still stands where I first saw it in August 1951, and my room at the Excelsior appears to be the one the Stravinskys occupied at that time, a thought that brings memories flooding back, one of them of Auden, when I checked in and asked for a room with a shower, saying, "Well, you really are an American."

We share the hotel restaurant's crude service—the waiters, when you want them, are assiduously not looking—and rude plenty with a refined and quiet Japanese couple. At intervals, gusts of laughter from a raucous, rasping-voiced "sorority" intrude from an adjoining private room. The booklet *Qui Napoli* informs us that "St. Guarisco, Bishop of Abitina, in Africa, who died in 451 or 452, arrived in Naples after Genseric the Vandal"—who had plundered Nola, birthplace, 1,100 years later, of Giordano Bruno—"stripped him of everything he owned and made him go abroad in an old ship which was then abandoned at sea." A sad story, but why is Guarisco a saint?

10. Our concierge's price for a small car to Bari, with English-speaking chauffeur, is three times what we consider reasonable, and the ride is harrowing. The bumptious teenage driver knows no English and is insolent in Italian. He chain-smokes, loudly jokes with friends on his cellular phone, maintains a velocity better suited to the Indianapolis races, and tunes his blaring radio to a soccer game, the Italian madness. At the outset he pretends to comply with our pleas—*"non fumare," "più lento," "troppo forte"*—but we are periodically re-enveloped in tobacco fumes, the radio gradually returns to full blast, and the speedometer is soon back to 180 kilometers. Worst of all, he has never heard of the places we want to see, and, as we realize after leaving the autostrada at Canosa, where he chooses the wrong directions at clearly-marked crossroads, he cannot read.

Naturalists and others who object to landscapes altered by human beings would not like the terraced slopes and acropoli cresting mountains of the wonderfully dramatic Apennine crossing. Nor would agoraphobes feel comfortable when this terrain transforms into undulating, deforested table-lands blanketed with red poppies and yellow daisies, the *pianura* and the granary of Apulia: wheat with the sheen of a young woman's soft golden hair ruffling in the wind. It is a land of Romanesque castles and churches, white hilltop towns, vineyards and olive groves.

Canosa's eleventh-century cathedral is famed, in part, for a marble throne borne on the backs of two small almond-eyed elephants. To judge from the transverse ridges segmenting their trunks, which are curled at the distal ends, as well as from the same eye-shape of an elephant in a mosaic at Ostia, the animals are of the African variety, *Loxodonta africana cyclotis,* the forest elephant employed by Hannibal, as distinguished from the larger bush elephant. But to judge by the small ears they are Indian, the *Elephas maximus, "Elephas"* being Homer's word for ivory. The source of ivory, the elephant itself, is not mentioned before Herodotus.

The first elephant in Italy seems to have been the prehistoric *Elephas Meridionalis,* found at Scopitto, and now in the Museo Nazionale at L'Aquila, its skeleton misguidedly hidden under a reconstructed body. The first of the proboscideans were Indian, brought from Greece in 280 B.C. by Pyrrhus of the too costly victory. (Macaulay: "The Greek shall come against thee/The conqueror of the east/Beside him stalks to battle/The huge earth-shaking beast.") A coin portraying one of his elephants—he used twenty of them in defeating the Romans at Heracleia—was minted at Tarantum in that year, and an Indian elephant of the same date, a cow with calf walking behind, mounted by a mahout and two archers in a howdah, appears on the painted dish found at Capena, now in the Villa Giulia. The other best-known Indian elephants in ancient art are the terracotta statuettes of a cow and calf found in the Sanctuary of Apollo at Veii, the one depicted on the silver-gilt phalaera disinterred at Sark (Channel Islands), and the ones on an Etruscan coin in the British Museum. But numismatic portraits often confuse the features of the Asian and African species, distinguished in the Indian by a convex and rounded back, abruptly sloping hindquarters, and a single "finger" at the tip of the trunk (*vs.* two for the African). The best-known pachyderms in Roman art, in the Piazza Armerina mosaics, the Naples terracotta figure, the fresco of four elephants in Verecundus's shop at Pompeii, are of the African variety, as Pliny noted, when he was attributing a "religious nature" to the beast, with which Montaigne concurred: elephants *"ont quelque participation de religion."* The Greeks were familiar with African as well as Indian elephants, but Aristotle's observations on the animal are thought to have come from his nephew, Callisthenes, who accompanied Alexander to the Punjab, where Porus, in Peter Green"s estimate, had about 130 of them. Aristotle must have witnessed a dissection, since he correctly notes that the creature has no gall bladder, and that its proboscis is a lengthened nostril. He compares elephants submerged in water, tips of trunks at the surface, to "divers with instruments for respiration," i.e., ancient snorkels. The painting of the diver in mid-air found on a coffin lid at Paestum symbolizes the plunge from this world to the next, but it also indicates that the sport was popular with sixth-century (pre-Aristotelian) Greeks.

At Ascoli Satiriano a small sign points in the direction of the "Battaglia di Pirro" (279 B.C.), but the intersections after that lack further indications, and the people we ask do not know what lies beyond the next hill.

The cathedral of Ruvo is a short distance away, but we find it only after much trial and error involving U-turns, backings-up, zoomings ahead—brrm, brrrm, and the scrunching of brakes—as well as other maneuvers conducted without regard for potential traffic beyond the last and next bends in the road. One of our direction-asking stops nearly startles an inebriated red-eyed shepherd to death; and the same can be said of the effect on ourselves of a not-quite stop when our driver overtakes a moving automobile, slows it with horn-honking and shouts of *"Dov'è Ruvo?,"* then "vrooms" around in the opposite direction. Most of this chasing is carried on at cyclonic speeds on bumpy back roads that wind between olive trees with black, barren, and weirdly contorted upper branches and the conical stone structures called *trulli.*

The Apulian plain was once covered with loose rocks from the rupture of the limestone crust that formed the surface of the land as it emerged from the sea. Over the centuries these stones were piled into innumerable dividing walls and *trulli,* which are compared to igloos, giant beehives, or anthills but are best described, or left undescribed, as an other-planetary apparition. Since mortar was not used, the flat slabs rising from the ground in concentric circles, successive layers diminishing in size and overhanging each other like fish scales, had to be fitted to a tee. The oldest of them, like the megalithic dolmens also found near Ruvo, are prehistoric burial crypts. In contrast, the *trulli* of tourist-trap Alberobello, whitewashed, joined together to form block-long rows, are relatively new. A few surviving old ones are thought to have been built about 4,000 years ago by Anatolians. The gold ball suspended above a cylindrical saucer at the pinnacle, symbol of sun cults, has been found in Assyrian territories.

The Ruvo façade is remarkable for the great height of its rose window and the enthroned figure above it, supposedly a portrait, like most such in the area, of Frederick II, the *stupor mundi.* Below this sculpture is a bifora window with a relief of Saint Michael in the lunette; an oculus surrounded by heads of angels; and, at street level, a pair of crouching telamones supporting the columns of the central portal. We are inside for only a few minutes when our driver runs after us pretending that the *polizia,* nowhere in sight and probably non-existent in this small, very poor town, is forcing him to move.

In addition to two stunning cathedrals, the treasures of nearby Barletta include the 15-foot-tall *"Colosso,"* a bronze statue thought to be of the Emperor Marcian; a museum containing a Cellini head of Bacchus; and a milestone from Roman Cannae. (The Roman mile, *mille passus,* a thousand paces, is roughly the same as the English, as are the Roman *leuga* and the league, the Greek and Roman *stadium*—610 feet—and the English furlong; the Persian parasang, in Byron's *Sardanapalus,* reckoned by Herodotus as equal to thirty *stadia,* is three and a half miles.) Farther south are the two beautiful Romanesque churches of Bisceglie and the museum containing the paleontological finds from the Chianca dolmen. Maps divide the coast from here to Bari into discrete towns, but it is a run-together congeries of super-markets, apartment houses, factories, used-car lots, seafood restaurants ("Marlon Brando *e figlio*"), remnants of ancient buildings. In Bari we go to the rufous red Teatro Petruzzelli[1] where, fittingly in this land of menhirs, cairns, and dolmens, *Norma* is on the boards.

The gates of Bari's Albergo Ambasciatori are closed when we reach them, and our baggage, though not quite all of it, has to be schlepped from street to lobby. We discover, a moment too late, that our *banditto* driver has skedaddled back to Naples with our camera. After taking an impression of my credit card, the reception clerk bows and, with a *"distinto saluti,"* tells us that we are to receive a matrimonial room, but this turns out to mean a very small one with a double bed and a wash basin that emits a sigh but no water. The hotel restaurant being closed for the Feast of Saint Nicolas, he recom-mends "Cesare's" on Rodeo Drive (!), calls a taxi, and, explaining that hag-gling is involved in every transaction here, hondles and chaffers with the driver about the fare without success.

Cesare, short, stout, oleaginous, wearing orange-tinted glasses, leads us past a profusion of wilted salads and gooey desserts to a table filled with samples of *"tipica cucina barese"*: a plate of deep-fried funghi, a pasta with the consistency of boiled linoleum, a wedge of cold, greasy omelette, a gen-erous helping of putty (pecorino?), a slice of an unidentified but revoltingly pinguid substance, a carafe of luteofulvous emulsion purported to be the best local white wine. But then, the really scrumptious regional delicacies are strictly for foodies: *sangiackju in fricassa* (fried pigs' blood), *cozzapinna* (raw fish fins), and *sciuscielle* (lamb-entrails soup). One wonders about the good meals mentioned in Evelyn Waugh's diaries of his sojourns in Bari between military missions in Yugoslavia in the winter of 1944-45.

---

[1] Burned to the ground not long afterward.

11. Bari was founded by Bronze Age Illyrians (the Daunii, the Peucetii, the Messapii), civilized by Greeks from Mycenae (the Messapii adopted the Greek alphabet), and commercialized by Romans. At the end of the fifth century it fell to the Ostrogoths, and in the sixth to Justinian. In 847 it became a Saracen emirate, and in 975 a Byzantine catepanate. By the eleventh century, under the Normans, it was a religious center and the script had become Beneventan Latin. Anselm of Canterbury presided at the Council of Bari in 1098, successfully defending the doctrine of the procession of the Holy Ghost. The Normans were succeeded by the Hohenstaufen, Frederick II and his son Manfred (Dante's hero), the Angevins, and, in the late *quattrocento,* the Sforza. It became Aragonese in the *cinquecento,* passing to the Kingdom of Naples in 1558, then to Austria, the Bourbons, Napoleon (Joachim Murat), and in 1943-45 the United States Army. Thus do we lope through history.

While changing hotels in the morning, we are struck by the many billboards in the city's nondescript new neighborhoods intended to appeal to male adolescents of all ages. In an underwear ad for the brand-name "*Intimo,*" a nearly nude young woman shares a roomy and transparent T-shirt with a young man clad in a jock strap. An ad for see-through *mutatire* (panties) displays the unclothed caudal attractions of a very fetching female, and in another for *reggiseni* (bras), a girl teasingly cups her hands in front of, but without concealing, her undraped udders. In still another, a partly undressed young man lying on his stomach balances a coffee tray on the small of his back, while a scantily dressed female lifts a cup to her lips, but whether the purpose of this is to sell undergarments, crockery, coffee, or just plain sex is not clear. The last of these commodities is unambivalently promoted at a cinema whose current "*solo adulti*" offering is promoted in English only as "Pretty Anal." At the same time, *suori* and Dominican *prete* and *frate* are far more conspicuous here than in any northern Italian city, and religious processions with elaborate floats are a feature of Holy Week and other observances, as are displays of peasant-art *presepi* (cribs) at Christmas.

In comparison to the Ambasciatore, the nine-room (only) Melograno, inland on a narrow road from Monopoli, which was a Venetian dominion, merits a whole galaxy of Michelin stars. But whereas high, fortress-thick walls, an electronic security system, and two mastiffs protect it from the outside, intramural dangers remain. The maze between the lobby and our outlying room is studded with invisible and unpredictable steps and lined with spiny cacti that threaten impaling, while the low-lying vines of the pergola at the end compel us to walk in a feral crouch. In the pluvial season, moreover, which appears to be now, floods engulf our beds to the depth of the casters. Still another peril lurks in the restaurant's cellars. Horace's Epode about the "*dulci vina*" served by the "*uxor Apuli*" neglects to say that whereas minute quantities of the liquid are an effective soporific, large ones could be lethal. The dinner music is soothingly strummed by an old man and a boy on small classical guitars.

In contrast to his Neapolitan counterpart, today's driver from American Express is patient to the point of urging us to stay longer wherever we go. But he does not know how to find the places we wish to see, nor do the pedestrians whose help he solicits ("*non so,*" and a shrug). The bulls of Bari's Basilica of Saint Nicolas and the façade of its Cathedral have provided models for numerous other Apulian churches, including Bitonto's Saint Valentine's. This is secluded in an opera-set *campo* of balconied houses with green shutters and a weedy Baroque monument to a bishop or saint. The feature of its beautifully spaced façade is a sculpture of a pelican pecking its breast to feed its offspring with its own blood, a Christ symbol. The portal arches repose on columns borne by lions at the base and by griffins near the top. The columns in the nave arcade alternate with piers in a rhythmic order of two to one, but the floor has been dug up to excavate an older church. The pulpit on one side of the choir, and the ambo on the other, display sculptures of skeletons, the standing ones like exhibits in a *teatrum anatomicum,* the seated, leaning forward, elbows resting on knees and chins on fists, like Rodin's "Thinker."

Trani, the twelfth-century cathedral on the edge of the Adriatic, white

stone against indigo water and azure sky, is the most famously photographed in Apulia, though rigidly symmetrical, and with a disproportionately large and tall *campanile* open at the base. The central window of the
façade is subtended by sculptures of large-eared African elephants. An
inscription over one of the lateral doors commemorates Richard Coeur-de-
Lion's participation in its construction, but the marble floor and the
coffered ceiling are quite new. A young boy detaches himself from a tour
group to ask if we are Germans.

Trani appears in the Peutinger Table, the earliest surviving *mappa-
mondo,* a 21-foot end-to-end cartographic projection of the world from
Britain to the mouth of the Ganges, plotted after the road system of the
Roman Empire. (According to Strabo, "the sea determines geography and
marks out the shape of the land. Rivers and mountains must be added.
These are the features which distinguish continents, peoples, and sites
appropriate for cities.") The Table is a medieval copy of Agrippa's *Orbis
Terrarum,* which in turn was based on Eusebius's *Onomastikon.* Drawn in
Colmar in 1265, it was acquired by Konrad Peutinger of Augsburg in about
1500, and is now in the Vienna Kunsthistorisches Museum. A facsimile was
published in Graz in 1976. It consists of eleven segments of parchment; the
missing twelfth represented the westernmost world. The perspective of the
viewer is from the south, looking north from the Sahara toward three beck-
oning emperors, in, respectively, Rome, Constantinople, and Antioch, even
though Constantinople did not exist in the first century A.D. What we know
about Agrippa's map derives from the elder Pliny, who says that it was displayed in the Porticus Vipsania and attracted crowds of spectators. The
Peutinger's chart of Palestine comes from the mosaic map in the floor of a
church still standing in Madaba, Jordan.

12. The peach-colored Baroque of Lecce is elegant and restrained, and the
curvaceous balconies and window frames of secular buildings are some of
the most beautiful in all Italy. The spacious *cortile del Duomo* is framed by a
profusion of architectural marvels, a Seminario, a Palazzo Vescovile, a tall

campanile, and the pale-gold Duomo itself. The statue of St. Orontius garnishing a Roman column in the Piazza Orontius celebrates the tradition that St. Paul, believed to have stopped here en route to Rome, appointed him Bishop of Lecce, which would have been about thirty years before Pliny the Younger's letter to the Emperor Trajan about the Christian problem, the first mention of it in Roman history. The Roman amphitheater is well preserved, but the best of the bas-reliefs from the wall separating the cavea and the arena are in the Museo Provinciale. The collections there include a showcase of terracotta whistles and tintinnabula for obstreperous children, excavated at nearby Rudiae, Ennius's birthplace (*pace* the *Oxford Classical Dictionary,* which locates it in Calabria).

Acáia, nearer the coast, is enclosed by Renaissance walls with a tower considered the crowning achievement of Aragonese military architecture. The road south is bordered by pine woods, marshes, dunes. At Badisco, the prehistoric wall paintings in the Cave of the Deer are contemporaneous with those of Magdalenian France, but the art, the representation of a hunter endowed with an inordinately large pizzle and holding an arrow in a taut bow, is primitive.

The Òtranto Cathedral's 750-square-yard mosaic carpet illustrates mankind's nightmare history from the Expulsion, Cain and Abel, and the Flood, through the "*giudizio finale.*" It extends from the entrance, where an allegorical Tree of Life rests on the backs of two Indian elephants, its branches compartmenting the individual scenes. Chronological confusions notwithstanding, the tableau should be viewed from the top, where a huge tarantula (Taranto is not far away) is poised threateningly at the center of a zodiac.

Immediately below the altar, the surprising presence of King Arthur standing next to the exit from Eden suggests that the order of people and events below may be hierarchical. Arthur would be closest to Eden, because he is a Christ figure in the earliest versions of his myth, which feature him carrying the cross of Christ on his shoulders. Stories from Geoffrey of Monmouth's *Historia Regnum Britanniae,* in which the legendary king is the conqueror of Western Europe, were brought to Southern Italy by Breton minstrels following Norman armies. Placement, otherwise, appears to be haphazard, except that Alexander the Great, wearing a medieval crown similar to Arthur's, is near the bottom of the picture. Not only do mythological, Biblical, and historical people rub elbows, but imaginary beasts consort with actual ones. The scenes of husbandry and hunting recall the Bayeux tapestry, woven a hundred years earlier but more "modern"— though not woven, of course, but embroidered in successive scenes. Here the carpenters building the Ark wield hammers, axes, and a two-handled double-bladed saw. Some of the workmen constructing the Tower of Babel stand on ladders, but others float weightless by its sides. In the Middle Ages, Òtranto was famed for its Talmudic academy, in the nineteenth century for Horace Walpole's Gothic novel.

The *trecento* frescoes of the Apocalypse in the church of Santa Caterina at nearby Galatina are the most astonishing south of Rome. Maria d'Enghien of Lecce, who became Queen of Naples, is thought to have commissioned them as a memorial for her first husband, Balzo-Orsini, whose tomb is in the choir. They are attributed to a painter of the Umbrian school active in Naples. The plaster is black.

According to Herodotus, Oria, a few miles north on the Appian Way, was originally a Cretan settlement, then a renowned royal city of the Messapians. It became a major Hebrew center when Titus brought captive Jews here from Jerusalem. In the year 4814 of the Hebrew calendar (1054 A.D.), Ahimsaz, the chronicler, wrote his book of genealogies here, telling us that his people prospered and grew in number and strength, and that the learned Rabbi Amittsi was among their descendants.

Manduria is famed for its Messapian necropoli, Greek-style walls, library of sixteenth-century medical texts, and a well in which the water level remains constant whatever the amounts drawn from it. (How far was this tested?) Ostuni, a stunning white city, overlooks the shimmering Adriatic from a panoramic height. Its cathedral has a tripartite façade whose tall central segment slopes concavely and symmetrically down from both sides of its pinnacle, while the flanking segments curve convexly, like padded shoulders. All three have beautiful rose windows and ogival doors. But a still more stunning window is the perfectly proportioned stone-lacework one of the Cathedral of Tróia, that glory of the Pisan Romanesque on a "windswept eminence"—Augustus Hare's phrase—near Lucera.

All that remains of Lucera is the Angevin circumvallation, the largest in Italy, containing Frederick II's citadel, but drawings of the interior buildings, made by the French architect Louis Jean Desprez in 1790, four years before they were destroyed, confirm that they followed Arab models in the application of the Pythagorean triples: 3^2 plus 4^2 equals 5^2 (9 plus 16 equals 25). Frederick populated Lucera with Saracens transported from Sicily after the war of 1222, and granted them freedom to worship as Muslims. All twenty-four towers are intact, though one of them on the western escarpment has had to be buttressed. Apart from peek-holes, the wall has been breached only by weeds growing in cracks in the masonry. The most intriguing object in the Museo Civico is the sculptured head supposedly of Frederick's Moorish slave, Johannes Morus: frizzled hair, large ears, popping eyes with large pupils, thick lips.

The First Crusade was proclaimed at nearby Melfi, but of greater concern to us is the need to find a W.C. Alva manages to convey our plight to a passing girl who conducts us through the cathedral to a room where a Catechism is in progress, and straight through it to a convenience beyond, albeit one without a door. Seen from below, Melfi is little changed today from the view of it, with the same perspective, in Edward Lear's lithograph.

Lear also did one of Venosa, whose present-day Duke, Alberico Ludovisi-Buoncampagni, married Letizia Pecci-Blunt, daughter of the Stravinskys' and my Roman friend Mimi Ginzburg Pecci-Blunt, niece of Pope Leo XIII (Cardinal Pecci). The capital of the largest Roman colony from 290 B.C., as Mommsen, who wrote part of his *History of Rome* here, tells us, Venosa is also the center of the richest archeological lode in Basilicata, owing to an inheritance of Chellean, Acheulean, Clactonian, and Jewish cultures. The renovated *quattrocentro* castle has been a museum since 1991, and the drawbridge over the wide moat leads to an air-controlled and well-lighted assortment of antiquities, in which the Roman collection, mutilated statues, ceramics, *cippi,* is less interesting than the Hebrew. In 1853, Jewish catacombs, dating from the fourth to the ninth centuries, were discovered cut out of the rock wall above the main road outside the city. The contents exhibited here include a frescoed depiction of a menorah and shofar, and a marble tombstone with menorah carved below an inscription in Hebrew characters: "Samohil deceased in 808 aged seven years seven months." Unlike the Jewish tombstones of the same period in Catania and Syracuse, one of them with two *menoroth,* no concordance is given with the Hebraic lunar calendar.

As we enter the castle museum, a video in the foyer is showing a documentary about Carlo Gesualdo, Prince of Venosa, accompanied by a CD of his madrigals and sacred music. After four centuries, the composer's principality has finally discovered him! A young female curator, seeing my signature in the guest book, recognizes my name in connection with Gesualdo, perhaps from the recent biography of the Prince by the local historian, Antonio Vaccaro, but it is closing time. She apologizes and graciously escorts us to the fifth- and sixth-century churches, the unfinished Romanesque basilica, and the Roman temple with Medusa's head in mosaics. But the stratigraphy is complex and the Roman and Cluniac walls are indistinguishable to us. We part company at the statue of Quintus Horatius Flaccus himself. "Venosa," Gibbon wrote, is "a place much more illustrious for the birth of Horace than for the burial of the Norman heroes."

13. Like "*Perfida Capua,*" Metapontum, a few miles west of Taranto, had sided with Hannibal. Before returning to Carthage, in 203 B.C., he rewarded the inhabitants by evacuating them, thus thwarting Roman revenge. The Romans had lined the road from Capua all the way to the capital with crucifixions.

Metapontum was a Neolithic sheep-raising center when Achaean colonists arrived in the sixth century with superior breeds of horses and cattle. As late as the fourth century A.D., the largest cattle in the Roman world came from here. The Greek settlers, males only, married local women, and analyses of the bones of both sexes show that syphilis was endemic. Fifteen Doric columns of the extramural Temple of Hera still stand, but the large stoa inside the walls, nearer the Ionian Sea, is richer in history than in surviving edifices, of which only two rise above foundation level, both pros- thetically: a Doric frieze inserted in the rebuilt wall of a theater, and three Doric capitals from the Temple of Apollo Lycius placed on Le Corbusier- style stilts. According to Justinus, the Temple of Athena here contained the iron tools with which Epeus constructed the Trojan Horse.

The Metapontines of the early Greek period made female ornaments of great refinement, as we learn from an exhibition in the Museo Archeologia, *Ornamenti Femminile in Basilicata*. The displays feature gold diadems, earrings, necklaces with painted pendants, armlets, buckles, bracelets, gold wreaths, gold fleece, unguentaries, perfume vials, and cosmetic implements. All were found in 300 excavated graves in the Pantanello necropolis north of the city, now a cemetery of lidless tombs. Before the arrival of the self-abnegating Orphics, women of superior social status wore a great variety of expensive jewelry, whereas the Hellenistic age is represented mainly by bronze mirrors. But the treasures of the museum are the marble head of a woman with hair raised above the neck, and a basin for lustral water found at nearby Incoronata, with relief sculptures at three different registers. In human figure sculpture, the artists apparently began with the anatomical structure, formal equilibrium being a later concern.

Cicero and Martial lived in Metapontum. Centuries earlier, long before Rome absorbed Greek Italy, Pythagoras moved there from Crotone, to preach vegetarianism—believing that all living beings had souls—mortifica- tion of the body (one of Dante's reasons for excluding the Neo-Pythagorean Virgil from Paradise), and metempsychosis.

Clowne: What is the opinion of Pythagoras concerning wild fowl?
Malvolio: That the soul of our granddam might haply inhabit a bird.

Universally known for his theorem, Pythagoras should be better remembered for having discovered the numerical ratios of the Greek scale and the aliquot parts—1:2—of the octave, not to mention his perception of music's cathartic powers. The idea of the reduction of all reality to numbers, of a quantitative reality, stems from him as well, and the mixture of scientist and mystic in him is part of the inheritance of Empedocles (of Agrigento), who went on to develop the notion of an incorporeal, nonanthropomorphic god. (Plutarch's claim that Empedocles's philosophy began in his belief in the doctrine of transmigration seems to be receiving support from the newly published Strasbourg fragments of Empedocles.)

In 387 Plato resided at Tarantum, from whence, as mentioned in the *Gorgias,* he may have pointed in the directions of Magna Graecia and Sicily when identifying the places where philosophical speculations and discussions of the soul flourished. The Thurii of Herodotus is not far from Metapontum, and across the peninsula, at Elea, dialectics (Zeno's paradoxes) and axiomatic reasoning (Parmenides's proem) were born. Bernardino Telesio, the first "modern," as Francis Bacon called him, who proposed to explain nature by following the testimony of the senses rather than preconceived and abstract Aristotelian notions, came from nearby Cosenza.

The survival of the Greek language and philosophical traditions in Magna Graecia into the Renaissance is another absorbing subject. John of Salisbury, Thomas à Becket's friend and the author of *Policraticus,* journeyed all the way to the Sila (crossing Theocritus's Neaithos River) seeking enlightenment from Greek scholiasts on abstruse passages in Aristotle. Cassiodorus was born in nearby Squillace, as were Leonzio Pilato and Barlaam, who taught Greek to Boccaccio in Florence and to Petrarca in Padua.

From Metapontum, we go inland to Neolithic, troglodytic Matera, most of whose narrow, meandering streets are impassable for motor traffic. The city's famous *sassi* can be reached only by clambering up a jagged and weaving goat path, whose loose stone retaining wall, on the edge of a sheer 1300-foot precipice to the sluicing Torrente Gravina glistening below, is only knee-high. The partly natural, partly hewn-out caves pockmark the ravine walls that divide the east, Sasso Barisano (Bari side), and west, Sasso Caveoso, sides of the city. Part of a ledge immediately below us is a cemetery of infant victims of a plague. Chiseled out of the porous tufa, their tiny tub-like graves are as close together as the compartments of a honeycomb.

The caves themselves are tenebrous, the floors dangerously uneven. Some were *rupestri,* rock churches, and to judge from crosses carved in their ceilings, at least two were Byzantine. Architectural devices have been carved on natural stone pillars to make them look like columns in a church. Traces of wall paintings are visible in Santa Lucia and Santa Maria di Idris, and more than traces in a thirteenth-century fresco of the Archangel Michael. On one wall, two earlier levels of fresco extend beyond the surface, the third beyond the second, like three tiers of time to which the trilobites encrusted in the outside wall add an infinitely older fourth. (Though Leonardo had correctly deduced that marine fossils found at Alpine altitudes were evidence of receding seas, Voltaire foolishly maintained that they were imprints of crustaceans left by pilgrims to Rome.)

Other caves were wineries. A fresco fragment depicts pairs of feet (only) treading on clusters of grapes in a torcularium, and fermentation rooms have been cut into the deep interior. Stone troughs indicate that the caves were stables and sties as well as human dwellings, which, given the foulness of these open-fronted but otherwise unventilated rock wombs when empty, beggars the olfactory imagination. Yet the closeness of man and beast helps to account for the prominence of mangers in the culture of the region.

Matera Cathedral's most prized artwork is a larger-than-life Nativity populated by wood sculptures of the Holy Family, the Magi, donkeys, cows, sheep, dogs. This magnificent Romanesque building at the summit of the city is remarkable for its rose window borne by angels. The columns in the interior are said to have been quarried in the ruins of Metapontum, but the color of the stone is different, and the capitals are not Doric echinus and abacus but Cluniac.

Like so many in Apulia, the church in the Piazza San Francesco below is part Romanesque, part Baroque. The nearby church of the Purgatorio is entirely Baroque and its art entirely dedicated to death, with stone reliefs of scythe-swinging skeletons on the façade, skulls and crossbones carved on the wooden portals. The treasure of the interior is an effigy of the deposed Christ lying on a bed of daisies, blood draining from his wounds.

Carlo Levi's *Christ Stopped at Eboli,* published at the end of World War II, deserves some of the credit for the De Gasperi government's efforts to resettle the *sassi* people in modern apartment houses—less than completely successful, as the television sets and refrigerators in a few still-inhabited caves testify. During the Abyssinian war, Levi was exiled to the nearby town of Aliano, "Grassano" in his book, for his anti-Fascist activities. His sister Luisa, a medical doctor like himself, coming to visit him from Turin—Primo Levi's birthplace as well—and stopping in Matera to obtain permission from the authorities, saw starving, diseased children, naked or in rags, faces yellow with malaria, heads crawling with lice and covered with scabs. She told her brother about people with tuberculosis, dysentery, and trachoma living in the *sassi,* side by side with cattle, mules, goats. Carlo Levi's own impassioned account of Matera refers to its "tragic beauty." How pleased he would be to know that a book of his paintings is on sale in a store in the new part of the city, alongside a book of Cartier-Bresson's photographs of the *sassi* people. (I knew Carlo Levi very slightly in Rome and Venice, after he had become a Senator, and greatly admired him for the *Eboli* book.)

Back at the Melograno I learn from Vaccaro that Gesualdo's ancestors have been traced to Benevento in the eighth century, that he corresponded with Philip II of Spain, and that in 1610, aged fifty, he pleaded illness in order to avoid the trip to Milan to attend the canonization of his uncle Carlo Borromeo. Thirty years earlier, the future saint had approved the Spiritual Testament, signed by John Shakespeare, the poet's father, and despatched it to England from Milan.

14. Golden coralite Castel del Monte, a Romanesque tower at each of its eight corners, crowns a lonely peak overlooking the Murgia plateau. From a distance it might be a modern space observatory in medieval disguise. Columns with couchant lions frame the main portal, which is made of *breccia rossa* and is in the form of a Roman triumphal arch. Beyond what was once a portcullis, the temperature drops about forty degrees, and the light, filtering through arrow slits, dims equivalently; a torch would be needed for an appreciation of the famous sculpture of a faun's head with pointed ears and tongues-of-fire hair at the foot of the stairs. The rooms, all the same shape and size, are trapezoidal, and all, on both storeys, are dominated by ribbed and groined vaults that rest on single columns of *breccia rossa* on the lower floor, and on three-column bundles of light gray marble on the upper. The downstairs walls were originally faced with *breccia rossa,* the upstairs with marble, but, as Edward Lear remarked in 1847, this has been stripped away. (Lear's diary, unlike his ear for versification, is not always reliable: he confuses Frederick with his Barbarossa grandfather and repeats folklore as fact.) The floors, too, were originally covered by a pattern of hexagonal mosaics with triangles between the touching points, hence on all six sides, but these survive only in Room VIII of the lower storey.

The upstairs rooms are slightly less gloomy, thanks to balconies, fireplaces, and travertine wall benches. A window over the front portal looks toward nearby Andria, where Frederick's second and third wives, Isabella of Brienne and Isabella of England, are buried. (He preferred his mistress, Bianca Lancia; Manfred, their son, was the only one of his many bastards—the insignia for which was a bend sinister emblazoned on his shield—to whom he bequeathed an appanage.) In the eighteenth century, Luigi Vanvitelli further pillaged the building by carting off the marble middle columns of the upstairs windows to Caserta.

Only one document connects Frederick to the castle, a dispatch of 1240 ordering the completion of an outside pavement. Yet he, incontestably, was its architect. The model for the building is clearly the Dome of the Rock in Jerusalem, which he had seen and admired, and which also rests on an octagon.

The mathematical regularity of the castle can be traced to Frederick's long-time patronage of Leonardo Fibonacci, the great Pisan mathematician, brought up in Algeria, who introduced Arabic numerals and algebra to Europe, and who dedicated his treatise on square numbers to the Emperor. (The Fibonacci sequence expresses the harmonic ratio of the golden section.)

Castel del Monte was conceived as a hunting lodge. One of its upstairs rooms was a mews for the imperial falcons; above it is an eyrie for breeding young falcons. (Frederick's book on ornithology contains a taxonomic survey of falcons, but does not say that they can dive at a terrifying 100 miles an hour.) One imagines the Emperor here, surrounded by a menagerie of monkeys and other animals, attended by a seneschal and several eunuchs (though his principal harem was at Lucera), and with an entourage of Arab astronomers—Frederick was as fluent in Arabic as in Latin and Greek—Provençal poets (Dante ascribes the birth of Italian poetry, and the first Italian sonnet, to Frederick's court), and a consort of musicians. (Leigh Hunt, rebutting Byron's denigration of music lovers as effeminate, named Frederick, Epaminondas, and Alfred-of-the-burning-cakes as macho amateurs of the art.)

The castle's most novel feature is invisible, a plumbing system that collected rainwater in cisterns on the tops of the towers and conveyed it through gutters and drainpipes to lavatories and bathrooms: Frederick believed in the cleanliness-godliness equation.

As the finest example of Hohenstaufen-Islamic architecture, it seems fitting that Castel del Monte was declared a national monument largely through the efforts of the nineteenth-century German historian Gregorovius.

The massiveness of the walls, the silence and emptiness become oppressive, however, and after an hour or so we fairly run outdoors into the blazing sunshine and open space, the olive groves and umbrella pines, the crocuses and thistles, the floribund world and the living one of skylarks and butterflies.

15. The turn-off to Cannae, the ruins of the hilltop city overlooking the scene (according to regnant opinion) of Hannibal's greatest victory, is not marked, and our out-of-date map shows no automobile road but only a railroad on the side of the Ofanto River. To the left of the narrow, winding, unpaved ascent to the citadel is a menhir.

The superficial strata of the dead city beyond the cyclopean stones of the outer ramparts have been excavated, and the digging equipment on the main thoroughfare, as well as a cordoned-off, chicken-wired dig-in-progress, indicate that archeological work is processual. The Antiquarium at the entrance houses the oldest ceramics found in Italy, along with Byzantine ivories, bronzes, earrings, coins, and an iconostasis. Of the Roman city, baths, temples, and mosaics have been unearthed, as well as two huge granite columns brought from Egypt, which must date from the period of the Roman reconstruction. When Horace, Virgil, and Maecenas were here, on their last night before continuing to Bari and Brindisi, it would have been a new city. Most of the ruins, including three basilicas built with stones plundered from the Via Appia, are medieval.

A Roman herm, erected by Mussolini and incised with quotations from Polybius (in Greek) and Livy, marks the city's highest viewpoint above the Ofanto valley, the locus, in Livy's words, "of the most famous battle in antiquity, and of a catastrophic Roman defeat." Livy makes the most of the debacle for the glory of Rome: "No other nation could have suffered such tremendous disasters and not been destroyed." He also tells us that the Carthaginians had appropriated so much armor from Roman casualties at Trebbia and Trasimeno that they might have been mistaken for Romans themselves. Hannibal had captured seventy Roman standards since the start of his campaign at Saguntum in Spain.

Though modern historians dismiss Livy as over-imaginative, they value his account of Cannae for its reference to the fleeing Romans as Trojans. Belief in the Trojan origin of Rome (the *Aeneid*) was widespread as early as Pyrrhus. With the second Punic War the Greeks allied themselves with Rome in regarding Hannibal as the common enemy, the "*alienigenae hostes,*" in the language of the Marcian Oracle.

After Trasimeno, Hannibal crossed the Apennines at Spoleto, marched to the Adriatic, captured Cannae, then re-crossed to Campania, where he spent part of the winter until, short of grain, he returned to Apulia, where harvests are earlier than elsewhere in the peninsula. It seems that after his victory at Trebbia his army subsisted principally on herbs (purslane, orach, amaranth) and vegetables (radishes, celeriac, salsify, samphire, cardoon).

Meanwhile, the Roman Senate sent an unprecedented eight legions to destroy him. Reaching the Ofanto below Cannae in late July 216 B.C., they were commanded by two generals with opposing views on military tactics, Terentius Varro, headstrong and pressing for attack, and Aemilius Paullus, havering and fearful of a snare. In fact, Hannibal is reported to have set one, leaving his camp wide open and pretending to have fled with his army while actually hiding in the hills and waiting to ambush the enemy as soon as they entered it. But the Romans suspected a ruse, so when the sacred chickens in their golden cage did not eat, the augury was interpreted as a presentiment, a warning from the gods. Aemilius, like Alexander refusing to cross the Oxus until his hepatoscopist could provide a favorable forecast from the color and shape of rams' livers, took no action.

The Romans established camps on both sides of the Ofanto, then withdrew from the right to the left bank. Hannibal followed, keeping his back to the river, and hence to the sun, the south-east wind, and the dust. Livy and Plutarch describe a cloud of dust blowing over the Carthaginian army into the faces of the Romans, but a map of the positions of the two armies in a seventeenth-century edition of Livy shows both the "Romani" and the "Poeni" on the right bank, and no backs to the river. This illustration also pictures them as equal in size, whereas the Carthaginians, with some 40,000 men, were outnumbered, two to one in some accounts, six to one in others. Both armies placed their cavalry on the flanks of their infantry, in Hannibal's case Celts and Iberians on the left, Numidians on the right. His front-line foot soldiers were Iberians and Gauls, the former naked from the navel up and wielding short, sharply pointed swords, the latter in white linen tunics with purple borders, wielding long, slashing ones. Trying to account for the absence of dissension in an army composed of men of different races, Machiavelli believed that the reason was "terror of Hannibal's person." Surely the explanation must be that his Afro-European army was free of racism.

The unimaginably sanguinary battle between the superpowers, August 2, 216 B.C., began with an encounter between Hannibal's left flank and the Roman right. The Carthaginian cavalry, which the Romans feared as invincible, was numerically superior, but the deciding factor was that the closeness of the combat compelled the Romans to dismount. According to Plutarch, Aemilius's horse, wounded early in the fighting, threw his master, and when nearby generals alighted to aid him, the infantry, seeing their commanders quitting their mounts, took it as a sign that they should charge the enemy on foot. In Livy's version, Aemilius himself was severely wounded by a stone from a sling and forced to abandon his horse. Whatever the truth, the grounded Romans were quickly crushed, thereby enabling the syntagmas of Carthaginian heavy cavalry to ride behind them and reinforce their own right flank. The remnants of the Roman cavalry galloped away to Canosa and Venosa.

Polybius describes the wedge formation of Hannibal's infantry as a crescent-shaped convexity, that of the Romans as a parallelogrammatic phalanx. Hannibal's center gave way when the Roman infantry attacked it, but by design. As the Carthaginians fell back and their line became concave, the Romans were drawn into, and were soon pouring into, the middle, where Hannibal's Lybian (Berber) veterans slaughtered them. Varro had foolishly ordered his centurions to close the distances between units (centuries), thereby depriving them of maneuverability and packing them so tightly together that they were unable to move. Scipio, "Africanus," who would avenge Cannae fourteen years later, learned from the battle to keep large lanes open between his maniples. But the deciding factor in Hannibal's humbling on his home ground—Zama, near Carthage—appears to have been the blare of Roman bugles, which frightened his elephants into turning against his own army.

Estimates of casualties at Cannae differ. A consensus puts the Carthaginian losses at 6,000-8,000, the Romans variously at 50,000 (Livy, Plutarch, Appian), 60,000 (Quintilian), and 70,000 (Polybius, who was closest to the events and could have talked to veterans, but whose unreliability in military censuses was exposed by Mommsen and, recently, by Arnaldo Momigliano). Three bushels of rings (Dante's "spoil heaped high with rings of gold") were reportedly taken from the fingers of the fallen and sent to Carthage, along with silver from harnesses and other booty.

The chief political consequence of Cannae was that most of non-Greek and non-Latin lower Italy rejected Roman rule and gave allegiance to Hannibal. Capua, the richest and most populous (300,000) city in Italy after Rome, welcomed him, and the Carthaginian army took up winter quarters there. This was Hannibal's undoing, though his greatest mistake, like Meade's at Gettysburg, was in his failure to follow the routed enemy and march on Rome (Richmond in Meade's case). Plutarch says that Hannibal's friends "earnestly persuaded him…that in five days' time he might dine in the Capitol."

Livy argues that Capua demoralized Hannibal's army! "When it came to the good things of life the troops lacked both familiarity and experience. These heroes who had resisted the assaults of adversity were undone by an excess of enjoyment.…The round of sleeping, drinking, eating, whoring, bathing, and taking their ease became sweeter to them each passing day." Livy was apparently unaware that, pursuing a policy of attrition, Hannibal undertook numerous marches in central Italy during the occupation.

The mystery of what became of the remains of the 75,000 dead is still unsolved. No cemetery has been found, and archeological evidence for the slaughter has vanished virtually without trace. In 1727, the Medici Museum in Florence acquired a Roman helmet said to have come from the banks of the Ofanto, and the British Museum purchased two more of them from a dealer in antiquities in Naples. The Taranto Museum exhibits a javelin disinterred near the river. But that is all. A grave uncovered in 1938-39, initially thought to be ancient, actually contained the bones and armor of

Lombardian and Norman soldiers defeated at Cannae by the Byzantines in October 1018.

Or did the great battle described by Plutarch take place somewhere else? (His account of Hannibal's oration to his warriors before Cannae—in Punic, Iberian, or Greek?—extolling their valor must have inspired Henry V's at Agincourt.) Some modern historians believe that the real location is the valley of Celore, in nearby Daunia, but others point out that the Ofanto is a meandering, vagabond, riven river that has had countless divergent and divaricating changes of course.

16. Tomorrow we return to the tourist-trampled north. Not to worry, Alva says. It's still Italy.

Piazza Armerina, Stilo, Noto

I was somewhere between Gela and Piazza Armerina with my friend Eugene Berman at dusk on the day of President John F. Kennedy's assassination. Motorcycle radio police stopped our driver, not to tell us that but to warn us that since the area was infested with bandits, we must go for our safety to Catania. I resolved to return and did, thirty-two years later, by which time Piazza Armerina had become Sicily's top attraction. New roads lead to it from Taormina, and a tourist-industry city has grown up around it. Our destination across the straits in Calabria was not Stilo but Sybaris, which proved to be too far. Noto and Lecce are the most beautiful Baroque cities I have ever seen.

October 11, 1995. Arriving at De Gaulle for our flight to Rome, we learn that it has been canceled, despite assurances to the contrary from Air France only an hour ago. Alva, not easily fazed or riled and without peer in expostulating, succeeds in switching us to an Alitalia flight, but this involves schlepping our book-heavy bags to another gate and waiting three hours on hard benches. Finally in Rome, we must traverse the airport from end to end in seven minutes for our connection to Catania. Our baggage is not on the flight with us, of course, and in Taormina we sleep in San Domenico Palace bathrobes. The renovated-monastery hotel has a beautiful cloister and gardens, but the food is greasy. The city no longer appears to be the world capital of pederasty, its reputation when Oscar Wilde, Anatole France, Maugham, Cocteau, Harold Acton, Capote, and Tennessee Williams were here, but the best writing about the place, not by any of these, is in Hermann Broch's *The Sleepwalkers.*

12. The very limited English of our driver to Piazza Armerina is even less comprehensible in the Australian accent of his tutor. Though we have come to see Enna above all, and the excavations beyond it at Morgantina, we will not trust him on that precipitous road.

The floor mosaics of the forty-six rooms of the "Villa Erculia," the work of North African craftsmen of the late Roman period, the largest in scale and best preserved Roman mosaics in Europe, cover 10,500 square feet. The visitor views them from elevated plank-board pathways under protective blue plastic awnings. Archeologists now assign the villa to the early fourth century of Diocletian and the Tetrarchs (the embracing figures in porphyry by the entrance to the Ducal Palace in Venice). The owner is now thought to have been Maxentius, whom Constantine defeated at Milvius, one of the subjects of the Arezzo frescoes. Built on the slope of the mountain that buried it under a landslide for more than a thousand years, the villa is terraced. On the lowest of the three levels are the baths and latrines, which emptied into the Gela River. On the next highest are guest rooms, service rooms, the kitchen, a vomitorium, and the Diaeta of Orpheus. And on the uppermost are the rooms of the Imperial family, with, between peristyle and triclinium, the "Great Hunt" mosaics. Two aqueducts supplied the complex from the Gela, presumably upstream.

The "Hunt" mosaics—the hunting horns are long, thin, and have detachable mouthpieces—picture the capturing of animals for exhibition in the Circus Maximus in Rome. Panthers are shown being trapped in Mauritania, hippos and rhinos being bound in the Nile Delta, and ostriches and a captured buffalo, dragged along by ropes, being loaded on a ship in Carthage. The tunic of a soldier engaged in this baiting and lassoing is embroidered with a swastika, which signifies the rotation of the sun-god of the four seasons. India, in one segment, is represented by a tiger, a phoenix, and an elephant. Strips of many-colored cloths tied to the branch of a tree behind the elephant are said to be part of the method of capturing it, but how? Hundreds of years earlier, in the victory parade for Julius Caesar on his return to Rome from Asia, his chariot was followed by "a herd of giraffes," which must have been taken in the same way. This was the event in which he chose to reveal his successor, for Octavius (Augustus, but that is a title, not a name) rode behind him.

The most famous mosaics depict ten "bikini" girls, so-called because of their scanty panties and narrow bras. They compete in discus-throwing, racing, playing with a ball and spoked wheel, and they crown the winner. But they are gawky athletes, with none of the grace of a Nausicaa.

The floor of the "Erotic Room" depicts a young man and woman making love while standing. To judge from their ecstatic eyes, intromission has been achieved, except that he is carrying what seems to be a heavy wine cooler in a hand that, by the laws of nature, should be fondling the voluptuously bared backside of his partner. In the music room, five Greek letters, each in circular frame, represent musical notes, and animals turn, enchanted, toward Orpheus's lyre, which is a blank in the mosaic, but a seven-string instrument is shown in the adjoining scene. The dining room mosaics depict the twelve labors of a Hercules whose genitals are incommensurately small for so bulgingly muscular a body. The rich blues, reds, celandine yellows, browns, greens (for Tritons) indicate recent restoration. Workmen clean and polish as we walk through.

13. The actual crossing to Calabria on the Messina ferry lasts only fifteen minutes, but the loading and unloading of trailer trucks and the clanky winding and unwinding of chains on each side consumes more than an hour. The road from Reggio lies between the soft blue Ionian Sea and the Aspromonte, the southernmost spur of the Apennines. White-clay soil on the mountainside gives way to decomposed, friable granite, the effects of erosion, earthquakes, and landslides evident as far as Monasterace. The closer roadside slopes have been strung with steel nets to catch falling fractile rocks, but most are already full to bursting. Near Locri, bougainvillea, olive, eucalyptus, and willow trees relieve the inland side, but the city, praised by Pindar for its good government, famed for its sanctuary to Persephone, is now a dreary summer resort. Motor traffic is non-existent, replaced by gaggles of racing-club bicycles, each team sporting its own color in clothes, caps, and sneakers.

The road from forlorn, indigent, sparsely populated Monasterace into the mountains and to Stilo is loopy and narrow, though the land is more fertile and the valleys filled with orange groves and vineyards. A statue of Tommaso Campanella, Stilo's native-son philosopher, stands at the center of the new town. How odd that two Calabrians, he and Bernardino Telesio, should have founded the scientific-rationalist, freedom-from-theology movement known as Neo-Platonism that had such a powerful influence on Michelangelo, though his direct sources were Ficino and Pico.

The tenth-century Byzantine church we have come to see is on the edge of a cliff 1,000 feet farther into the empyrean, at the end of a vertiginous dirt road. The square basilica measures only 14' x 14', with three apses and five cupolas, whose windows flood the room with light. In its fragmented frescoes, John the Baptist, John Chrysostom, St. Nicolas, St. Basil (in the bay of the left window) are identifiable, as well as the Madonna and Child, and the Christ in the ceiling vault, but of one figure only lips and eyes remain. The most impressive picture is the most complete, an Assumption of the Virgin in which her body is being hoisted heavenward by angels. Fleurs-de-lis decorate the outer layer of one panel, testifying to Angevin or Norman rule. Most heads in the frescoes are blonde. Greek letters are visible in some, and an inscription in Greek is carved in one of the four stone pillars.

The panorama from the sedgy, cactus-studded hillside above the church extends to a monastery on a distant mountain and to the sea. Remote as Stilo is, the guest book contains 3,000 and more Italian, German, French, English, and Japanese names. Stilo and, to the east, Rossano, were centers of Greek culture as late as the *trecento*.

In consequence of the 1908 earthquake, the streets of Reggio Calabria are some of the widest in Italy. Many signs are in English ("chewing gum," "video clubs," "computer office"). The Museo Nazionale contains most of the excavated treasures from Sybaris and Locri, including the Dioscuri, but the most famous object is the ruminant of Papasidero, or, more exactly, the cast of a *graffito* of it, the only artifact of the Upper Paleolithic period so far disinterred in Italy. The Riace bronzes, the two stupendous male nudes, attributed respectively to Phidias and Polyclitus, discovered in 1972 in an ancient shipwreck near Riace and first exhibited in Florence in 1980, are believed to have come from Delphi, and to have commemorated the victory at Marathon. We return to Charybdis (Messina) on the ferry from Scylla (still called that).

15. Driving from Siracusa to Noto on old, narrow, stone-fenced roads, we encounter the only donkey cart we have seen in Sicily, whereas on my last visit they comprised most of the traffic, automobiles being the exception. At two intersections German concrete anti-tank "pill-boxes" still stand against the American landing at Gela in 1943. Though Noto is architecturally homogeneous, having been entirely rebuilt after the earthquake of 1693, its greatest sculpture, Francesco Laurana's *Madonna della Neve,* in the Church of the Crocefisso, dates to 1471. Since the earthquake of 1990, so many edifices have been propped up and surrounded by scaffolding, including the beautiful Palazzo Ducezio, that those who know the city only from Antonioni's *L'Avventura* would not recognize it.[1] The *passeggiata* on this sunny Sunday afternoon is so thickly populated that we choose to watch it, from a park of palms and monkey-puzzle trees, rather than to join in."*Noto*" means "unknown," but does no one know when and why the city acquired the name?

16. Arriving at the Catania Airport far ahead of time, we learn that our flight to Rome has been canceled because of an Alitalia strike. This means not only a four-hour wait but also the uncertainty as to whether the scheduled later flight will happen. It did, and, finally in Rome, we dine at Sans Souci, a pretentious and expensive *Dolce Vita*-style restaurant. My son Alexander comes tomorrow for my birthday.

-

[1] Five months after this was written the roof of the Cathedral of St. Nicolas fell in.

La Serenissima

Beginning in 1951, I spent more time in Venice than in any other European city. It could be called my home abroad during my years with Igor Stravinsky, who in the late 1950s and early 1960s composed his Gesualdo motet arrangements, his Dufy Canon, and a considerable part of Agon, Threni, *and* Abraham and Isaac *there. The premieres of his* Rake's Progress, Canticum Sacrum, Threni, *and the* Monumentum Pro Gesualdo *also took place in Venice, and I introduced his* Requiem Canticles *to the city, as part of his funeral service in the church of SS. John and Paul. Shortly after, I assumed responsibility for his grave, in the island cemetery of San Michele, and, eleven years later, of his widow's as well; I still journey to San Michele every year to see to the upkeep of their tombs. The Venetian diary that follows includes accounts of some bizarre experiences in that capacity.*

After Stravinsky's death, his widow returned to Venice from New York quite regularly, the first time only two months after his burial, the second six months after for the installation of his tombstone. She was present at all the occasions described here from the 1970s, but during the last five years of her life, 1977-82, was not able to make the trip. In September 1982 I attended her funeral in the Church of San Giorgio dei Greci, then arranged for the placement of her pietra.

In the 1980s and 1990s I was in Venice several times on my own account, to conduct concerts, see friends and art exhibitions, some of them, notably of Canova, organized partly by these friends, as well as to show the city to my son and his mother, then to my second wife, and, lastly, to give recorded BBC interviews on Stravinsky history in Venice. My descriptions include revisits of those originally undertaken with the Stravinskys, to nearby cities, villas, churches.

June 1973. Venice has escaped death by drowning for another winter, but succumbed to a Japanese invasion—aerial units only, thus far, to judge by the 747-size contingents in the Piazza, though heavily armed with cameras and yen. "The Americans of the seventies," the Italians call them, except that the Japanese reportedly clean their own rooms and make their own beds.

11. The "Widener" Canaletto of the *campo* of the Church of SS. John and Paul shows a now-missing wooden bridge near the church of the Mendicanti, and a well-head on the *campo* side of the Ponte Cavallo that is no longer there. (Since the Church of John and Paul is centuries older than Verrocchio's statue—the building is prominent in a map showing Marco Polo's route out of Venice—couldn't *"Cavallo"* refer not to the statue but to the earlier period when gondolas had not yet superseded horses as the city's main means of transportation?) Less conspicuously, the façade of the great *chiesa* seems to contain more paterae now and definitely does contain two more sarcophagi in the arcades. Otherwise the scarred epidermis is much the same, and less faded than that of the neighboring buildings. The gondolas in the Canaletto have *felzi* and are flat, not crescent-shaped, the gondoliers wear red bloomers and red fezzes, and the green of the mossy *campo* is nearly the same tint as that of the canal.

A measure of the decline from the century of the equestrian to that of Canaletto is in the painter's treatment of the Colleone monument, the city's most powerful secular image.[1] In the picture, the Bergamasque mercenary, "one of the first to make use of cannon," Rembrandt Peale tells us, is less important than the dark windows and shadowed bays of the church. The *magnificenza* of the sculptured equestrian figure (the ferocity and brutality, rather, of the imaginary portrait of the real Colleone, whom Verrocchio never saw, having been something of a wimp) is asserted only by the horse and the plinth. Nor is Canaletto's *campo* exactly bustling: a pair of mantilla-ed churchgoers; two marketers with baskets; a few idlers and onlookers; a masked man; a man and woman in black, he, to judge from his wig, a prothonotary or procurator, she a widow, perhaps, but if so a merry one,

---

1. Panofsky calls the statue "overbearing" and remarks that it surmounts both the secular and the religious.

veil-less and décolleté. The remaining two figures are tourists, those most ominous portents of decadence, or so I take them to be, since one of them is pointing to an architectural feature of the church for the edification of his companion. A puppet booth appears to be setting up in front of the Scuola di San Marco, but this part of the picture is clearer in its Dresden version, which also shows a blue curtain covering the door of the church. Did the painter use the *camera oscura?* What was his perspective? He could not have been positioned on the next bridge, the view from there having been blocked by buildings, as Bellotto's *Scuola di San Marco* in the Accademia confirms. Which leaves fantasy, the realm of Marieschi's engravings.

14. To Torcello, via the *rio della Pietà,* a sewageway of empty bottles and assorted offal, the lees of the last minstrel. In the lagoon, boys are diving from a barge girded with old rubber tires against bruising by stone corners. In the Torcello canal, weeds writhe behind our boat, "like souls in torment," as Stravinsky's widow remarks, no doubt thinking of that other island, San Michele, where "all flesh is grass." The beautiful mosaic floor of Santa Maria Assunta is now invisible under pews, and the walls are defaced with dial-a-lecture telephones.

October 7. Many *campi* are cluttered with "art objects," a legacy or aftermath of the Biennale. What resembles a mammoth tuning fork faces the Hotel Baur like a threat in the Jericho sense to its Fascist-mausoleum architecture. A huge metal "construction," a bronze outhouse, perhaps, and so used by late-night male pedestrians, occupies the Campo Santa Maria del Giglio. But the most bizarre of these alfresco exhibits are the sculptures in bread by Enrico Job. Featureless except for heads, torsos, handless arms, footless legs, they horrifyingly suggest victims of thalidomide, or partly baked bodies recovered from death-camp ovens. Pigeons and small birds crawl like maggots over a distribution of these monstrous figures near the Accademia bridge, pecking at them warily.

In Luca Ronconi's production of the *Choephoroe* in a theater near the

Arsenale, the stage itself, though limited to raisings and lowerings, see-sawings and squeaks, is both the center of attraction and a more compelling performer than any of the actors on it. The size of a badminton court, this mobile arena would have been more suitable for a play about Sisyphus—its side-to-side roll keeps the actors climbing hills—than for Aeschylus. The dipping of the stage also exposes the "backstage" under it, where a prompter follows the text, workmen read newspapers and eat sandwiches, and members of the chorus prepare to go on, all of them competing favorably for audience attention with the tragedy unfolding above their heads. The stage is divided in the middle and each half departs periodically for the ceiling or basement like a freight elevator.

Ronconi apportions the chorus part polyphonically by having small groups enter and exit in canon, and in overlapping rotation. A great deal of howling and screaming takes place as the players writhe on their stomachs and fling "ordure" about, some of it landing in our row. The props include a phantom staircase, armillary spheres with fire at the core (Ptolemy's geodesic world), and some of Enrico Job's bread people (a groan from the audience), one of them representing Iphigenia's corpse, whose limbs the Elders of Argos break off and munch with more appetite than the Accademia pigeons. The most dramatic moment is also the most repugnant, an ax falling on a sacrificial lamb that may not have been dead, and from which a haruspex withdraws a handful of entrails.

Enunciation is over-deliberate, words like "justice" being dissected ("*gee-ewe-steet-tsee-a*") as if the theater were a speech-therapy clinic. Suffering from *mal de mer* brought on by the tilting stage, I leave long before the end.

6. After the Panikhida [memorial service] for Stravinsky in San Giorgio dei Greci, I unsuccessfully explore the *sestiere* for more traces of the great Greek colony that numbered about 5,000 when Domenicos Theotocopoulos (i.e., El Greco) lived here, studying with Titian, and was the same size in 1499 when his fellow Cretan, Iacharias Calliergus, the famous printer, discovered a technique of melting gold leaf to blend with gold type for large initial letters.

August 7, 1975. Stravinsky's tomb was desecrated yesterday afternoon by a member of "NAP," the "Nucleus of the Armed Proletariat," who daubed these initials on the stone in red paint. According to *Il Gazzettino,* a party of tourists surprised the vandal, but could not stop him. Shocked though Vera Stravinsky is, she and her friends are thankful that she did not witness the incident herself. Francesco Carrara tells us that the acronym stands for "Nono, Abbado, Pollini, Italy's wealthiest communist musicians." The Mayor of Venice promises to have the tomb repaired immediately, but we leave on an afternoon flight for Munich.

July 10, 1977. The perspectives of the city from the canals reveal fewer perfectly perpendicular belltowers, and more loose bricks and stones, more cracked and crumbling walls, more eroded intonaco facings.

The cynosure at Harry's Bar this noon are two starlets, a *bruna* and a *bionda,* their fingers, wrists, and weasands jewel-bedecked, their blouses open to the waist, their pants tourniquet-tight, their eyes hidden behind bug-eyed sunglasses. A fat man with them pitchforks spaghetti into his mouth without bothering to wind the skeins. We walk to the Ponte dei Baretèri (hatters) and to a shop selling the glass that looks like cellophane wrap.

12. To San Michele. The dome of SS. John and Paul, undergoing restoration, is boxed in wicker as though for shipment. The lagoon's normally paludal odor is mixed with the stench (*"spussa"* in the dialect) of coagulating refuse.

On the island we walk past a row of graves with quadrangular granite frames and metal inscriptions, black wooden crosses, wax wreathes. The lapis lazuli on Stravinsky's tomb has lost its luster, and for some reason the letters seem more cramped and in need of the bullet that separates the first and last names. Did Manzù (who designed it) add it because he recognized that he had miscalculated the spacings? A newly occupied neighboring plot has acquired a pompous monument framing a passport-like photo of the deceased, as if to identify him at the Resurrection. A toe shoe has been placed beneath the cupola on Diaghilev's tomb, like an offering on an altar, but the waterlogged and moldy slipper seems to symbolize the death of the dance rather than its rejuvenation.

A prefab wooden bridge is being erected across the Grand Canal from the Campiello del Zobenigo, the same place where, in the eighteenth century, pontoon bridges were built for the celebrations in honor of the Madonna della Salute, as in Luca Carlevaris's painting in the Hartford Atheneum. This new bridge provides a shortcut to the Zattere for the best view of the Festa del Redentore fireworks. A dozen sections, with railings and lamps attached, are assembled like a large toy, hoisted from anchored barges to a high, steeply arched framework. The chief engineer in spiffy white and gold-braid uniform directs the water traffic like an opera conductor, dramatically flagging down each approaching boat to a *molto ritardando.* The fireworks begin at midnight, when upward arpeggios of colored light burst into umbelliferous clusters, loiter a moment, dissolve.

September 22, 1982. Dinner in a café with my friend Baron Ernesto and his wife, Marie Thérèse, after drinks at their Palazzo Albrizzi, which, in the interior of the Dorsoduro far from the San Tomà dock and not on a principal canal, is difficult to find. The narrowest street in Venice, the Calle Stretta, debouches into the Campiello Albrizzi, where one of the walls, struck by an Austrian shell in World War I, displays a marble plaque inscribed by D'Annunzio over the scar. I arrive at the Palazzo early enough to see its treasures inside and out: the lantern from Admiral Emo's flagship at the entrance (*fanale de galera*); the Baroque plasterwork on the *piano nobile*; the twenty-eight *putti* holding up a white drapery in the cubical ballroom; the high, walled garden that was the site, so important in the history of opera, of the early-seventeenth-century Teatro San Cassiano. Ernesto's young children and especially their mother are remarkably beautiful, their manners exquisite.

April 27, 1983. Beyond Marghera's permanent pall of oil-refinery smoke, the Venetian sky is flocculent and our landing smooth. The tide is low in the lagoon and fish are jumping, but as our boat approaches the cemetery island, I can hardly bear to look in that direction. We enter the city via the Misericordia, where, in the last house on the Fondamente Nuove, a young boy sits in a windowsill sunning himself. The niches for statues in the monastery's walls are untenanted, weeds sprout from bridges, coppices flourish in the courtyards of empty palaces, buildings are flaking, their ornaments crumbling, their colors fading—the Fondamenta dei Tedeschi, russet when I last saw it, is now ghostly white—and the general decay seems to have progressed several years in the last eight months. Mercifully, my hotel room is in a wing unknown to me high over the Albero Canal.

In the Piazza, gold-lettered red banners announce an exhibition, "WAGNER E VENEZIA." Not Wagner but *Tootsie* is playing at the Cinema San Marco, and though I am tempted to see what the film is like dubbed in Italian, the thought of its "location" in the Hurley and Stone Ridge of my native Ulster County, New York, deters me: I cannot, at this point, allow my memory to exhume that even deeper past. The young female fashion in Venice this spring is the highest-hemline miniskirt, with matching hose and shoes in scarlet, indigo, gamboge, purple.

28. To a Panikhida service at S. Giorgio dei Greci, the first for both Stravinskys. I stand and kneel alone.

30. Francesco Carrara comes to tell me that George Balanchine has died, an expected and prayed-for release but also a shock. When I first met him, April 5, 1948, in the Stravinsky suite in the Ambassador Hotel, New York, he was forty-two years old. Thirty-five years have vanished.

Realizing that I cannot avoid visiting the Stravinsky graves, I buy red roses at the cemetery's flower stall and follow the path of last September 22. At Stravinsky's tomb a guide is lecturing tourists in German. Finally alone, I plant the roses in the soft mound of earth over Vera Stravinsky's grave. Then turning to walk away, I am drawn back as if by a magnet, remaining there all afternoon until the loudspeaker announces closing time. "A pair of locked caskets," Isak Dinesen wrote, "each containing the key to the other."

September 17. A Panikhida service in S. Giorgio. The archimandrite beckons me into the sanctuary, where I hold a candle a few inches from the iconostasis as he intones prayers in which the names "Igor" and "Vera" recur. Afterwards he tells me that the Greek congregation no longer exists, and that the church will become a museum next year.

After the service Dottoressa Chiara Carrara takes me to the shop of a stone mason on the Fondamente Nuove. He will copy Manzù's Stravinsky's stone (*tagliapietra; taiapiera* in the dialect) for his widow. On the walk back she explains that a *ruga* is a street, larger than a *calle,* lined with shops, and a *salizada* larger and more important than both, having been paved at an earlier date.

The baby-angel carver in Campo San Stefano tells me that *putti* are naked boys, cherubs are heads only, with a pair of wings, *angeli* are fully robed and of indeterminable sex, and cupids are always armed with arrows.

19. Jacopo Sansovino's Villa Garzoni at Pontecasale is now called Villa del Bosco, thanks to poplar avenues, chestnut trees, and umbrella pines, all enclosed by two miles of ancient crenellated wall. The entrance to this former summer residence of the doges is a ramp gently sloped for palfreys. The statues adorning the loggia and the banisters above the open courtyard are gold and green with fungus. More surfaces are red than white, the marble having been stripped from the brick and the cladding, but this does not lessen our pleasure in the perfect proportions of the architecture. The interiors might better have been left bare: the furniture is too small for the room space, the mirrors are cracked, and the "Veronese" *Marriage at Cana* is a gross forgery filled with idiot faces. The columbarium and the stables also date from the Renaissance. The twenty racehorses being trained here eat and drink from sixteenth-century stone troughs and are shod in a blacksmith's shop of the same period.

22. Vera Stravinsky's tombstone is installed this morning in the Russian section that, newly cleared of weeds and tall grass, reveals a stretch of ground large enough to contradict Auden's "Island Cemetery":

> This graveyard...
> though new guests keep crowding in,
> Must stay the size it's always been.

(Does "guests" come from Donne's "The Relique," "Where my grave is broke up againe/Some second ghest to entertain"? In any case, the image of the cemetery as an inn occurs in one of the last *Winterreise* songs, with which Auden was well acquainted.) The poem contains one of his best couplets:

> Wherever our personalities go
> (And, to tell the truth, we do not know)

Next to the discolored marble, blackened lazuli, and tarnished gold of Stravinsky's stone, his wife's looks sadly new. Ezra Pound's grave, near the rows of filing-cabinet tombs, is marked by a small disk flush with the ground. His wishes,

> Where I lie let the thyme rise and basilicum
> Let the herbs rise in April abundant,

have not been fulfilled, but this is the wrong season.

23. In view of the last-minuteness of the event, the audience for my memorial concert in La Fenice is surprisingly large. I address it, explaining that Stravinsky's 1915 arrangement of the *Firebird* "Berceuse" is being played in his memory, the lullaby from *Le Baiser de la fée,* "The Eternal Dwelling Place," in Mrs. Stravinsky's.

January 7, 1985. The lagoon is frozen for the first time in fifty-six years, but Venetians seem unconcerned, unlike their disbelieving, astonished ancestors in Guardi's *Lagoon Frozen Over,* in the Ca' Rezzonico, in which people cavort on the ice, while an improvised gondola-like ice-breaker slowly cleaves a path through it. As the Gritti's only guest, I am installed in the Royal Suite, in whose draughty, high-ceiling rooms I am never out of my overcoat. We rehearse in the icy winds of the Teatro Malibran.

11, 12, 13. In spite of a blizzard, my concerts in Padua (Teatro Verdi) and Mestre (the Toniolo, a cinema) are well attended. In the one at La Fenice the electricity fails during the second movement of the Violin Concerto, bringing Rolf Schulte's and my performance to a halt for about three minutes, destroying our feeling for the piece.

August 7, 1986. Long before the home stretch at the Futurism and Futurisms exhibition at the Palazzo Grassi, the viewer wonders about the techniques by which a fringe movement, more pamphlet and poster than artistic accomplishment, is presented as the vortex of early twentieth-century modernism. Soon after the first laps, slogging past a batch of Balla's "Iridescent Compenetrations," one begins to ask what Futurism is not. Seurat, Munch, Picasso, and Kandinsky are here, insidiously presented as ancestors. "Toward Futurism" is the heading above the Seurat, but was he ever on a road leading to *this?*

The exhibition exploits claims of kinship and interaction with numerous artists of modernist tendency, some of them tied-in with little justification. Apollinaire, for one, dismissed the Futurists as "childish," Duchamp, for another, never locked arms with any movement for long, and Léger's and Delaunay's only connection was in protesting that they had any. In truth, the Futurists fed on more artists than they nourished.

The show emphasizes the Futurists' restrictions against the Surrealists. But the two movements resemble each other, and nowhere more conspicuously than in their intolerances, the Futurists as anti-feminist Fascists, the

Surrealists as gay-bashing Communists. Where they are most unlike is in the quality of their artists, the Surrealists having produced several estimable ones, the Futurists only Antonio Sant'Elia, that early casualty of the Great War. Chirico, who inspired the "mystery" in Surrealism and was the only major Italian painter of the period, is not represented. So, too, Pirandello and Svevo, contemporaries of Marinetti and incomparably superior writers, are as unfindable in the exhibition catalog as is Trotsky in Soviet history books. Another unaccountable omission is any reference to the performance by Diaghilev in 1917 of Balla's and Stravinsky's *Fireworks* in Rome, which was "staged" entirely by fuse-blowing electric-lighting effects. The exhibition confines Futurist music to notation: a Pratella manuscript, opened to a page-long and most un-futuristic B-flat-major chord; and an "enharmonic keyboard instrument" (as if all equal-tuning pianos were not enharmonic). Edgard Varèse, the only significant composer who used some of the same instruments as the Futurists, and who shared some of the same ideas, is not mentioned. *Je m'en fous*-turism.

Visiting the Frari with Alexander to see Donatello's *John the Baptist,* I am reminded of the acoustical testing here in May 1955 with Stravinsky and part of the Fenice orchestra, in the event that the *Canticum Sacrum* concert could not be held in the Basilica of San Marco. After ruling out the round and resounding Santa Maria della Salute, we came here in three motorboats, only to discover that the boom and echo in the straight-up Gothic church lasts even longer.

9. Où sont nos amoureux
    Elles sont aux tombeaux…

A shock at San Michele: the gold cross has been stolen from Stravinsky's tombstone, apparently chiseled out. But why am I so surprised? The robbing and desecration of tombs is thousands of years old, after all, and in all likelihood the thief never heard of the incumbent. Still, I will provide a replacement only if it can be protected. On second look, a refill might not be the most desirable solution. The gold always seemed miserly in proportion to the size of the marble slab, and the empty frame makes the grave part of the history of Venetian ruins.

July 29, 1988. Japanese tourists photograph everything. Thanks to their currency exchange rate, they are the only gondola passengers, a less than joyful experience for them, if I read their supposedly inscrutable faces rightly. At night, in gray and black clothes, filling flotillas on the Grand Canal but not responding to the concert of accordions and wobbling sub-Mascagni tenors that are part of the fare, they make a somber spectacle. How do these visitors from a country mercifully free of tipping adjust to one that blocks every possible escape from it? The Venetian tactic, a waiter at Harry's tells me, is to augment all charges for *servizio* like a hidden tax.

30. To San Michele. Since my last visit, the gold cross has also disappeared from Vera Stravinsky's tomb. Is the City of Venice unable to protect the graves even of those who honor it? Should I have the Stravinskys reburied elsewhere?

31. In the exhibition of Pre-Colombian sculpture from "Messico" at the Doge's Palace the huge stone figures consort oddly with the portraits of Doges and Venetian bigwigs. Gold work is not shown, no doubt because of inadequate security.

August 3. To the Villa Malcontenta and Pisani. The former, home of my old landlady the Baroness d'Erlanger, is now a state museum, the latter a major tourist stop mysteriously offering free admission to South Koreans and Dutch!

Padua. Despite claims that an airlock antechamber will be added to the Scrovegni Chapel entrance, the large door opens directly into the polluted atmosphere, remaining open during the entire time we are here. Lacking an air filter and any form of climate control—the temperature is not adjusted to seasonal changes—damaged by the new materials used in each subsequent restoration, and exposed to the corrosive chemistry exuded by malodorous overcrowds of viewers, Giotto's frescoes are not expected to survive the first decade of the chiliasm.

What strikes me most in them today are the "interposed heads" of Judas and Christ, the witheringly penetrating eyes of the Christ as He looks at those of the Judas puckering to kiss Him. Meyer Schapiro compares the "coarse, tilted profile" of the one to the "noble features of the other" and remarks on the encounter of two men who "look into each other's eyes and in that instant reveal their souls"—though the revelation of Christ's to Judas seems improbable. Schapiro describes the scene as the "first example of a painting in which the reciprocal subjective relations of an I and a you have been made visible through the confrontation of two profiles."

Giotto's great humanity informs every scene: the impertinently curious fish observing the Baptism, the pot-bellied wine-taster in the Wedding at Cana, the clenched fists of Christ expelling the merchants from the Temple. And Giotto's colors, the verdigris and raspberry-sherbet of the garments, the livid Lazarus, the mazarin blue of the star-spangled heavens, have never been surpassed. It is true that Dante damned Enrico Scrovegni as a usurer. But surely it is time to pardon the shade of one who so overwhelmingly controverted Ezra Pound's: "with usura/hath no man a painted paradise on the wall of his church." After all, Shakespeare's father was twice convicted of the same crime.

The discussion of the Annunciation scene in the new Guillard monograph fails to mention the two symbols in the Saint Anne panels, the serving woman's distaff, representing motherhood, and the kiss of Joachim and Anne on the bridge, a metonomy for intromission. It also fails to note that the executioner is a black man; or that the sexes are separated in the Baptism scene, females on the left, males on the right, in which direction, pubic area uncovered, the Savior modestly turns. The sexuality in Hell is anal, as it is in the "Slaughter of the Innocents," both in the promiscuous pile of babies' bodies in the foreground, and in the infanticide by skewering between the buttocks about to be carried out by soldiers at the center of the picture.

April 20, 1989. San Michele. The Stravinsky tombstones have been restored with what at least look like gold crosses.

We drive to Pomposa, where Giotto and Dante met. A derelict church and tower in swamp grass when I was here with the Stravinskys and Eugene Berman thirty-three years ago, it is now a *"centro turistico"* with fifty or more buses and hundreds of cars in a vast parking lot, and long lines at the door of the abbey. According to an inventory dated 1093, Seneca's *Phaedra* is one of many manuscripts copied here.

The towers of the Castello Estense in Ferrara, visible from far away when I was last here, are now hidden behind miles of gentrified new city, and the Schifanoia frescoes behind souvenir booths. What would European civilization have been without the ducal dynasties, the Estes, Gonzagas, Medici, Sforzas, and the rest, tyrannical and cruel as they were, and what will today's democratic governments leave? (cf. Toqueville, or, better, Max Weber).

October 1. After two hours in a purgatorial transit lounge in Munich, we continue to Venice and the hair-mattresses and fine linen of the Gritti.

West African vendors have set up in front of the stores that line the Calle delle Ostreghe and the Via XXII Marzo selling imitations of the merchandise fetching vastly higher prices inside. What appears to be the same luggage displayed in the Louis Vuitton window in Campo S. Moisè is hawked in the street outside at a fraction of the price. But the Senegalese salesmen here, unlike their huckstering counterparts on Fifth Avenue in New York, are gentle and soft-spoken.

Perfumes of autumn: the aroma of roasting chestnuts in the streets, and of white truffles in restaurants.

3. The *mostra* of *Italian Art 1900 1945* in the Grassi is one of the least buoyant exhibitions of any kind that I can remember, but the stair-climbing to see eight marvelous Chiricos of 1912-15, pictures of absence, loneliness, solitude, and empty space, repays the exertion. Long shadows, not always cast from what seem to be the sources of light, dominate the outdoor scenes

(*Ariadne, Melancholy,* the *Gare Montparnasse*) and, indoors and out, black is the predominant color, as in *Perspective with Toys* (black ground, black windows, black arches); the one-eyed *Astronomer* (black walls, black painting on an easel); and the pyramidal and claustrophobic *Enigma of Fate* (with the robot hand, or vambrace, touching the checkered black and white board). The *Child's Brain* (black table, walls and archways) is an astonishing picture, and so is the *Premonitory Portrait of Apollinaire* (the black glasses of a blind man on a classical statue-head with the coiffure and features of a young, contemporary man). No wonder Chirico could not sustain this powerful world of feeling for more than a few years!

June 4, 1990. To San Michele with flowers for the Stravinsky graves, thinking of Pound's

> They will come no more,
> The old men with beautiful manners,

and of Claudel on Mallarmé: *"le resumé exquis d'une race urbaine, d'une société courtoisie."* Stravinsky's manners were courtly and gallant, with bows and sweeping arm movements. The poet's plot, in the adjoining north section, is overgrown by bushes, probably to protect it.

5. In the Titian exhibition at the Ducal Palace, the theatrically religious pictures attract me least, especially the *Assumption* that bewitched Wagner and in which Rembrandt Peale saw "animated, vigorous, sun-burnt mortals, miraculously sporting among the clouds"—baby angels without diapers, rather—and those with rapt heavenward gazes (*The Pentecost*). But the canvas of San Lorenzo on his grill is the stunner of the show. Seen close up, instead of on the left wall of the Gesuiti, its home church, the stratification of light is powerfully dramatic, the white of the supernatural rays (*not* "lightning," as Vasari and the catalog describe the beams) outshining the dark reds of the burning coals and the bright reds of torches that Panofsky believed to be archeologically correct.

One other religious picture, the *St. Sebastian,* seen in Washington three years ago on loan from the Hermitage, is one of the artist's most affecting works. Bound to a tree, the seven-foot figure spellbinds the viewer. So sparing was the painter with arrows that they are scarcely relevant, and instead of writhing in agony, the body is comparatively reposed, the left knee gracefully, balletically bent. Apart from the luminous body and the transcending face, nothing in the picture is legible, least of all the amorphous mass next to Sebastian's right foot and the distant area of light (a hillside city?).

Referring to Titian's late-in-life boast that a good painter needs only three colors, black, white, and red—this was long after he had renounced green even for grass—Panofsky astutely remarks that in all late Titians we have an impression of a colorful tonality without being struck by any particular color. But in this very late, indeed posthumous picture, the smoldering red background is unforgettable.

Close up, and thanks to the excellent lighting, we can appreciate Titian's impressionism—in scumbled backgrounds, in the texture of St. John the Almsgiver's white surplice—as well as his *vedutismo*: the St. Christopher fresco is a postcard view in the sense of Guardi.

For me the great Titians are the portraits with wonderfully intelligent eyes, above all the two *autoritratti* and Pope Paul III, who fathered the Farnese. Or powerful eyes: Isabella d'Este—whom the scapegrace Aretino described as having ebony teeth—Andrea Gritti, Francesco Maria della Rovere. In another category, the *Venus with an Organ Player* strikes me as unintentionally droll. *Intentionally*, the picture is said to demonstrate the Neoplatonic idea of the inferiority of the aural to the visual sense, beauty made incarnate in the nude figure. But the rivet of the musician's eyes on the goddess's pudenda argues the more urgent priority, if not the superiority, of the sense of haptic manipulation, and then some. The eyes of the fluffy dog beneath the Venus's dangling left arm look out of the picture at us, as if in skeptical complicity. Panofsky detects an influence of Michelangelo's *Venus* (*"alla Michelangniolesca"*), noting that Vasari's copy of it was in Venice and in the collection of Don Diego Hurtado de Mendoza from 1541, after which date Titian painted it.

October 2. Most of the photos in the Edward Weston exhibition at the Mariano Fortuny y de Mandrazo Museum are the same small size, with subject matter scarcely less uniform: eroded California beaches, close-ups of peppers, gnarled Point Lobo trees, portraits of Robinson Jeffers and the 1930s Mexican muralists. Weston's trademark clarity is most effective in photos of slender nudes reclining in the sand, contours outlined like silver-point drawings. So too, Fortuny's nudes, more buxom than Weston's, are displayed in dank, dusty rooms otherwise devoted to his fabrics and *objets d'art,* which include plaster and bronze copies of Wagner's death mask.

In the Van Gogh-to-Picasso, Kandinsky-to-Pollock show in the Palazzo Grassi, the unique picture with a social message, unless Giacometti's "lobster" (*Woman with Her Throat Slit*) has one, is Kirchner's 1915 canvas of naked showering soldiers overseen by a uniformed officer whose Wilhelm II mustache is all that distinguishes this picture of humiliation and obliterated individuality from those of the concentration camps of World War II. The most intriguing work is Tanguy's *Promontory Palace.* On all levels of a butte-like, multi-tiered, corrugated construction, and on the surfaces beyond, bulbous, blobby, pinniped shapes glide, secrete, melt, become transparent, deflate.

3. To Torcello, by way of the channel between S. Erasmo and the Lido, an unfrequented passage to judge by the flutterings of the pin-tailed ducks. On the island, the towpath by the canal leading to the basilica is a gantlet of touters; inside we are alone with the Last Judgment mosaics, now, finally, restored. They are thought to date from the eleventh century, but the space must have had mosaics long before, since the foundation stone of the cathedral reads: "In the reign of Heraclius Augustus, 639 A.D." From the center of this six-layered tableau a river of fire flows down to a compartmented, hier-archized Hell. Each sin is punished in a separate fascia: pride, lust, envy (skulls with imps in the eye-sockets), indolence, miserliness (eleven severed heads, four of them female), gluttony (naked, bloated men nibbling their own hands, which could have been suggested by the pagan tale—Ovid—of Erisychthon, who devoured his own flesh). The wings of the Seraphim are, as Ezekiel describes them, quilted with eyes.

The blue peplum with gold fringes of the Madonna in the apse of S. Donato in Murano is virtually a copy of the one in Torcello. When I was here with Stravinsky in September 1951, what struck him most was the floor mosaic of a bound reynard slung from a pole shouldered by two birds. He was annoyed that no one could explain the presence of the fox in a church in the first place, but did not need to be told that the braces of peacocks are a resurrection symbol. Like those in the *pluteus* in the Torcello iconostasis, these are shown drinking out of marble and jasper urns.

6. Driving to Asolo, we find all streets closed in order to accommodate two wedding processions. In Padua, the confessionals in the Basilica of S. Anthony are occupied (red lights switched on), and the queues outside are as long as those at the cashier's in a *supermercato.*

June 20, 1991. The *Celti* show in the Palazzo Grassi is highly dramatic. The feeling of an ancient forest is evoked in a room containing a darkened grove of artificial trees. The refulgence of gold objects in the showcases of another room provides its only lighting. According to the catalog, all European cultures trace roots to Celtic origins, the aim of the *mostra* being to explore the traits and features of a civilization that, creating no architectural monuments and no written, first-hand accounts, is all but invisible today.

The Celts emerged in Bavaria and the Danube valley at about 600 B.C., migrated over the whole of Europe, and disappeared about A.D. 1000—through assimilation, historians contend, but to judge from the space given here to bronze and terracotta wine flagons, Wagnerian drinking horns, stirrup cups, the real cause may have been alcoholism. Miners and metal-workers, the Celts minted coins, made phalerae and fibulae, buckles, linchpins, tools and the appurtenances of war: swords, shields, helmets, war trumpets (carnyx); Strabo described them as "war-mad." They were coopers, carpenters, fletchers, ceramists (carnated pottery) who liked highly adorned small things, being especially fond of ornamenting with coral from the Gulf of Naples. Farmers, warriors, a practical people, their religion was animistic. (The principal historical source is Caesar's *Gallic Wars*.)

21. We visit the Ghetto hoping to see the eighteenth-century painting of a circumcision belonging to "the Baali Berit confraternity" (i.e., the Jewish community), but are unsuccessful. The description of the rite by the Marrano Giulio Morosini fits the picture exactly: the empty chair for Elijah, who must witness all circumcisions; the scalpel held by one of the matrons; the Rabbi holding a receptacle for the prepuce, which will be ceremonially buried; a vestmented figure bearing a tray of bandages; and finally the mohel, leaning over the uncovered infant. Rebutting St. Bernard's sermon against circumcision, Aquinas argues that not only is it necessary as a sign of the faith with which Abraham believed that the Christ would be born of his seed, but that it also helped diminish the "fleshly concupiscence which thrives principally through the organ of generation because of the intensity of venereal pleasure."

Aquinas explains the choice of the eighth day of Christmas, January 1, for observance of the rite because of the delicate condition of the infant during the first week of life, but Richard Crashaw provides the crucial link:

> And till my riper woes to age are come
> This knife may be the speares *Praeludium.*

In the Museo Ebraico, the Scroll of the Law itself, the parchment Pentateuch, is not exhibited because of its sanctity, but only its ornaments, exquisite seventeenth- and eighteenth-century silverwork. The viewer is nudged with reminders that none of the objects is primarily aesthetic, the artist's only intention being to honor the Law of God. The showcases display Hanukkah lamps, Seder plates, amulets, *ketubah* (marriage contracts), tallith (prayer shawls), *mappah* (drapes for the reading platform), and *rimonim, tass, besamim* (spice boxes).

The doors of the Sephardic Synagogue (*"sesandei"* in the Judeo-Venetian dialect) are closed to us because of a lecture in progress there for a tour group from New York. We learn that Venetian Jews were not required to live in the Ghetto until 1516, and that money-lenders there could charge no more than 5½ per cent. But the area was small, hence the tall tenement buildings which remind New Yorkers of, well, New York. Why did Carpaccio choose the Ghetto as the setting for his *The Calling of St. Matthew?*

22. The Stravinskys' tombs are already covered with fresh flowers when we bring ours. Diaghilev's has been scrubbed, the lettering newly gilt.

April 26, 1992. The Canova exhibition at the Museo Correr is a lifetime event in that so many large marbles are not likely to be brought together again soon. The Correr might have been built expressly for the show. The rooms, culminating in the vast balconied ballroom, have the right amplitudes and the ceilings the right height. Best of all, the wall-mirrors, although some of the oldest are blind and no longer reflect, enable the viewer to see the sculptures from different perspectives at the same time. The Correr appertains in yet another regard: Canova lived here for a time in the Procuratie Nuove.

Since more of the sculptures come from the Hermitage than from the Louvre or the Vatican, the occasion is an incidental display of early-nineteenth-century Russian taste, or, more specifically, the taste of Nikolai Yusupov and Alexander the First. (Canova had declined Catherine the Great's invitation to visit her at the end of the previous century.) Nothing is on loan from England, surprisingly, since the British government had sought Canova's opinion of the Elgin marbles before purchasing them, and prior to that Elgin himself had shown drawings of his Grecian booty to the sculptor in Rome. Moreover, after Waterloo, when Pius VII sent Canova on a mission to Paris to request the return of the art that Napoleon had looted from Rome and placed in the Louvre, the artist's English connections, extending as high as Wellington and Castlereagh, prevailed on the French to effect the restitution. (Back in Rome Rossini composed a cantata to celebrate the occasion.) Among the pieces from Venice are the early *Daedalus and Icarus,* and two from the Albrizzi Palace; Canova had given the greatest of his *"teste ideali," Helen,* to the Corfiote Isabella Teotichi Albrizzi, who provoked Byron's line, "What nature could but would not do, beauty and Canova can." She published a four-volume monograph on the sculptor in 1821-24.

For Canova, sculpture meant carving, not modeling in clay and casting in bronze. His bronze *Napoleon* in the courtyard of the Brera in Milan was cast without the artist's knowledge, and he took no interest in the bronze version of his equestrian Charles III in Naples. White marble, the idealized color of flesh, is the material of his most celebrated works, meaning the nudes with fluidly undulating contours of backs, buttocks, bellies.

A contributor to the exhibition catalog notes that the soiling of certain areas on sculptured female bodies is a result of human handling, which is hardly surprising. After all, Herder's *Plastik* argues that sculpture appeals as much to the sense of touch as to the visual sense, and Burke's *Sublime* says that smoothness is part of the ideal of beauty. Hegel noted that his fellow academic, Böttinger, fondled "the voluptuous parts of marble statues of female goddesses" and the poet Ugo Foscolo confessed to Contessa Albrizzi that he had "kissed and caressed" Canova's Venus. The *Cupid and Psyche,* also in the exhibition, excited Flaubert to the extent of kissing her armpit. Canova's finishes, the patinas that give his marbles the illusion of transparency, add to their erotic attraction. But if the sexuality of his Eurydice in her moment of bereavement is more explicit than that of any of his other women, the explanation is in the whirls of smoke that veil her lower body.

Statues of the same subjects completed at different periods have been placed side by side, helping the viewer to see why, for example, the later of two versions of *Mercury,* the one with gold inlay in the helmet, is the stronger, the pedestal of clouds in the other being a backward look to the Baroque. The most powerful pieces in the show are the nude pugilists Creugas and Damoxenos. The weakest are the friezes in low relief, including the *Death of Socrates,* which, like Canova's Titian monument in the Frari—a copy of the Cestius Caesar pyramid in Rome but with figures outside approaching the door—bring to mind the narrative sculptures in the cemetery at Genoa.

Hugh Honour's catalog essay contains a vivid description of Canova's Rome studio. The rough hewing was done by apprentices and assistants in the front rooms, which were also used as showrooms: workmen would revolve statues on plinths so that potential customers could see them from all angles. Canova himself labored alone in an inner sanctum, "chips of marble flying about him like snowflakes." He worked concurrently on several *opera,* taking infinite pains over the finish. Many rooms were stacked with clay *bozzetti,* the artist having made models of everything he did.

In the Rome of 1806, Canova ranked as the *premier artiste napoléonien,* and his absurdly idealized bust of the Emperor, exhibited here, was copied forty times for French adulators. Having neither a political philosophy nor any scruples, Canova was on good terms with the Corsican, as well as, immediately after him, Metternich and the Austrian Emperor.

The reputation of "the most sought after artist in Europe" declined rapidly after his death. In 1830 Rembrandt Peale saw Canova's right hand exhibited in a vase in the Accademia. After that the Italian art establishment continued to ignore and even deride the sculptor's Anacreontic art. Then in the late 1950s, Mario Praz's participation in conferences devoted to Canova in Venice and Bassano helped to swing opinion the other way. The publication of Praz's *L'Opera completa del Canova* in 1976 began a new era of appreciation.

April 20, 1994. At La Fenice, the house lights are lowered for *Tristano e Isotta* several minutes before the conductor appears, thereby provoking protest applause from the upper balconies that destroys the intended reverential, Bayreuth-like, atmosphere. When the maestro, Marek Janowski, finally enters, his unfleeced crown, featuring two prominent warts and a Ritz Brothers rim of hair, is spotlighted throughout the *Einleitung*. This is too briskly played, the small string section being unable to sustain, let alone intensify, Wagner's volumes. Orchestral and vocal intonation is consistently off, and the Isolde, shrill as well as flat, is overpowered by both the Brangaene and the Tristan (Siegfried Jerusalem). The histrionic range of all three is limited to lurchings and sinkings-to-the-knees. No one seems to be reading the Italian translation projected on a screen high over the proscenium.

21. The Tintoretto exhibition at the Accademia disappoints, with the exception of some portraits, the *autoritratti* most compellingly. The group portraits are like school class photographs, all heads and eyes trained toward the painter. Some of the Madonnas are goitrous. Incredibly, many of the windows of this great gallery are open to the intense morning sunlight and the thickly polluted air. The dampness of human exhalation can start the process of decomposition, yet no picture is protected by plexiglass, ultraviolet filters, Lexan fiber-optic cables and the like, nor do we see a hygrothermograph.

22. At San Michele many of the old graves in the center of the Orthodox section have been removed, the cleared space being prepared for more recent ones; the rentals here are for twelve years only, after which the remains are taken to a mausoleum or island ossuary. Visitors to Stravinsky's grave come and go in a steady stream, and a trash bin for dead flowers has been installed nearby. A metal plate the size of a credit card, with the legend *"Bruna a Igor 7/12/93,"* has been attached to the stone directly above his name. We dislodge it but cannot imagine what it means, Stravinsky never having known anyone called Bruna. If she is a young admirer, why the first-name basis? Next to the north wall, not far from Diaghilev's tomb, I notice for the first time the preposterously ostentatious monument to one Romeo

Supparcich and his wife. A bronze head of the incumbent, identified as a *"maestro di suoni,"* reposes on the top of a pedestal with a bronze relief on each side, one of them a portrait of Signora Supparcich, who looks like Liszt in old age, the other a scroll-like score with five staves of bad music in A major.

The exhibition "Architecture from Brunelleschi to Michelangelo" at the Palazzo Grassi, and above all the fifteenth- and sixteenth-century wooden models for churches, should be made permanent. Sangallo's for St. Peter's, the largest of the thirty or so that survive, nearly fills the huge main floor. After seven years in the making, by the carpenter Antonio Labacco, it was not yet finished when the architect died, whereupon Michelangelo condemned it as having "too many hiding places for scoundrels" and proceeded to make models of his own, seven in all, two of them in clay.

Michelangelo is portrayed in two paintings showing one of his St. Peter's models to, respectively, Paul IV and Leo V. His model for the façade of San Lorenzo in Florence is also here, as well as Buontalenti's, and three by Giambologna for the Duomo in Florence. My favorites are those for S. Maria della Consolazione in Todì, and the richly colored and finely carved one for the Pavia Cathedral. The viewer can compare, in minia-ture, the Gothic arches and flying buttresses of San Petronio in Bologna, and the curling ones of Reggio Emilia's neo-classical Cathedral. In the eighteenth century Juvarra and Vanvitelli still worked from models, after which the practice was generally discontinued until Gaudi, Mies, Le Corbusier, Wright.

The most curious painting in the *mostra,* Piero di Cosimo's *spalliera* panel, *The Building of a Double Palace,* comes from Sarasota. In it, oxen-drawn wagons haul timber from a forest and stone from distant mountain quarries. Masons and carpenters wield mallets, chisels, two-handed saws, set-squares, vises, and hoists for raising statues. The foreshortening and per-spectival inconsistencies in the foreground can only be intended to show that the activities there are unrelated. Vasari remarks on the large number of horses in the picture, but only three appear in the foreground, the cavalcade at the back being a blur.

24. Though beyond our powers of appreciation, countless objects in the Palazzo Ducale exhibition, "Islamic Art in Italy," seem to me breathtakingly beautiful, but the intricacy of the geometric patterns and floral abstractions as well as of the culture's highest art form, calligraphy, are eye-straining. Of the Abbasid period, which interests me most, only a single page from a Cufic Qur'an in black ink, chrysography, and red vocalization dots, is on display. In it, moreover, because the letter forms of the Alif and Mun are almost all curved, the picture lacks the balance of vertical and horizontal in the great Abbasid Qur'ans in the mosques of Cairo, Kairouan, and Damascus. Even the qualities of the finest rugs, one of which fills a huge room, are not fully apparent to me. Some of the English captions, moreover, are strictly for lexicographers ("proficuously"). The literature makes claims for the superiority of Islamic carved quartzes, but are they really "more transparent than glass"? From the catalog I learn of the Islamic influence on Byzantine pictorial and sculptural techniques in churches in the Mezzogiorno, particularly in the *rupestri* of Matera, in Santa Maria Le Cerrate in Lecce, and in San Marco at Massafra.

26. In a music store near S. Maurizio, where Canova had a studio, we trade an armful of CDs for a lute, which we will have to carry like a baby all the way to Florida.

September 29. Arrigo Cipriani accompanies us by traghetto and on foot to his son's apartment on the Dorsoduro, which they would like to sell. Nearby on the Zattere is the walled garden of the destroyed Incurabili, one of the four great musical sororities of the sixteenth-to-eighteenth centuries. A *putto* on its Rio Vio corner perch sings from an open part-book.

30. The Carraras drive us to Padua to see the exhibitions of drawings by

Sanredam and Van Wittel, and, in the Palazzo Raggione, Luca Carlevaris's Venetian *veduta* paintings. Pictures here by Cimaroli show that corridas were held in the Piazzo San Marco, and that a grandstand was set up on the porch of the Basilica itself, which, in view of the four pagan-period horses over the portal, should not be all that surprising. The Arena (Scrovegni) Chapel still lacks an instrument to measure temperature and humidity, but today it is so loud with restorers' hammers that we flee to the Museo Civico to see Giovanni Bellini's *Portrait of a Young Senator.*

October 2. Arrigo Cipriani fetches us in his motorboat for a visit to Contessa Tana Contini Bonacossa in her Palazzo Vendramino on the Giudecca. Now in her late eighties, she is vivacious, elegant—in a Fortuny-period dress—and a considerable actress. Recently widowed, she wishes to dispose of this comfortable, modernized residence and move permanently to her winter home in Milan. But though we could never have afforded it, wouldn't we feel marooned here?

January 13, 1995. In anticipation of flooding, planks have been piled in the Piazza and arterial streets, but today's water level is so low that our motor-boat scrapes the bottoms of canals.

15. In bitter cold and leashed to a BBC recording machine, I go to SS. Giovanni e Paolo, the location of Stravinsky's funeral and traditionally those of the doges. In San Michele the tombstones of the Stravinskys, like the others in this corner of the necropolis, have been submerged and are dirty and stained with alga. In 1830, Rembrandt Peale noted that "the vaults of those who could afford it were raised above the high water mark." Darkness gathers early in the cemetery.

16. Some of today's interviewing takes place in loge 29 at La Fenice during a distracting stage rehearsal of a ballet, *Il Profeta.* Since no cats are "hanging out" or on the prowl at Stravinsky's feline-feeding end of San Fantin, we move to the Baur Grünwald, first in his 1951 suite, then in the basement, a nightclub when he worked there in 1957, now a warehouse. This visit to the hotel bothers me more than all the others. Now, after forty-four years, it is both too familiar and too alien: I have been forbidding my memory to stray into our rooms, the porches, and the lobby presided over by the unforgettable Luigi Tortorella, "the most famous hall porter in Europe," as Hugh Honour calls him. Our next stop is the Cardinal's palace, which we enter from the canal side, as I did from a *motoscafo* in August 1956; this time I am poled by a gondolier sporting a striped red and white blouse and a borsalino with bright red ribbon. No new light is shed during our colloquies in the Basilica, but at least the bells peal, a perk for Andy Cartwright, our recording engineer.

April 22-3, 1996. Venice is cold and rainy. The roofless, burned, and gutted Fenice, a sickening sight, has become a tourist attraction; to prevent souvenir hunters from sifting the debris, carabinieri strut in front of the building and on the back and side approach bridges. Our Venetian friends blame the conflagration on arsonists, saying that it can only have started in several places at once. The rest of the city is repairing, polishing, cleaning, dredging —guiltily, it seems to me.

25. The emphasis in "The Western Greeks" exhibition at the Grassi is didactic, all upper wall space being filled with maps, drawings, photos, and texts. But the sculptures are unforgettable, above all the seated, legs-crossed female flute player, an undamaged relief fashioned on the Sicilian island of Mozia, *c.* 460 B.C., now part of the altar known as the Ludovisi Throne, for the art-collecting Roman cardinal. Another of the Throne's friezes, the birth of Aphrodite from the sea, clinging wet clothes and hair, is less appealing only in that her two handmaidens have been decapitated. The other wonder of the show, one of the Dioscuri from Reggio Calabria, exemplifies the Greek glorification of the human form. The young horseman has dismounted but not yet touched the ground, a uniquely unstable posture for a sculpted figure. Obviously intended to be seen from below, the tableau is assumed to have been designed for an acroterial perch. The Greeks began to colonize the coasts of Sicily and Southern Italy from about 800 B.C., for commercial rather than political or territorial motives. They brought civilization with them, founding their city-state *poleis* wherever they settled. The Etruscan thalassocracy formed a naval barrier against them, assumed to be Scylla-Charybdis, but at about 770 B.C. permitted the establishment of an emporium at Pithekoussai on Ischia, from which they trafficked in Eastern goods. The cruelest of Mediterranean peoples, binding their prisoners face-to-face with cadavers, the Etruscans apparently encouraged their pirates to practice cannibalism.

26. The new Holland-America cruise ship, launched yesterday from Marghera and anchored by the Riva degli Schiavoni before embarking on its maiden voyage, is so large that it makes Venice itself seem toy-like and, at night, compared to the glitter of the boat, appear to be in a blackout.

August 18, 1997. *This Week in Venice* announces a series of conferences on the music of Luzzasco Luzzaschi at the Cini Foundation, an Anselm Kiefer exposition at the Museo Correr, and, at last, the opening of the Palazzo Labia to the public, albeit with thirty days' application notice. The restored Wagner rooms in the Palazzo Vendramin Calergi can also be seen, but also by appointment. And, after more than a century, the "Burchiello" (wherry) has resumed service to Padua via the Brenta canal. Francesco Carrara warns us that the now-motorized ride lasts two hours, during which a multilingual lecturer endlessly explains that Mozart, Goethe, Shelley, and everyone else came to Venice this way. But the island of San Giorgio in Alga and Palladio's Villa Malcontenta are on the itinerary, and I would like to see them again if only because both belonged to the Baroness d'Erlanger, my long-ago Hollywood landlady.

In this high tourist season, gondola tours with tenors and accordions begin not at moonlight but in the blaze of early afternoon. The sudden outburst at 2 P.M. of "O solo mio," or the wail of "Santa Lucia," can only mean that the passengers are still on Tokyo time.

August 20. We are late for our visit to the Wagner museum because of a wrong turn from the San Marcuola dock and a mistaken attempt to enter the Palazzo by its Casino door. When finally we catch up to Signora Pugliese, the guide, and a group of nine, she greets me as "Maestro," which sets the others eyeing me with puzzlement for the rest of the tour. Later she reminds me that in September 1983, under her WASP maiden name, she sang in the concert that I conducted at La Fenice, and that Nuria Schoenberg came to the rehearsal.

The proportions of the rooms are Wagnerian: a symphony orchestra could be seated comfortably in the main reception hall. The smaller room in which Wagner died was also the one in which he composed, and his living presence there still permeates the place. Guy de Maupassant, who visited Wagner's rooms in the Hotel des Palmes in Palermo shortly after he vacated them, testified that the closets still smelled of his eaux de toilettes. Having damaged his olfactory sense by snuff-taking, the composer became addicted to the stimulation of strong scents.

La Pugliese recounts the story of Wagner conducting his teenage Symphony at La Fenice using a score reconstructed from orchestra parts found in Dresden. He rehearsed it himself on December 22, 1882, in the foyer of the Fenice—where I rehearsed Stravinsky's *Requiem Canticles* for his funeral—and led the performance, a private one for Liszt, Humperdinck, and a few other friends, on Christmas Eve. Thenceforth he ventured outside the Palazzo rarely, the last time being on February 6, 1883, when he threaded his way through the masked crowds on the final night of Carnival.

Death, apparently from a ruptured blood vessel in the heart, came just before three o'clock on the afternoon of February 13. A moment after he had rung a bell for the maid and told her to fetch Cosima and a doctor, his manservant burst into the adjoining room saying, "The master is dead."

Cosima held him in her arms for twenty-five hours, then cut off her hair and placed it on his breast in the coffin.

The record of Wagner's later medical history left by Dr. Friedrich Keppler, the city's resident German physician who tried to revive the heart-beat by friction, parallels some of Stravinsky's: "an inguinal hernia, greatly aggravated by an unsuitable truss…disorders of the stomach and bowels, and a bad habit of taking, promiscuously and in considerable quantities, many strong medicines that had been prescribed by physicians he had previously consulted."

A Venetian woman writing two months after the death detailed the contents of the room as she found it; the present refurbishing claims to follow her inventory and description. Showcases contain photos, facsimiles of manuscripts, originals of letters, and the Wagner collection from the Fenice archives, which includes an account book for the local premiere of *Der Ring des Nibelungen*. Payments for gas-lamps and candles are entered, as well as fees for singers, walk-ons, and orchestra players. One major gaffe in the displays is a grotesque "composite portrait" of Wagner by a still-living Venetian painter "based on all photographs of him during the *Parsifal* period," but resembling none of them. Another is a recording of *Tristan* seeping in from somewhere in the distance, the wrong music for this palazzo.

August 22. Francesco lends us his Lexus and driver for an excursion to Mantua, a ninety-minute ride now, versus four hours on a back road when I drove the Stravinskys here in 1957 (and in 1461 nineteen hours on horse-back from Milan by the fastest Sforza courier). The three of us were alone in the Ducal Palace in 1957, and mercifully unguided. The difference in incentives then and now is that forty years ago we came chiefly to see the (not-yet-restored) Mantegnas, whereas today it is the sinopias and frescoes of Pisanello's Arthurian cycle, discovered in 1969. In my first glimpse of them, in June 1973, only the two golden-haired ladies sheltered by a baldachin had come to light, but today the upper walls of the huge Sala del

Pisanello, the first room on the *piano nobile* of the Palazzo del Capitano, expose full panels, as well as fragments of what must have been magnificent pictures. For certain, Uccello's *Battle of San Romano* owes much to Pisanello's illustrations of "Bohort and the tournament near the castle of King Brangoire," as the melée is now thought to depict, except that four or five knights are shown as dead or dying, whereas fatalities were rare in the sport of jousting. Still, whether a battle or merely target practice, Tristano and Lancellotto are somehow connected with the action; Henry VI of England bestowed heraldic collars of the House of Lancaster on the Gonzagas, and Mantua is a Grail city, by reason of the relic of the Holy Blood in Sant'Andrea. Pisanello's drawing in the Louvre of the head of the young Moor seems to me far superior to the same head in a group of *cavalieri* here in the fresco.

The palace's tour traffic is divided into groups of about thirty according to language. The allotted time per room, corridor, staircase depends on the speed of the groups ahead as they shuffle along the endless enfilades. Our Italian guide, more security guard than culture-vulture, has never heard of Poliziano and Pico della Mirandola, let alone of their philosophy, pedagogy, and translations from the Greek, though both were in the train of Cardinal Francesco Gonzaga, Marquis Lodovico's most famous son. Nor does the name Monteverdi mean anything to her, though his *Orfeo* was performed *al fresco* in the courtyard; nor even Mozart, who, aged thirteen, inaugurated the Castello's concert hall. But she does take us to see Isabella d'Este's music room, with its notations in many shades of blond, light and dark brown intarsia woods. The canon by Johannes Ockeghem, square white notes close together and all stems pointing upward, suggests the spires of a Gothic city.

Thinking of Huizinga's argument about the greater intensity and effect of sound and color ("gules, gold, argent") in the unpolluted *quattrocentro,* we try to imagine the Camera Picta's splendiferous frescoes at the time they were finished (1474): Lodovico's red gown trimmed with bands of yellow, the white fur collar, vermilion *berretta,* heraldic hose—right leg white, left leg red—Cardinal Francesco's red *cappa* lined with white, and his blue stole; his brother Federico's brocaded gold tunic over a red doublet. Lodovico's grooms and servitors wear green hats, and the lappets of his horse's saddle have gilt pendants. Mantegna himself wore a crimson and silver *gonnella* at court.

The monograph by Ronald Lightbown on the painter is helpful on the *di sotto in sù* perspective of the outdoor scene. We learn from it that a chamberlain is identified by his gloves, a sign of rank, that peacocks were prized denizens of the Gonzaga gardens, and that the portraits of Emperor Frederick III, Lodovico's suzerain, and of Christian I of Denmark, who had married Lodovico's sister-in-law, were inserted after the picture was finished.

But the Gonzagas, especially droopy-lidded, long-nosed Lodovico, were overbearingly proud and selfish, and Barbara of Brandenburg, his wife, was cruel, retaining her female dwarf solely to amuse the court with the poor creature's deformities. As for Cardinal Francesco, his thick lips and flushed face are part of what must be one of the most sensual visages ever painted. How much nicer are the greyhounds and horse; Lodovico, wearing spurs, is apparently about to ride. It seems to me that the fortified hillside city in the background is not "fantastic," as art historians say, but a quasi-naturalistic representation of the Soave castle, much as it looks today a few miles north on the road to Verona.

The most powerful face in Mantua, the high-relief bronze head of Mantegna, is in Alberti's Sant'Andrea, where it is twenty degrees cooler than the piazza. The Romanesque rotunda of Matilda of Canossa is very similar, if not identical, to a Byzantine building depicted in the Utrecht Psalter. As for Giulio Romano's frescoes in the Palazzo Té, the naked lovers dallying on a couch display ample qualifications for the business at hand, but having to show front- and back-sides in full at the same time is awkward for the female.

Mantovan drawbacks unchanged since my last visit are the oppressive humidity of the low-lying city—

And the frogs (O Mantuan) croak in the marshes.

—the hobbling cobblestone pavement of the main piazza, the kilometers of staircases in the 500-room *castello,* and the lack of latrines—Alva finds one in the basement floor of a trattoria in, of all places, the Palace of Reason. (Voltaire, with his obsession about *la chaise percée,* would have appreciated this, except that it lacks the *chaise*.)

August 24. The one-time Venetian colony of Aquileia, now a village of two or three thousand in the midst of extensive excavation sites, was a city of 200,000 when Caesar Augustus received Herod the Great here. It remained one of the world's largest cities until razed by Attila. The Emperor Constantine died in Aquileia some thirty years after proclaiming the Edict of Milan, and in 381 Jerome and Ambrose attended the Council of Aquileia together. The claim that the Basilica is one of the most remarkable of all Paleochristian monuments is more believable now than when I saw it in 1956, the 2,100 square feet of floor mosaics and the crypt frescoes having been luminously restored. The mosaics date from the fifth century, which explains the mixture of pagan and Christian symbols. The Good Shepherd, a lamb over his shoulders, charms his flock with pan-pipes like a Christian Orpheus. Another pagan survival is the confrontation of the cockerel, the bearer of light, and the tortoise, the symbol of "Tartarchos," "outer darkness."

The aquarium depicted in the Jonah mosaics, and the aviary and zoo in those of the Garden of Eden, are wonders of the world. The whale spews Jonah from its hot, dark, and damp gullet after three days, which, according to Matthew, is Christ's foretelling of His entombment and resurrection. IKTHYS, the Greek for fish and the acronym for "Iesus Kristos Theu Yos Soter," is found here as it is in the catacombs in Rome. The pavement mosaics include scenes of anglers with rods and lines in long boats curled upwards at the prow like gondolas; of a heron with an eel squirming in its beak; of jelly fish, lobsters, giant sea snails, an octopus, baskets brimming with clams, scaly fish with yellow eyes, white underbellies, and red gills. Waves are evoked by undulating black lines, as well as by an intentional roll in the floor.

The twelfth-century crypt frescoes are thought to be the work of a returned Crusader, because of a representation of the Holy Sepulcher in Jerusalem. The waves here, red lines, are confined to the columns. The most curious tableau is a descent from the Cross in which the dead Christ is being eviscerated, His intestines stored in a pot with a lid. (What is the tradition for this?) On the upper level, near the Bishop's throne, is a low-relief portrait of Thomas à Becket, believed to have been made soon after his martyrdom in 1070. The Baptismal font is hexagonal, the "X" intersected by "I" being another symbol of Iesus Xristos.

July 31, 1998. The gouging marks of a chisel or awl have defaced the marble around the gold crosses on the Stravinskys' graves, yet another attempted theft. A handwritten letter in Italian has been left, partly hidden, by the shrub at the head of Stravinsky's stone. The text, still legible despite blurring rain, expresses the woes of an old woman from St. Petersburg, the loss of her family and of "the great city of the Neva." The paper is unsigned but mysteriously inscribed *"Stravinsky e la Vecchina, un Colloquy con Stravinsky da R. Craft."*

In the adjoining *Evangelisti* (Protestant) cemetery, the remains of Olga Rudge have lately been interred next to those of Ezra Pound, the love of her life, in a new, elevated, attractively shaped plot. Signs direct visitors here from the boat dock, but without including the name of this remarkable woman, violinist and musicologist, more responsible perhaps than any other single individual for the rediscovery, in 1939, of Antonio Vivaldi. On a sign at the entrance to the *Reparto Greco,* someone has written the name "Brodsky" underneath the names of Stravinsky and Diaghilev.

August 1. The exhibition, *"Tibet oltre la leggendra,"* at the Palazzo Querini Stampalia is hardly worth the long walk. The masks are spooky, and the huge scarecrow is frightening. The collection of musical instruments includes long Himalayan horns, lutes with large frets, tiny rebecs, but most of the wall space is filled in with photographs.

Milan, Bergamo, Castelseprio, Castello di Canossa

During my matinée concert in the Teatro alla Fenice, Venice, on January 14, 1985, a blizzard began to rage outside. I had air tickets to Copenhagen for the next day, having promised to visit my son, but the lagoon was frozen over and Marco Polo Airport closed. Since traffic was said to be moving on the autostrada, and thinking that I stood a greater chance of finding a flight from Milan, I hired a car and driver, and headed there. The journey took eight hours, one of them waiting in a queue at a gas station. The blinding snow fell for two more days.

I went to Bergamo the following year at the invitation of a friend from Padua and in his Lancia. Alexander accompanied me. In 1991 both he and Alva were with me at Como, en route to, respectively, Copenhagen and New York. The trips to Castelseprio, Castiglione Olona, and Canossa, again with Alva and Alexander, were fulfillments of old dreams.

January 15-17, 1985. Snowbound in the Principe di Savoia Hotel, I discover that Sophia Loren occupies the room next to mine, also a prisoner of the weather. She is surprisingly shorter than her movies have led me to expect. But if she is the best of the experience, the worst is that "Elvis Presley Month"has monopolized Italian television. Whereas he speaks in monosyllables, and, to judge by his lip movements, not many of them, the over-dubbed Italian, in a voice remarkably similar to his, tumbles out in torrents.

18. My taxi to Linate Airport takes more than an hour and never makes it all the way, unremoved snow and other taxis blocking the entrance, reducing the road to a path: *"Tutto bloccato,"* the drivers relay down the line, superfluously. I lug my two heavy suitcases to the SAS counter only to learn that the Copenhagen flight has been canceled for the fifth time. The company has provided a bus to Zurich, however, and, hoping for a connection there, I join a cargo of alcoholically embalmed Swedes and Danes. Flares along the highway, a lurid sight in the dense fog, mark several accidents on the way to the St. Gotthard tunnel, but the road on the Swiss side has been plowed. Near the exit, helicopters are dropping supplies by parachute for stranded mountain villages. In Zurich at midnight I manage to find a seat, but on a flight to London.

August 6, 1986. An excursion with Francesco Carrara to Bergamo and the Oratorio Suardi at Trescore, to see Lorenzo Lotto's frescoes of scenes from the lives of Saints Brigid and Barbara. Lotto's intarsias in Bergamo's Santa Maria Maggiore are difficult to make out in the dim light; the long-winded guides, alone permitted to lift the felt flaps protecting the panels, insist that we hear their spiels to the end. Berenson maintained that the subjects, allegories, and symbols in these pictures are so "suggestive" that they detract from the appreciation of their qualities of composition, but he praises the *intarsiatore*'s faithful transferral of Lotto's "line" to materials so different from pencil and paper. One of the subjects is the *Apocrypha*'s "Family Who Preferred Death to Eating Pork."

At Trescore, Christ Himself is the vine, a literal representation of John's words: "I am the vine, ye are the branches." The huge Christ figure dominates the wall facing the entrance, while the donor, Battista Suardi, his wife, and sister kneel at His "feet," or, rather, the trunk of the vine. The "ye" are saints, each one portrayed in a roundel formed by the curled end of one of the branches that stem from His upturned fingers. The ceiling frescoes picture a host of chubby *putti* romping in vineyards, clutching grape clusters, and exposing their genitalia, while making a pretense of concealing them behind the leaves. Withered vines, bearing no fruit, represent heretics whom Ambrose and Jerome, disguised as gardeners, push into perdition. But Christ as a vine is eerie — "revolting" is Berenson's word — as if He had overlong, Fu Manchu fingernails. Berenson awards high marks to the animation and the distinguishing of class and characters in the groups, and he rates the vow-taking scene in the *Legend of St. Clare* among the most valuable of Lotto's works.

The gory events of the Santa Barbara narrative are depicted in linear left-to-right succession from the far left north wall, where Barbara, in a blue and yellow robe, is imprisoned in her father's tower. Her poses are said to be indebted to some of those in Raphael's *stanze,* but, compared to them, Lotto's figures are clumsily drawn, his backgrounds and spatial limbos crudely perspectivized. A Brueghel-like circle of children plays in an area separated from other space in a cartouche and in radically unrelated scale. In one sequence, a terrier, sharing the same plane as the saint, upstages her, apparently for no other reason than to prove that every dog has its day.

Barbara's expression is not tortured, as Mantegna would have portrayed it. After flagellation, burning by torches, and sledge-hammering, her body sustains only minor bruises, this in contrast to the realism, when suspended upside-down, of her hair hanging toward her halo. For the decapitation, in a faded scene opposite the altar, the artist shows her in the raiment of a queen.

June 22-24, 1991. The sign "ADAGIO" at the gate of the Villa d'Este in Cernobbio seems to establish the languorous pace of life inside. Reception treats us as VIPs, not required to sign papers, show passports, surrender plastic cards for impress. The supreme luxury of the hotel is the total absence of TV. A smaller convenience is that toilet seats have been designed to accommodate the anatomical differences of the male from the female.

The Villa's plastic swimming pool floats in Lake Como, moored to the hotel dock. To judge by the oiled and tanned, primping and combing young men reclining on its deck, the redistribution of male and female sexual roles among affluent Italians has reached an advanced stage. Outdoor dinner entertainment is provided by water-skiers. Towed by speedboats a hundred or so yards from shore, they glide up a ramp and jump from it without a spill. As lights on the mountain across the water turn on, we follow a lakeside rose-path under magnolia and chestnut trees. A soft, perfumed, still night.

November 15. Milan is the capital of *tartufo bianco,* now in high season. The head-waiter at the Principe di Piemonte brings a sealed glass jar containing a dozen lumps of the misshapen vegetable, removes the moist cloth from the uppermost of them, and with his thin-bladed *tagliatartufi* shaves it over our risottos. The odor, powerfully redolent of humus (and rootling pigs?), lasts longer than the taste.

Also in peak season are the fashion shows: tall, teased-hair mannequins sashay the catwalks for Valentino, Versace, Armani, but we manage to see them only on television.

16. To Castelseprio and Santa Maria Foris Portas (outside the gates), after telephoning the custodian to meet us at the entrance. The lobed-cross, *tricona* church is situated at the top of a low hill, a walk of 500 or so meters on a muddy path through a grove of poplar, oak, and birch. The stillness and sense of remoteness so short a distance from Milan's madding crowds help to explain why, in 1944, partisans hid out here in the partly ruined building, thereby discovering its marvelous frescoes of Joseph's dream and the journey to Bethlehem, the Nativity in which Salome assists the midwife!, the Adoration of the Magi, the Annunciation, the shepherds, and, above the arch, the Etimasia, the empty throne of the Last Judgment. The paintings have been restored (1980-85) since the publications of Kurt Weitzmann's thesis attributing them to a tenth-century Byzantine or Near Eastern artist, and the more convincing studies by Meyer Schapiro, who classifies them as seventh- or eighth-century Lombardian.

The church could hardly be simpler: a flat roof over the center, horseshoe arches, coarse masonry, no vaults or niches, and it is so small that the modest tomb of G.P. Bognetti, one of the first to examine the frescoes, nearly fills the right lateral apse. The ceiling of the main apse has been rebuilt, but below it some of the original wood beams are still in place. According to the Soprintendenza Archeologica's mimeographed script, evidence of frequentation during the Bronze and Iron ages was discovered in the church, which explains why part of the floor is a planked-over excavation. Whereas the Castrum Sibrium, in the same archeological zone, is mentioned in the itinerary of a seventh-century traveler from Ravenna, no reference to the church has come to light.

Schapiro attributes the "deeply felt, passionate frescoes" to a much greater master than the artists of the Joshua Roll in the Vatican and those of the Paris Psalter, both of which, to an extent, they resemble. He cites the "command of atmospheric perspective, landscape, architectural form, light and shade," the "rhythmic sweep of line," and the naturalness of the shepherd's dog in the Nativity. And he draws attention to the light on the beard, hair, and face of the iconic Christ, the only frontal head in the frescoes, forming "more active and varied patterns" than the light in the Roll and Psalter. In the Nativity, he goes on, "the arms of the Cross at Christ's head project beyond the translucent nimbus, suggesting the sun and its rays rather than the Crucifixion." And he invokes the metaphors of the Pseudo-Dionysius the Areopagite, the Syrian mystic: "essences emanating from a superessence," and "blinding blissful implosions of dazzling rays." I, for one, feel the painter's ardor despite the dark, damp, marrow-freezing church and the drizzling, dispiriting autumn morning.

At nearby Castiglione Olona, the custodian of the Gothic Baptistry of the Collegiata is a hospitable young ordinand who will accept no perks. Masolino's frescoes (1431-35) can be glimpsed only during intervals of scarcely a minute, after coins inserted in slots bring electric light, but the blaze of color between the blackouts is worth the frustration. After working in San Clemente in Rome (the Chapel of St. Catherine, in which her wheel is shown in two different stages of construction), and with Masaccio in the Brancacci Chapel, Masolino accepted a commission from Cardinal Branda di Castiglione, who was born here, to decorate the Baptistry with frescoes depicting the life of The Baptist. A new biography of the Cardinal identifies him as the second figure from the left in the scene of Herod's feast. In view of the clerical robes, who else could it be, though scholars argue that no dignitary of the church would agree to be portrayed in such company? The tradition that Leon Battista Alberti is a member of the audience in the scene of John hailing Christ has also been challenged, not because no face resembles the one in his self-portrait medal, but on grounds that the painting is more decorative than Alberti prescribes. Yet another of Alberti's dicta was that historical pictures may include famous faces.

At the feast, Salome sits opposite Herod. In an inspired interpretation of the next scene of this sequential narrative painting, she is dressed as a bride, with flowers in her hair, which does not stop her from kneeling before Herodias and, to the horror of the female attendants, dumping John's head in her lap. Though perspectively inaccurate, the receding arcade that stretches behind this scene expands the depth of the Baptistry many times. The picture of John looking out of his barred prison window is painted on a real window embrasure, the actual source of light for both the room and the fresco. The other most strikingly conceived and executed scenes are of John rebuking Herod and Herodias for their incest; of the Baptism itself, in which the river Jordan seems to be flowing from the upper apse into the room, until the font becomes visible; and of Rome, the new Jerusalem, in which Trajan's Column and the Pantheon are conspicuous landmarks. The one-room museum next door displays three enormous parchment music manuscripts.

17. The exhibition *Le Muse e il Principe,* at the Poldi-Pezzoli in Milan, contains a model *studiolo,* that creation of mid-*quattrocento* Ferrarese Humanism, the private retreat in a country palace in which the Duke could listen to music while savoring his collection of antique art. Here are illuminated manuscripts, some of the earliest printed books, a gilt tabernacle of the Madonna and Child; numerous medallion portraits including six of Leonello d'Este by Pisanello; hand-colored tarot cards; crystal flasks with Venetian enamel mounts; small boxes with plaster appliqués of classical subjects; and Mantegna's *Adoration of the Shepherds* from New York, this last for the reason that its wattle fence and gourd were Borso d'Este's preferred heraldic devices. The reconstruction of Borso's *studiolo* at Belfiore, the prototype for those of Isabella d'Este at Mantua and Federigo da Montefeltro at Urbino, is the centerpiece of the show.

The treasure-filled vitrines are placed close together, forming walls and corridors with the intention of recreating the intimacy of a private retreat. Also on exhibition are four of the six panels that once adorned the Belfiore, all of them carpentered from the same tree and decorated with portraits of Thalia, by Michele Pannonio, and of Terpsichore, Erato, and Uranio, by a collaborator of Cosmè Tura. Thalia, holding a vine with pendant grape cluster and sheaths of wheat protruding from her hair-do like feathers in an American Indian's headband, is more goddess of agriculture than Muse. Her mincing expression, too-heavy left arm, too-small and too-high breasts, and over-opulent, jewel-encrusted throne are unappealing; if I had come across the picture in a provincial museum, I would have attributed it to a Mannerist of a century later. Moving on to the Jacopo Bellini, the Rogier van der Weyden, and the no less marvelous portraits by anonymous painters of Francesco I Sforza and Bianca Maria Visconti, we climb the stairs to see Holbein's Luther and Frau, on loan from Basel.

August 4, 1998. In October 1959, when I drove with the Stravinskys from Bologna to Milan, most of the tortuous 25-kilometer climb from the autostrada to bleak, romantic Canossa was on a dirt road, without fences or guide railings. We encountered no other car on it, and I do not remember seeing a habitation, barn, or shed. The pinnacle was covered with snow, as can be seen in Mrs. Stravinsky's home-movie, but no matter, since at that time the ruins of the mountain fortress were fenced off. Today the turnoff road, just west of Reggio Emilia, has been widened, is solidly paved all the way, and abutted in two places by restaurants. The footpath to the summit of the castle is a broad stone staircase, and the ground at the start has been levelled for a parking lot. The flow of ascending and descending people is surprisingly large for a historic site so remote, and the majority of them seem to be German, despite Bismarck's promise to the Reichstag (in 1872): *"Nach Canossa gehen wir nicht."* A small museum displays objects found in the Monastery of St. Apollonio (the patron of dentists), which was protected by the original fortifications.

The abrupt rise of the Apennines from the Lombardian plain always astonishes me. Steep from the very beginning, quite suddenly deep ravines gape on the sides of the road. The hills that pile up behind hills, many of their peaks extended by towers and castles, are more varied in shape than in other mountain ranges. Great vistas open up at every turn, and rock formations change, from quaternary pebbles and sand at the lowest elevations to cretaceous clay at the highest, the latter forming the base under the rock of Canossa, or so my geology- and orography-minded son tells me. Unexpectedly, since Canossa is on the second ridge of the Apennines, the temperature is as warm as it was on the plains below.

The Castle of Canossa, bastion of the Countess Matilda of Tuscany, is the site of the submission of the Holy Roman Emperor Henry IV to Pope Gregory VII in January 1077, an event that seems to have marked the beginning of the Guelph and Ghibelline wars; Matilda's second husband, a certain "Guelph of Bavaria," was an opponent of the German Emperor. But she, rather than the Pope or Emperor, is the central figure in the conflict, partly because, as a close relative of Henry IV, she is credited with having induced him to bow to the Papal authority, thereby lifting the decree of excommunication against him.

Born in Mantua in 1046, Matilda is perhaps the most famous female between Augustine's mother and Joan of Arc, whom, as a warrior and leader of armies, she much resembles. William the Conqueror unavailingly sought her hand in marriage to his son Robert, and on her reburial in St. Peter's, Bernini designed the sarcophagus. More importantly, she is the lady who answers Dante's question as to how there can be wind in a place free from all atmospheric changes, as Statius assured him was the case in Purgatory — she tells him that its origin is in the movement of the universe — and who, after Virgil's departure and before the appearance of Beatrice, acts as Dante's guide in the Terrestrial Paradise. In fact, she leads him through the river Lethe to the place where Beatrice is standing on the opposite shore. (Dante scholars do not unanimously accept the identification of his "Matelda" with the Countess of Tuscany, but the "no's" have not been able to provide a credible alternative candidate.)

On the death of Matilda's father, Pope Boniface III, she inherited his lands and immense wealth. But a few years later, at age eleven, she was forced to marry Goffredo the Hunchback, by whom she had a short-lived child. Fleeing Goffredo, whom she eventually succeeded in having poisoned, she returned to Canossa. Meanwhile, hostilities between the Papacy and the Holy Roman Empire escalated. In 1073 Hildebrand of Soana, elected Pope Gregory VII, reasserted the supremacy of the Church over the Empire. Henry IV responded by convening an assembly of German bishops at Worms to depose the Pope, on charges of his adulterous relations with Matilda. Gregory excommunicated Henry and, accompanied by Matilda, set out for Germany. In Mantua, learning that Henry had arrived in Turin with an army, they retreated to her Castello at Canossa.

On Saturday, 26 January 1077, despite snow and weather so cold that the Po River was frozen, Henry reached the gates of Canossa "in humble attire and barefooted." The actual course of events seems to have been that he arrived on the 25th, the day celebrating the conversion of St. Paul, and was admitted to a sequestered place within the walls, where he fasted and prayed while an agreement was mediated between his representatives and Matilda. When the Emperor emerged, after three days, and petitioned for a pardon, the sacraments were administered to him by the Pope.

Only a year later the situation was reversed. Henry rebelled again and was again excommunicated, but this time he appointed an antipope, Clement III. Henry conquered Rome, drove Gregory from the city — he died in Salerno shortly after — and Matilda found herself alone defending the Papacy. She then won a decisive battle against Henry, and killed his son Corrado by poisoning. This paragon of virtue then had her last husband, Zenobio, beheaded, in spite of which all of the literature is strongly biased toward, not to say worshipful of, her.

A gift shop beneath the great rock sells a de luxe edition of the Latin poem *Vita Mathildis,* composed between 1112 and 1115 by a Benedictine monk Donizo, abbot of the St. Apollonio monastery. The manuscript illuminations reproduced in the volume are admirable as color and art but confusing as history. One of them from the Vatican Library, for instance, shows Matilda, not Gregory, on the throne, and Henry, with only one knee bent, dressed not as a penitent, but wearing regal raiments of the same design and the same gold, green, and blue as Matilda's. The Abbot of Cluny, a well-documented witness to the 1077 act of submission, is present in all portrayals of the scene, and always comfortably seated.

The panorama from the crest of Canossa includes five or six other fortress towers at lower altitudes, thick forests, eroded slopes and valleys, and the plains of Lombardy. After winding back down the mountain, and trying to fast-forward our perception of historical time, we visit Modena, best known today for its balsamic vinegar, which the Lords of Canossa sent to the Ghibelline emperors in a silver keg, and as the birthplace of Fallopio, the *cinquecento* physiologist, Bononcini, Handel's rival in London, and Luciano Pavarotti. The fields between Reggio and Parma are stacked with bales of hay rolled up like carpets and wrapped in plastic.

To my tastes, the Romanesque Baptistry and Duomo of Parma are among the greatest treasures of Western civilization, and Benedetto Antelami's sculptures there of the archangels, and of David and Habakkuk, the supreme masterpieces of the art before Ghiberti and Donatello. The controversial restoration of the Baptistery has been completed since my last visit, but I have no quarrel with it, and I now think I prefer the façades of both buildings even to those of Pisa, the slanting uppermost third arcade of the Duomo to the four piled-up, flat-based ones of the Pisan.

After the harsh, gloomy, mountaintop Middle Ages, what pleasure Parma is, its tree-shaded avenues, elegant domestic architecture, wrought-iron street lamps. Alva is reading the *Charterhouse* for the third time and wants to see the actual *trecento certosa*, but that will have to wait.

Florence, Perugia, Rome

Florence

The first two visits to Florence were undertaken by myself, Alva and Alexander, the first primarily to help rehabilitate me after the implantation of my prosthetic aortic valve. Step-climbing in Italy would be the test, and I mounted the staircases in Caprarola, which I could not have done at all before my surgery, with ease. We came by air from London to Venice and by train from there.

April 23, 1989. The Villa La Massa at Candeli, mentioned in D.H. Lawrence's letters as an appealing residence, is now a restored, modern-convenienced fifteenth-century hunting lodge on the south bank of the Arno below San Miniato al Monte. It is also a combination of Palazzo and Fawlty Towers. We reserve a table at 7 in its "Verrocchio" restaurant, but at that hour are told to wait until 8, at which time the manager calls, apologizes that the chef is not ready, and asks us to spend a few minutes at the bar. The Massa's nine other guests, formally dressed Germans, are already there and, having been told the same thing, plainly annoyed. At 8:30 we stroll by the cypresses and the river, which at this altitude and in freshet season sounds like a rushing Rocky Mountain stream. Eventually, at about 9:30, the high-vaulted Gothic restaurant opens and a maître d'hôtel in an orchestra conductor's *frack* takes our orders in German; or, rather, enumerates the limited selection of available dishes, prices unlisted, or unascertained, or unknown. A piano, semitone flat in the upper register, loudly serenades us with sentimental German songs.

24. On the way to Arezzo we stop at the hill town of Poppi, from whence the exiled Dante wrote to the Ghibelline Henry VII, urging him to "hew" the rebellious Florentines "like Agag, in pieces before the Lord." Piero's Arezzo frescoes could be seen only from ladders or scaffolds placed in the choir, which is cordoned off, limiting our view to an impossible angle. The low-wattage lights are turned on for only two-minute periods, the pay-station telephones with recorded lectures distract, and the pushing throngs thwart any attempt at more than a few sideways glimpses of the miraculous pictures.

At Orvieto, we join a queue in front of the cathedral, only to find that Signorelli's *Last Judgment* in the San Brizio Chapel is still under wraps and behind restorers' scaffolding. On a back street a tabby cat sleeps curled up in a doorway next to a beldame shelling peas. A monk strolls by, brown robe belted with rope, bare feet in sandals.

South of Orvieto the green undulating landscape is broken by tufa-colored towns growing out of, or mortised into, the summits of hills, hard lines of massive stone fortifications, medieval grafted on to Roman grafted on to Etruscan. The exit road for Caprarola is lined by cane brakes, groves of hazelnut, and haystacks "fluted" into polygons with wig-like thatching on top. The Zuccani brothers' frescoes in Vignola's Villa for Alessandro Farnese contain a portrait of the great architect and leafy landscapes.

From the gap-toothed, crenellated walls of Viterbo we go to Villa Lante della Rovere. Where I wandered alone thirty five years ago, hundreds of people, many of them carrying cameras and light meters, wait in the adjoining park to be admitted in batches for claustrophobic 45-minute periods, during which the iron gates are locked, and exiting, as well as entering, is forbidden. Inside, the watercourse, a feat of hydraulic engineering, passes through five terraces top to bottom, each with progressively larger sculpture-filled fountains. The parterre, Four Moors Fountain in the center, is a symmetrical arrangement of gravel paths outlined by boxwood in green curlicues and volutes. The gray stone statues of giants, dolphins, a Pegasus, and the links of a descending chain of small pools, are enhanced by moss and green-and-gold fungus. With its ancient oaks, tall cypresses, hedges, its view of medieval Bagnaia below and of the valley beyond, this surely is the most splendid of all Renaissance gardens. Montaigne, on a visit in 1580, concurred, but Carlo Borromeo thought it a great waste of money. How odd that this part of Italy should have Shakespearean resonances! Duke Orsini, who stood behind Queen Elizabeth at the first performance of *Twelfth Night,* lived a few kilometers away, while Francesco Maria della Rovere himself, a *condottiere* in the service of Venice at the time of his death (1538), was believed to have been murdered by a Gonzaga pouring poison in his ear.

April 30, 1992. Our rooms in the Grand Hotel overlook the Arno, where boys are swimming in what must be bone-chilling water.

The trompe l'oeil ceiling in the Ognissanti is so real that one expects the figures "outside" the painting to fall. At Santa Maria Novella, we are able to see Masaccio's Trinity fresco only because of the powerful lights being used to photograph it for an art-book. The Ghirlandaio frescoes behind the altar are lighted only periodically and very briefly, and the odor from the tightly packed bodies in front of them is more powerful than our desire to peek at the paintings.

2. Florence is loud and noxious from vespas and autos in narrow streets, and Florentines, waiters and taxi drivers especially, are ungracious at best. But then, the city is seething with tourists, all of them complaining about "tourists," and they outnumber natives thirteen to one. The graffiti on a wall of the Via degli Strozzi Banca d'America reads: *"Bush L'Assassino De Bambini Irachi."* After jostling in the white-sneaker herd in front of the Duomo, we escape to Fiesole, where the view of the Val d'Arno from the convent of S. Francesco is almost worth the highway-robber fare. Stravinsky claimed to have had a seismic religious experience here in 1925, during a detour on his return to Genoa and Nice from Venice.

I would like to examine the Lucca Choirbook, that treasure of illuminated music manuscripts from fifteenth-century Bruges, given to Lucca Cathedral by the banker Arnolfini, whose face, as rendered by Jan van Eyck, may be the most familiar from all Europe of the period. The thirty or so bifolia that survive from a codex of some 300 folios are in the Lucca

State Archive, but no one there has heard of it and my accreditation is questioned. We go instead to see the controversially restored tomb of Ilaria del Carretto.

The Villa Puccini in tawdry Torre del Lago is at the end of the Via Giacomo Puccini, which is intersected by side streets called Via Schicchi, Via La Rondine, Via Tosca. The home of the century's most popular serious composer, on the shore of Lake Massaciuccoli, is a museum in which music manuscripts are exhibited side by side with the composer-*cacciatore*'s guns. Not on view is the letter Puccini wrote in June 1922 to "Dear Margit," on Ruegen in the Baltic, saying that "if Stravinsky pleases, the sun of Puccini has gone down."[1] The view of the lake and, on the far shore, of the gashes and scars of the quarries on Carrara Mountain, is partly blocked by the "Butterfly Ristorante and Bar." The nearly life-size bronze statue of the maestro all but conceals the handsome face between the fedora and the upturned coat collar.

The snow-white cathedral of Pisa is closed, but the exterior is even more beautiful, the four registers of façade, arcades, the twelfth-century columns, cornices, and capitals with sculptures of lions, dragons, humans, and the tall bays with lozenges, circles, and inlays, reminiscent of Islamic art. The bronze reliefs in the doors, though only half as old as the beginnings of the basilica (1064), are difficult to make out, apart from the disconsolate rhinoceros and the quizzical stag. In contrast, the restored bronze relief sculptures in Bonanno Pisano's twelfth-century Porta S. Ranieri on the south side are distinct in all twenty-four panels. Bonnano's Sicilian (Monreale) background is apparent in the turbaned prophets between palm trees, and in the Baptism in which a dozen rolling waves cover the Christ from head to feet like a blanket.

The road out of Pisa, from the great white buildings on open expanses of green, passes a still-active U.S. military base (half a century after the war!).

1. He had called on Stravinsky in his sanatorium in Neuilly, ten days after hearing the *Sacre*, and was on good terms with him at a later date than this letter, even inviting him here.

Is this where Ezra Pound was caged? Four World War II U.S. prop planes are parked at the edge of the modern airport nearby.

4. To San Gimignano and Siena, the former totally tourized (the main attraction is a *"Museo Di Criminologia Medioevale Strumenti Di Tortura"*), the latter, great city of the Piccolomini and Aldobrandeschi, slightly less so, but its hills are steeper and its crowds denser.

April 18, 1994. The Villa San Michele, Via di Doccia, Fiesole, a monastery converted into a hotel, lacks elevators, TV, and light stronger than low candle power. The rooms are cell-like, and the canopied bed, the museum-piece dark-oak desk, the rusted iron window bolts date from the *cinquecento.* The W.C. is equipped with a quiver of long-stemmed wooden matches to dispel emphytic odors, a down-to-earth touch. If the rain were to stop, the garden, the cloisters, woodland walks, and the views of the *viale* from the loggia, might be worth half the price. The concierge's brochure indexes Florentine art by subject matter: Adorations, Annunciations, Circumcisions, Crucifixions, Descents from the Cross, Entombments, Journeys of Magi, Last Suppers, Resurrections.

19. At Monterchi, the Madonna del Parto has been removed from its cemetery chapel to a bleak room in a new building on the main street where it is exhibited with photos, diagrams, and a video of the stages of its disastrous restoration. Not merely the color but also the drawing, as shown in the 1911 photos of the Madonna's crooked finger, is grotesquely wrong.

Luckily for us, an exhibition devoted to Luca Pacioli at Borgo Sansepolcro draws off some of the Piero traffic. The steep road to Caprese Michelangelo, the artist's birthplace, commemorated by a modern museum at the top, crosses both the Tiber, a *torrente,* and the Arno, a *fiume.* Chiusi La Verna, much higher still, is a haunting and, in its rock formations and trees, other-worldly place, so close to heaven that on the crag where tradition locates Francis receiving the stigmata—surely the picture of it in Uccello's

Thebaid in Florence was painted from "life"—our ears crackle and our hearts pound. The monastery at Vallombrosa displays a plaque commemorating John Milton's stay in 1638, his description of the Etrurian Shades in *Paradise Lost* supposedly having been inspired by the surrounding woods, but Milton scholars today contend that he did not visit or even see the place.

20. To our inexpert eyes, and in spite of complaints that the colors look like Day-Glo, the Brancacci Chapel restorations are successful, but the only other viewer during our forty minutes here is a woman who never removes her sunglasses. The area of Masaccio's *Saint Peter Healing with His Shadow* has been identified as S. Felice in Piazza, and the cut-stone building as the Palazzo Vecchio on its Via della Ninna side. But the perspective seems askew between the foreground figures, the most memorable of them the kneeling old man with crossed arms, and the windows of the nearer overhanging house. In the *Raising of the Son of Theophilus,* the five figures to the left do not have enough feet to go around, Filippino Lippi having overlooked the requirement in the case of the Carmelite friar. Among the real people portrayed in the picture are Botticelli, Pollaiuolo, Lippi himself, and the father of the historian Guicciardini, but the features of the one identified as Cardinal Branda are utterly unlike those of the Branda in Masolino's Castiglione Olona portrait.

Perugia

I had shared a concert with Stravinsky in Perugia in October 1962, a memorable one, since he heard his 1910 instrumentation of Beethoven's The Flea *for the first time ever. The reason for the 1994 visit was the same as that for a visit in September 1960: the impossibility of finding lodgings in Rome, blamed in 1960 on the occupation of the city by the Olympic Games.*

September 19, 1994. The Brufani Hotel brings back memories of dinners with the Buitoni (pasta) and the Perugina (chocolate) tycoons, not here but in their homes. To judge by the absence of any renovation in the Brufani in the intervening third of a century, we assume that hotels in the smaller Umbrian towns are also not likely to have been upgraded since Smollett and Hazlitt griped about them.

20. The huge basilica of Santa Maria degli Angeli in the Tiber valley below Assisi was built to enclose the tiny church of the Porziuncola, whose walls are traditionally reputed to contain a stone from the tomb of the Virgin. Saint Francis died here in 1226, after, but not as a result of, throwing himself naked into the rose garden outside his small cell. His blood is supposed to have left a perpetual scarlet stain, but the roses bloom every spring, and the thorns have disappeared (miraculously).

All but a few of Assisi's pilgrims today are Japanese, which might have amused Goethe, who refused even to look in the direction of the double-decker basilica but went out of his way to visit the Temple of Minerva and the house of Propertius. On the lawn before the entrance to the upper level, flower-beds form the letters *"PAX."* Standing next to us, an old man who cannot read asks his granddaughter what they mean. She looks at us, embarrassed, before saying *"pace."*

On the ancient approach to Todì, one wall is the back of a Roman amphitheater. In the years since the superstrada bypassed the town, brigands have preyed on travelers on the narrow older road, which passes the beautifully domed Santa Maria della Consolazione begun by Bramante. The piazza, the highest Roman forum in Umbria, is the only level ground in this otherwise steeply canted city. Its southeast corner is formed by mer-loned but otherwise severely unornamented palazzi. (Square crenellations signify Guelph sympathies, the swallowtail Ghibelline; Todì was continually switching allegiance from one to the other.) The thirty or so steep steps of the dramatic stairway from the street to the first floor of the Palazzo Capitano are without railings, which means for me, nowadays and in however many or few later ones, that I can climb them but would be nervous about the descent. San Fortunato, repository of the bones of Jacopone da Todì, author of the *Stabat Mater* (and of a line in *The Waste Land*), is high above the street, but the zigzag paths up to it are flanked by protective hedges. Its much-praised Gothic interior attracts me less than the Romanesque interior of the Duomo (more but broader steps). Vignola designed the episcopal palace in the piazza, the younger Sangallo the Cesi palace next to it. Paolo Rolli, Handel's librettist at the Haymarket in London, spent his last years in the Cesi.

Todi would be an ideal starting place for a first visit to Italy: Medieval, Renaissance, and Baroque are harmoniously juxtaposed, all three in stunning examples. Tacitus and Pliny the Younger lived and wrote here. Pliny the Elder praised the local wine, Benvenuto Cellini drank it to cure an illness, and, as sampled in the Brufani, it induces deep slumber.

The nearby ruins of Carsulae, on the road to Spoleto, are presumed to have inspired Browning's *Love Among the Ruins:* "the site once of a city great and gay/(So they say)/Where a multitude of men breathed joy and woe/Long ago."

21. Perugia's Sant'Angelo is a circular, Pantheon-like fifth-century church whose roof rests on a ring of Corinthian columns. It is set in a lush green lawn on which scores of student couples are amorously entwined.

At Cortona, olive groves and vineyards extend up the hillside to the city walls. The treasure in the Museo dell'Accademia Etrusca, whose members included Montesquieu and Voltaire, is the 16-wick bronze tomb-lamp, decorated by satyrs and winged sirens, visible from all angles, thanks to an ingenious arrangement of mirrors. The showcases display a paleo-Christian glass chalice, ancient votive statuettes, fifteenth-century ivories, and Pisanello medals. One room here is incongruously devoted to the Futurist painter Gino Severini, a native son (and friend of Stravinsky). The city's greatest paintings are in the Museo Diacesano: Signorellis, Pietro Lorenzettis, Angelico, but only one by Sassetta, a native, for whom one must go to London.

We return to the Brufani by way of Lake Trasimeno, once Imperial Rome's naumachia for mock naval battles. Leon Battista Alberti tried to raise a sunken ancient ship here, a feat carried out successfully by Mussolini's engineers in the 1930s. Its hazy blue waters are famed for the flavor of its eels, irresistible to Pope Martin V, who died from eating too many of them, the Sixth Deadly Sin.

After Hannibal's victory at Trebbia, a tributary of the Po, 60,000 Gauls defected to his side. In the spring of 217 B.C., after spending the winter on the transpadane shore, he crossed the Apennines with the hope of gaining Etruscan support as well. The expedition lasted only four days, partly because rains had flooded the middle Arno and turned the land into marshes. The fording took a heavy toll of his army and of Hannibal himself, leaving his right eye blind from exposure: the "one-eyed commander," Juvenal calls him. According to Cato the Elder, he now rode his last surviving elephant, "Surus" ("Syrian"). Having outmaneuvered the Romans at Arezzo and Cortona, Hannibal hid his Carthaginians in the hills north of Trasimeno, keeping his Numidian and Iberian troops visible in the Sanguinetto basin as a lure. Flaminius took the bait and advanced through Borgetto to attack them, whereupon the Carthaginians swooped out of the hills, fell upon the Romans from their rear, and annihilated 15,000 of them. (Most of Hannibal's 1,800 casualties were Gauls.)

Mass cremation pits containing ashes and charred bones indicate that he feared a plague, but Carthaginian skeletons with all their teeth have been disinterred as well as the tombs, yielding cataphracts as well as bones, of thirty Carthaginian nobles.

22. Spello, the most appealing of the Umbrian hill towns, is still enclosed by Roman walls with five gates, the main one bearing the legend *"Splendidissima Colonia Julia Hispellum"* over the arch. According to Spellan tradition, a phallus carved in the inner wall of the Porta Urbica does not celebrate Orlando's (Roland's) amatory prowess but the range and perfect arc of his *actus mingendi.* Spello is noted for its restaurants and truffled cooking, its steep, winding, and narrow streets—all one-way only—its Roman towers and amphitheater. A *Vocabolaro del Dialetto Spellano,* compiled by Nicoletta

Ugoccioni and published here last year, contains, at a thumb-through guess, 20,000 words in current usage—by a population of only 6,800.

At Spoleto, the Lippi frescoes in the Cathedral apse have been restored, but I like them, and the city, a lot less than Montaigne did, or Dryden, Goethe, Byron, Shelley, James Fenimore Cooper, H.C. Andersen, and Gian Carlo Menotti. In the church of SS. John and Paul, a fresco depicting the Martyrdom of Thomas à Becket is thought to have been painted shortly after his death, in 1170.

Poplars and dark green oaks grow on the slopes of Montefalco, vineyards and barley fields in the valley. We compete with a party of Dutch tourists for a peek at Benozzo Gozzoli's newly cleaned St. Francis cycle, in which the walled cities, towers, landscapes are virtually the same as today's reality. Scholars still cannot agree about how good a painter he is, and the restorations do not help. The main room of the former church has been turned into a museum of dressmakers' dummies clothed in late-nineteenth-century gowns with trailing skirts. Frederick II's double-headed eagle seems overly menacing in this sleepy town, especially since he did *not* conquer it.

23. Perugia's Palazzo dei Priori is one of the great buildings of the world, but the *passeggiata* on the Corso Vanucci, which extends from the parapets next to the Brufani to the entrance, is impenetrably dense, and at present the marble fountain with Pisano's three bronze nymphs is invisible under restorers' wrappings.

24. By 9:30 P.M. the audience head-count for the announced Vivaldi-Geminiani concert in the Teatro Moriacchi comes to only five, with no sound of even one warming-up musician floating in from offstage. We retreat to a restaurant.

25. At Gubbio, en route to Urbino and Venice, I think of the ordeal, on a rainy date in September 1960, of climbing those steep streets with the

Stravinskys, and, then, bedraggled as we were, of having to return to Borgo San Sepolcro, the forward road being impassable. Since then, the place has become famous for the Nobel Prize-winning discovery (Physics) by Luis Alvarez that the iridium content in a layer of clay found here was too large to be anything but the result of a meteor impact. But in 1960 the countryside was still as wild as in Sassetta's painting of St. Francis subduing the wolf, with the circle of crows above.

At Urbino, tractors replace the yoked pairs of white oxen that I remember in the fields below Urbino, where tourist buses now clog the streets, and their passengers the stairs and loggias of the Ducal Palace. Piero's *Flagellation,* without frame, and *Madonna di Sinigallia,* both much smaller than I remember them, have been moved to a sunless corner and placed so far behind a cordon as to require binoculars. Uccello's well-lighted *Profanation of the Host* is anti-Semitic by any definition and should be shown only on request. The worst of it is that the great painter amplified the gory story after accepting the commission from a confraternity dedicated to the Eucharist. The narrative begins in Paris at Easter 1290, when a Jewish moneylender persuaded a Christian woman to give him her wafer after a Sunday communion service. When he pricked the host, it began to bleed, but remained intact, as it did when nails and a spike were hammered through it. When he boiled it, however, it was transubstantiated into a crucifix, whereupon the Jew was arrested and burned at the stake. His family then converted to Christianity, and a church at Saint-Jean-en-Grève was consecrated to venerating the mutilated relic. Uccello shows the Christian woman hanged and the wife and children of the Jew burning with him.

Near the exit to Padua on the superstrada, neon signs flash not only the day, month, and year, but also the hour and minute.

Rome

Arriving in Rome from Bangkok at the end of January 1990, I experienced a sense of euphoria at the sight of the umbrella pines, the perfect architectural proportions of an old farmhouse, the ruins of a medieval tower. We spent most of our time in the city simply recovering from the flight and adjusting to the change. But we did see Caravaggio's St. Matthew *triptych in San Luigi dei Francesi, or as much of it as possible in the thirty-second installments purchased by inserting coins that slowly switch on the ceiling lights. Alva and I were back in the city in May 1992 on our way to Magna Graecia, of which I knew little more than Paestum, visited with Stravinsky in 1959. My objective in 1995 was to see the Villa Giulia, which had been closed for many years. In April 1954 the Stravinskys and I explored the Etruscan tombs and their frescoes systematically, going almost daily to Tarquinia and the other great sites in a car provided by the Rome Radio, and no less frequently to the Villa Giulia. A madness for things Etruscan was afloat at the time, and the King of Sweden, one of its victims, lived above me on the top floor of the Hassler Hotel at night, but worked in an excavation during his days.*

May 5, 1992. In the Hassler roof restaurant at sunset, a waiter points out the unique views of the great domes and bell towers to an American couple at the next table, but they are impressed only by the Vittorio Emmanuele eyesore. He then tries to interest them in the wine list, but after a puzzled flipping of pages they decide to continue with more vodka, after which the oaths they aim at each other become increasingly vitriolic. Nesting swallows circle over the Trinità dei Monti and the area directly below, sacred to the memories of Poussin, Claude, Piranesi, Juvarra, Corot, Ingres, Berlioz, Mendelssohn, Wagner, Byron, Keats, Shelley, Goethe, Gogol, Stendhal.

6. The exhibition of drawings by *"Raffaello e i Suoi"* at the Villa Medici contains too much work by *"i Suoi,"* variously identified as "followers of," "shop of," "anonymous French," "school of Giulio Romano," but the corridors, staircases, galleries, are rewarding in themselves. The copies by Rubens are remarkable both for their fidelity to Raphael's originals and for the survival in them of the later painter's ebullient personality. But the point of the show seems to be in the demonstration of lighting and climate controls by "Thomson Consumer Electronics."

So, too, pictures by *"i Suoi"* swamp the Caravaggio exhibition at the

Palazzo Ruspoli. Here again, the underlying appeal is in the buzzword "technology," in this case the highlighting of details of pictures during brief blackouts. Maps are provided for routes from the Palazzo to Caravaggios in thirteen museums and churches.

October 17, 1995. The Villa Giulia itself, Vignola's masterpiece, together with its fountains, bowers, and pergolas, is as great an attraction as its artifacts. The "Seven against Thebes" relief and the three gold-leaf plaques from Pyrgi are once again on exhibit. The writing on one of the latter is bilingual, Carthaginian and Etruscan, evidence of trade between the two peoples. (In Etruria, writing, from right to left, seems to have started in the seventh century.) The collections of dice include some with the six numbers incised in Etruscan letters, instead of dots. Some are made of ivory, all are much larger than the Las Vegas kind, and two are "loaded" in the modern sense. We spend most of our time in the first five rooms, whose contents, ninth to fifth centuries, come from the 15,000 tombs uncovered at Vulci. Beyond them, the Apollo of Veio's smiling face and braided hair are mask-like.

The Giulia fosters the impression that Etruscan civilization was Eros-devoted and heavy-drinking. The most popular subjects are satyrs and inebriated figures, and the proportion of vessels used in the consumption of wine—*skyphoi* (drinking cups), *kylixes* (ditto, with stems), bowls, jars, rhytons, psykters (wine coolers: a thermos vase kept within a vase of cold water)—is much greater than that of any container or implement employed in any other activity. One scene picturing a nude girl reclining on a panther skin is remarkably like a *Playboy* centerfold. Here, too, are artifacts from the Temple of Diana at Nemi, the sanctuary of the Golden Bough in the sacred wood beside the Lake of Nemi. They include painted pictures of flutes and lyres, and real ivory plectra for string instruments. The Etruscans were passionate music lovers.

20. A walk on the Gianicolo to S. Pietro in Montorio (with its beheaded body of Beatrice Cenci), partly for the view of the city from the Spanish

Academy, partly to see Bramante's Tempietto, that most beautiful building of the early High Renaissance, which I have visited every time I have been in Rome since 1951. Back on the other side of the river we walk from the Palazzo Farnese to the Campo dei Fiori, San Andrea della Valle, and the Barracco Museum, which has an exhibition from Magna Graecia. With Alva and Alexander, I celebrate, and bemoan, my birthday at "Giorgio's" (truffled risotto and pheasant).

April 28, 1996. The first stop on our Rimini-to-Rome route, Alberti's San Francesco, is closed. This is no great disappointment, since I do not like the exalting of Malatesta in the interior, nor very much like Piero's Sigismondo. The severe façade and the arch, more elegant than Augustus's at the other end of town, are worth the detour. The Rubicon, with its ancient bridge, seems even smaller than when I last saw it.

At Recanati, we are not admitted to the already thronged Leopardi house, and at Loreto the frescoes by Signorelli and Melozzo da Forlì, let alone the Santa Casa, are impossible even to approach because of the crush of pilgrims. (Why did Velázquez, who painted only four religious pictures, come here? And why Montaigne? Descartes's reason is well known, of course, to fulfill a vow to the Virgin for having received the inspiration of analytical geometry, even though he must have realized, as clearly as Noam Chomsky, that Euclidian geometry is innate. Carlo Borromeo's visit, the last fifty miles of the journey on foot, may be attributed to piety and curiosity.) According to Torsellini's *Historia dell'origine e translatione della Santa Casa,* after the Fall of the Kingdom of Jerusalem in 1291, the sacred dwelling was airlifted from Nazareth to Tersato by an angelic host, and, later, from there to Loreto by the same agency. The contemporary archeologist Nanni Monelli contends that the stonework of the Casa is similar to examples found in the Holy Land in the time of Christ, and he claims that the measurements of the structure and of the thickness of the walls fit the place that adjoins Mary's grotto in Nazareth from which it was taken. He also affirms that crosses and graffiti in Aramaic have been found in the Santa

Casa. The transportation is now acknowledged to have been seaborne, the boatmen being returning Crusaders.

The encasement of the Casa—the original protecting church was completed in 1350, the present basilica in 1468—consists of some of the most sumptuous architecture and art in the world. Bramante's marble screen is embellished with low reliefs by Sansovino, Raphael, and Francesco da Sangallo; Bramante and the two Sangallos built much of the sanctuary. Vanvitelli's bell tower is a surprisingly harmonious addition to the Renaissance buildings.

No doubt the suppliants feel uplifted. Their faces suggest a thaumaturgical "happening," but the sight of so many wheelchairs, crippled children, and mentally retarded people disturbs us.

We inquire to no avail about the tomb of Richard Crashaw, appointed *beneficiatus* here by a Cardinal in Rome in 1649, and canon of the church from April of that year until his death in August, after which he was lamented by Abraham Cowley:

Angels (they say) brought the fam'ed Chappel there
And bore the sacred Load thro' the Air.
'Tis surer much they brought thee there.

The views of the valleys and the Adriatic confirm the top quality of angelic taste in real estate.

Like Crashaw after him, Lorenzo Lotto dedicated himself to the religious life. The words *"pittore oblato"* are inscribed next to his name in the Santa Casa register, and, like the poet, he died here. In Berenson's opinion, the *Presentation in the Temple,* Lotto's unfinished last painting, now in the Apostolico, is one of his greatest achievements, as well as "the most modern' picture ever painted by an Italian old master," whatever that means (he mentions a Manet). In my opinion it certifies him as insane: the four invisible legs of the low table in front of the altar end in four bare masculine feet. But then, Lotto's *Annunciation* in the Recanati museum is also crazy: the future Mother of God turns her back on the angelic messenger, and the center of the picture is a frightened cat.

Much of the drive in the snow-mantled Gran Sasso to Rome is in tunnels, and the landscape is the highest (*sic;* not the Tyrolean Alps) and bleakest in Italy. L'Aquila, in the Abruzzi, founded by Frederick II, but better known for the rule of the condottiere Braccio Fortebraccio, is the only significant city en route. The treasure of its Museo Nazionale is the Elephas Meridionalis (from Scopitto), not the skeleton, but a misguided reconstruction of the whole animal. The statue of Caius Sallustus Crispus, who was born at nearby Amiternum and is still readable for his terse, direct style, is academic twentieth-century sculpture at its unbeatable worst. The drive from the Ultima Thule of the Apennines to springtime Rome, to which all roads lead, lasts only an hour. Our room at the Hotel Eden overlooks the gardens behind the Trinità dei Monti and the Villa Medici, which are home to me.

29. The newly reopened Villa Borghese, after thirteen years in restoration, is still not exhibiting the Caravaggios, the Bernini, and Canova. Returning through the Pincio, we shortcut through a secluded area littered with condoms and testifying, evidently, to an orgy.

May 1. A Bank Holiday: absolutely nothing in Rome is open.

Cities

Oslo, Copenhagen, Amsterdam

Oslo

I came to Oslo in December 1975 to conduct Stravinsky's Perséphone, *with Vera Zorina (Mrs. Goddard Lieberson) as* diseuse, *in concerts and in a studio-made videotape. At the time, too, I was writing a critical essay about Munch and wished to see the Munch Museum, which was not yet open when I visited the city in May 1963. I also hoped to see my then three-year-old son, Alexander, in Copenhagen, to which it was necessary to fly in order to transfer to Oslo, but this proved impossible.*

December 1–7, 1975. Seen from my hotel room, the pedestrians in Karl Johansgate seem to be walking as they do in a Munch picture, all at approximately the same pace and without glancing to left or right, though whether they are also silent and grim-looking is impossible to tell in the subfusc of late morning. I am constantly struck here by scenes out of Munch that tend to reclassify him as a realist. The sightless windows in an old house resemble those in *The Red Vine,* the sky evokes the early *Starry Night,* and the blank faces—I have yet to see any of his entirely featureless ones—recall some of his people. Munch-like, too, are the unhopeful heavens that turn deep blue in the early, moonlit afternoons, with, just before the abrupt lights-out, a squirt of cold pink. Some acquaintance with the artist's physical world, and its psychological effects on the inhabitants, are indispensable to an approach to his work, although by virtue of his themes Munch is much more than a regional painter.

The Oslo National Gallery should be visited before the Munch Museum on any itinerary. The older institution owns more of the artist's greatest work, as well as contemporaneous pictures, notably by Hans Heyerdahl, whom Munch admired, and Christian Krogh, whose classes he attended. A visit to the National Gallery reveals that in his beginnings Munch was not an isolated phenomenon, that a related style and recurrent subject matter already existed. His preoccupation with illness and death is less morbid in the context of so many other sickroom and deathbed scenes, the result of the high incidence of tuberculosis in the Christiana of the time. The creaky floors and the gloom of the old building evoke the atmosphere of the artist's early years, and the passionate posturings of the Rodinesque sculptures in halls and on landings are evidence of the sexual repression of a society in which Munch was exceptional only because of his genius.

The Munch Museum is better lighted, offers comfortable seats, and presents its collections in ample, uncluttered space, all of which is in conflict to a degree with the turbulent emotions in the art it exhibits. Graphics are the main attraction, and the lithographs, woodcuts, and drypoints of the same subjects presented together with the paintings of them provide supplements, clues, variations, simplifications. In Munch's case the graphic work is not merely ancillary, only a few of the more than 700 examples on display exactly duplicating paintings. To compare the canvas of *Puberty,* suggested by Félicien Rops's *La plus belle Amour de Don Juan,* with the lithograph, *The Young Maiden,* the same picture executed in the other medium a year later, is to discover that the expression of the nude girl in the lithograph, hands crossed in her lap, increases the erotic element.

The most formidable obstacles in books about Munch are the radical differences between color photographs from volume to volume, as well as between these and the paintings themselves. The white-ish head in blue-ish space in *The Scream* on the cover of Reinhold Heller's monograph is reddish brown in the picture as reproduced inside the book, as well as in the monographs by Thomas Messer and Jean Selz, in whose publications the tones are utterly different. Heller defends the use of black and white for one of his illustrations on grounds that the colors defy the camera. But his verbal descriptions of tints and shades here and elsewhere are even less helpful than distorting photographs. Colors and their relationships are instruments of Munch's composition and essential to the meaning of a painting.

My rehearsals with the Oslo Philharmonic and chorus take place in the Aula, the University's assembly hall, in full view of Munch's *Frieze of Life* murals. With a single exception these pictures face each other on the sides of the rectangular room in symmetrical frames that are part of the architecture. Having seen them only in photographs, I am astonished by their magnitude, by the extent of Max Beckmann's indebtedness to them, and by Munch's debt to Gauguin, especially in the harvesting women and the figure of the girl in *The Chemistry*. The exceptional, unforgettable picture, *The Sun,* stands by itself at the end of the room, behind and above the orchestra. Broken rays of color, like spokes from an aureole, emanate from a white, borealis disk, for which Munch's first sketch was a pillar of naked men climbing toward the light, similar to his lithograph of a pillar of naked women bearing a coffin over their heads. *The Sun* is the most arresting painting from the artist's post-breakdown, rehabilitation period.

The guests' stolid countenances at a post-concert reception provoke the question of whether they conceal tempestuous emotions like those openly portrayed in the National Gallery sculptures. The conversation, at any rate, centers on the scandal of Fru Ø., who has left her husband and eloped with A., the famous director and actor. The gossip about this liaison predicts that it will not last, too many other women having preceded Fru Ø. in what is said to be the actor-director's pattern. Such affairs apparently flourish in this indoors country, where the climate is blamed for driving people to the bedroom and its blankets.

Adventitiously, I am invited to the Holmenskollen home of Fru Ø. and the actor-director. It is next to one of King Olav's lodges, and Fru Ø. tells us that her aunt, His Majesty's resident cook, says that the monarch is so lonely he sometimes comes to the kitchen and dries the dishes for her. After the inevitable aquavit, smoked salmon, and sweet brown goat cheese, I venture into the Munch winterscape in borrowed fur-lined stovepipe boots that might have been designed as gyves for Siberian convicts, though they also help to keep the wearer upright in the fierce sub-Arctic wind. Lacking ear baffles and a face-guard, I retreat indoors after about five minutes.

Copenhagen

My son Alexander first began to visit me during his summer vacations from school in his eleventh year (1983). From then through 1988 he spent most of July and August alone with me in Europe and the United States (Florida, New York, the Hamptons, Santa Fe, Chicago, Minneapolis, Boulder). This tradition came to an end when he left school, and partly because I was spending more time with him in Copenhagen. On an early trip there, the first one described below, I arrived from steaming Bangkok, and promptly caught cold.

June 25, 1984. Windowsill geraniums. Bicycles; the main street has a bicycle lane of its own. Flaxen hair and pigtails, a reminder of the marlok. Cobblestones. Equestrian statues on high pedestals of kings, Frederiks and Christians alternating. Canals. Gulls. Fishing boats, masts, sails, rigging. The eponymous name Hans Christian Andersen. Gleaming spires —one of them twisted like a narwhal's horn—copper roofs, tall gables, and the gold dome of a Russian church. Seventeenth-century Dutch architecture transmuted. Eighteenth-century architecture and brightly colored buildings. The city bespeaks nothing of Berlin but something of St. Petersburg.

The foyer of the Thorwaldsen Museum, housing Brobdingnagian sculptures of humans and horses, resembles the artist's vast studio in Rome, except for the black dandruff (soot) here on high elevation heads, shoulders, backs. The light from the single windows in the centers of the enfiladed small rooms extends to only one object, the wrong one in Byron's case, the risibly Romanticized full figure, seated. Whereas this basks in the comparative glare of the occasional break in the Scandinavian weather, the fine neo-classic head, which he disliked—too much focus on the dimpled chin?—is at the limen of the visible.

The *Three Graces,* smaller than life-size, have a room to themselves.

Their most carefully observed anatomical feature is the buttock contracted by the muscular pull of the weight-bearing leg, though the "bottom line" of its flaccid partner is scarcely less well done. The first-century-B.C. Greek relief of the threesome in the Louvre is more satisfying. There the left leg of the Euphrosyne (?) between Aglaia and Thalia is broken off at the knee, but enough of the femur remains to indicate the full line of the entire raised leg, and the headless bodies of the Greek sculptures are wonderfully differentiated, as Thorwaldsen's are not.

The artist's personal collection of antique erotica is on display in the basement, behind glass and under guard. These cameos, coins, medallions, sculptures, pottery paintings, and a gargantuanly engorged, provolone-like priapus attract more viewers than any opus by the sculptor himself.

The magazine *Copenhagen This Week* advertises more palpable gluteal and mammary forms and virtually guarantees satisfying convulsions; but then, escort-service call-books are as much a part of hotel room furnishings today as Gideon Bibles were in my youth. One of the agencies leasing out "understanding Aphrodites" is "The Little Mermaid." H. C. A. must be twirling in his tomb.

May 1987. To Lejre and Roskilde to see the reconstructed iron-age village, the tumuli with mottes, and the Viking Ship Museum. To protect their fjord, the Roskilde Vikings sank five ships weighted with stones at the entrance to the channel. Discovered in the late 1950s and raised by means of cofferdams, the waterlogged wood was treated with a synthetic wax, and in the course of thirty years the vessels were reconstructed from millions of splinters. The only perfectly intact part is the prow, sleekly carved—Brancusi would have admired it—from a single piece of oak. It resembles an eagle's wing, the curved, overlapping "feathers" diminishing in size from bottom to top. Except for bone needles, everything in the boats, cleats, rivets, strakes, was made of wood. Four of them are of the merchant and cargo class, while the fifth is a long, low, narrow warship, resembling those in the Bayeux tapestry. The museum space is confined, but the viewer regrets not seeing one of the ships mounted with its broad, square sail and clew lines. We leave wondering about the navigators, the men who provided no shelter for themselves and who slept under hides.

The City Museum's Kierkegaard Collection is on the second floor of an attractive eighteenth-century palace. Here are the philosopher's stand-up writing desk, his meerschaum pipes, his engagement ring, the palisander cupboard made for his fiancée, Regine Olsen, caricature portraits, and foreign-language editions of his writings. A model of Copenhagen in 1500 has been constructed in the front garden, a toy town, not surprising in the land of Lego, of steep-sloping thatched-roofed houses, churches, a castle, harbors, moats, canals.

June 7, 1990. Dinner at Krog, beginning with soused herring, takes me back to a lunch here with the Stravinskys in May 1955, before our polar flight to the west coast of Greenland, Winnipeg, and Los Angeles. The menus, in English then, are now in Danish and Japanese only. At Tivoli afterward we watch a Pierrot pantomime, then brave the roller-coasters and a whirling, bronco-busting ride that leaves the young people pallid, and me…well, able to walk unaided, to the evident relief of the attendants who had been nervous about admitting me.

September 26. We walk from the Frederiksberg Gardens to the Glyptotek, a museum of Prehistoric, Roman, Egyptian, Etruscan, and French nineteenth-century art. Gauguin's Danish-period paintings are here, as well as two fine Cézannes and several Degas horse and *danseuses* sculptures, the best, to my mind, of the thirty-odd versions of *The Little Dancer*.

The Lavender Street home of Constanze Mozart and her second husband, the Danish diplomat Georg von Nissen, has become a tourist stop, and the artist Constantin Hansen is perhaps better known as Constanze's godson than for his paintings of Paestum. In the evening, we go to the Royal Theater to see and hear her first husband's *Trylleføjten*. To think that Kierkegaard, Andersen, Bournonville, and Købke, who painted oils on canvas of Thorwaldsen's *Night and Day* reliefs, could have witnessed the opera here on the same day raises the question of whether the culture of any other city of the size, north of Berlin, rivals that of Copenhagen's Golden Age. Tonight's most satisfyingly staged scene is that of the flute-enchanted F.A.O. Schwartz animals—more Lego. But the Danish language blurs the musical articulation. This becomes especially apparent with the Queen of Night's arias, which, sung in German, provide the performance's only true *staccato*. Some of the voices are mismatched, Tamino's, for one, being much too small for the bellowing Papageno's. Perhaps a case could be made that just as the falling seventh is Wagner's "passionate" interval, so Mozart's is the upward major-sixth: F to D in Pamina's scene with Sarastro, C to A in her *"Tamino mein,"* but also in the last chorus of *Figaro,* the slow movement of the *Jupiter,* the beginning of the second movement of the A-minor Piano Sonata, etc., etc.

Danes detest Swedes and suffer from a national sense of inferiority vis-à-vis the large neighboring country. National pride is the favored subject of Danish humor, *viz.* the jokes of Victor Borge and Piet Hein's "Grooks": "Why not let us compromise/About Denmark's proper size/Which will truly please us all/Since it's greater that it's small." Small-country self-congratulation and patriotism pervade conversation here, and the word "Danish" in tourist books precedes every mention of the person, object, or place, no matter how firmly established already. Item: "Denmark's world-famous philosopher Søren Kierkegaard has made Gilbjergstien even more famous, for the reason that the Danish Søren Kierkegaard got his inspiration here." One wonders how far the fame of Gilbjergstien, "alive with sun-tanned people"—sun*lamp*-tanned, surely—extends.

Danes, moreover, bask in the pomp of the monarchy, with its tin-soldier, operetta-like changings of the guard, tattoo ceremonies, mini-parades. Nor have the mitre and crown been completely separated. The salaries of the clergy and the upkeep of the churches are paid by state taxes, and the Lutheran confirmation ritual, while not compulsory, is still observed in state schools. The throne is supported by a socialism sinking under 70 per cent taxes, yet the Queen owns the country's largest properties, including several Royal Palaces. Moreover, she still has the power to appoint the Prime Minister if no clear parliamentary majority has been established in an election, and she must sign every bill into law. Whether the socialism or the monarchy is to blame, young people from working-class families do not aspire to higher educations but only, in this country of high unemployment, to pension-promising blue-collar jobs. Many in the welfare state are content to live on social security and do nothing. The lack of initiative and ambition, the rigidity and inflexibility of the society, are stultifying. True, Danes do not jaywalk or cross a deserted street against a red light in the middle of the night, but this seems less like civic virtue than the force of habituation (read absence of imagination).

The lake-island castle at Frederiksborg, in a landscape of hills and tucks, is a Renaissance-style brick structure with round towers, corbiestepped gables, Gothic windows, and tarnished copper-green roofs. The interior, partly destroyed by fire in the 1850s but restored by a Carlsberg Beer baron, exposes beautiful vaulting and wood-paneling, and a chapel so heavily ornate in the Counter-Reformation manner that it must inhibit the Lutheran services still held here. What do the Danes think of all this gilt, let alone the tour groups of Russians, few of whom can have been abroad before? Frederik II, for whom the castle is named, was the patron of Tycho Brahe, who discovered a supernova even before the invention of the telescope. Nor has modern science been neglected: one of the escutcheons in the chapel is dedicated to Niels Bohr.

Amsterdam

The Dutch Radio had invited me to conduct a concert in the Amsterdam Concertgebouw in April 1988. The program that the orchestra proposed was long and difficult for someone who does not conduct regularly, and who, doing so after a long interval, feels like an out-of-training athlete. My concert was undoubtedly too strenuous for me, not because of the length or the music, but because of unrelated circumstances described below. Together with an experi-

ence in Vienna six months later, it led to my decision to undergo surgery for the replacement of my aortic valve. My son was with me in both cities.

My next trip, in June 1991, was at the request of the Dutch film-maker Frank Scheffer, to publicize the premiere of his documentary, The Final Chorale. *Based on Stravinsky's* Symphonies of Winds, *and scripted by Scheffer and Pay-Uun Hiu, a young musicologist, the film includes an interview with me in my New York apartment. This time I was accompanied by my wife, Alva. We flew to Amsterdam from Vienna.*

April 16, 1988. At the approach of the three-car yellow trams, swathes miraculously open up through the dense bicycle traffic like the Red Sea on another occasion. Pedestrians, too, nimbly sidestep joggers, but no paths are cleared for the gridlocked automobiles on the principal streets and the glass-topped boat-buses in the canals. The motorcycle police are female, not distinguishable as such from a distance because of helmets, goggles, padded jackets, man-size revolvers in hip holsters. At close range lipstick glistens in their rear-view handlebar mirrors, as I note from a taxi that offers a choice of rock-music cassettes.

Tonight the streets are quiet, in harmony with the reflections in the canals of spires, gabled brick houses, bridges. A late stroll: in a block of *maisons mal famés,* couples embrace against walls and loud-voiced pimps in doorways solicit in English.

17. A rainy Sunday; I have never seen so many umbrellas. I dine with my friend the musicologist Elmer Schönberger and an official from the Dutch Radio Orchestra. My Taiwanese room waiter at the Hotel de l'Europe replies to my complaints about slow service and the missing items from my order with "Typical of the West."

18. The drive from Amsterdam to the rehearsal studio at Hilversum might have been designed for a class in plane geometry. The dykes, ditches, bicycle paths, and roads form parallel lines; the polders are perfect rectangles and squares, some with quincuncial arrangements of trees; the roofs of the farmhouses are triangular; and bicycle fellies and hubs are (of course) circles. Hilversum is a town of tall trees, attractive villas, pleasant parks. The orchestra players, more experienced in rhythmically difficult twentieth-century music than those of any philharmonic in the United States, learn my program quickly. But they are susceptible to humor only of the broadest sort, to which they overreact.

The road back to Amsterdam is bordered by fields of tulips, windmills, dunes, and concrete "pill boxes"—German anti-tank fortifications, now vine-covered and preserved as historic monuments. Flocks of baa-ing sheep and dappled cows *à la* Cuyp graze in fields as much as twenty feet beneath the elevation of the canals. We stop to photograph some newborn lambs, but their camera-shy and suspicious mothers shield them, as if we smelled of mint sauce. Whole cities of houseboats float in the Amstel River. Back in Amsterdam, the older streets seem remarkably crooked after the Euclidean countryside.

At Monnickendam, halfway to Edam and near the fens of Markenmeer, Alexander and I eat too much smoked eel at "De Posthoorn," an attractive sixteenth-century tavern.

22. I conduct a four-and-a-half hour rehearsal in the newly reopened red-plush Concertgebouw. However famous its acoustics—a whisper on stage can be heard in the remotest reaches of the balcony—the response of the wind instruments seems late from my position, and the chorus, some fifty yards away and all on one side of the centerpiece organ grilles, is a half-beat behind. Names of composers are embossed on the base of the first tier of loges around the hall, and, comfortingly, "Strawinsky" is the closest to me. "Mozart," "Bach," and "Beethoven" are above the orchestra, and "Mahler" is at the back center beneath the Royal Box near "Debussy" and "César Franck." But what are "Spohr," "Niels Gade," and four Dutch composers of whom I have never heard doing in this company?

At 2 A.M. my son and I awake with cramps and nausea and during the next eight hours take turns in the lavatory. At 10 A.M. I call Jan Zekveldt of the Dutch Radio, tell him we have food poisoning, and ask him to send a doctor. At 1 P.M., weak, groggy, and heavily dosed with paregoric I go to the Concertgebouw for a "radio rehearsal." The worst of the concert, two hours later, is the entrance. The conductor must descend a steep red-carpeted staircase behind the orchestra and from near-ceiling height. Applause begins as he appears and continues until he reaches the podium, thus making him seem to have enjoyed a success before doing anything. I start the concert feeling feeble and scarcely able to raise my arms; more-over, I must reascend and redescend the stairs between pieces. At some point during the Symphony in C adrenaline begins to flow, and the perfor-mances hold together. At intermission, a doctor, waiting for me in the "green room," an attic turret another steep climb above the staircase, says that my pulse is 180.

June 17, 1991. The Pulitzer Hotel amalgamates five contiguous canal-side buildings of different heights and proportions and therefore unaligned floor levels. For this reason the corridors are an obstacle-course of staircases, like Max Escher's puzzle-pictures in which stairs cross, overlap, mysteriously disappear. In every hallway we encounter a bridge of a few steps up and as many, or more, or fewer, down, since they are irregular. The room next-door to ours, which has a view of the Prinsengracht, now with pedal-boat Sunday traffic, is about ten steps lower. In the restaurant, only four tables are on the same plane, and ours, number 4, is perilously close to the steeply spiraling descent to the wine cellar.

The screening of the film is preceded by an interview with me, wittily conducted by Elmer Schönberger, but the questions are largely about my impressions, or memories, of Glenn Gould. The film, like the music, stitches together a number of fragments, cutting back and forth to demonstrate the evolution of the instrumentation, piano to harmonium to winds, to a sketch for violin and viola of what became the flute-clarinet duets; the string combination leaves me thirsting for more. Stravinsky is its star per-former, in excerpts from the 1963 Canadian and 1965 Rolf Liebermann footage of him. Asked to identify a *Noces* sketch, he removes his spectacles, and, face lighting up, begins to sing the music. After reading the text in Russian, he adds, sadly, that like all his possessions when he moved from Europe to California, the book from which he took the song was "lost, probably sold."

Another interview, with Elaine Flipse, is for a film documentary on Arthur Lourié, but having seen him only once, in Tanglewood in 1946, and knowing nothing about him apart from his work as Stravinsky's musical assistant, I am able to contribute little. She says that Lourié was not converted by Maritain, as I had supposed, but had become a Catholic in Russia shortly after his Bar Mitzvah.

We dine (raw herring, ceviche, boiled eel) *chez* Louis Andriessen, the composer, and Jeanette, his companion, a therapist and bass guitarist, in their cozy apartment on the Keizersgracht. The three flights of stairs to his unpainted wood floors are nothing compared to the ladder from there to his studio loft, from which I would have preferred to descend by abseil or slow rappelling. Both hosts speak excellent, if not always idiomatic, English: "savage flowers" means "wild" ones. Tall, with long slender legs supporting a Heldentenor's torso, Louis moves quickly and lightly, and thinks the same way, a twinkling mind. Gentle and considerate, he is also straightforward and wholly his own man. He talks about life as a professor in Buffalo, New York, and about Messiaen's *St. Francis* on which we agree that the orchestral music is interesting, the vocal parts, except for the choral clusters, much less so, and in the case of the protagonist, not at all. Apropos his collaboration on Plato's *Republic* with Robert Wilson, he concedes that "Wilson can be difficult. You say something to him and he does not respond. Two days later he lets you know that he heard you." When I describe the period-instrument exhibition heard last week in Vienna and remark that in America the movement now has more cons than pros, he says, with no rectitude, "I am pro. I like authenticity above all and in all things and I like the difficulty, the struggle of the old horns. Beethoven mustn't sound simple and smooth, just as *Sacre* must not seem effortless. What I most dislike in any form is cynicism," this last apropos Thomas Bernhard, I think, whose plays draw full houses here.

We traipse along the rim of a canal and across it to a second screening of *The Final Chorale*. Like Louis, many of the men in the all-Dutch audience are blue-eyed with red hair and reddish complexions. Some have faces like Escher's in his 1920s self-portrait (in which Escher, in turn, resembles Van Gogh). Louis, if not his music, brings to mind the great old composers, like Sweelinck, and those of the time of Margaret of Austria's Regency, Jacob Obrecht and Johannes Ockeghem (who is portrayed in a miniature of 1523, in Rouen, wearing dark glasses).

Brussels, Bayreuth,
Prague, Vienna

Brussels

I went to Brussels to hear a performance of The Rake's Progress, *hoping to find singers to complete the cast for my forthcoming recording in New York. Disappointed in this, I revisited places that I had known with the Stravinskys. Alva and Alexander were with me.*

April 21, 1992. The four immaculately groomed hasideans who checked through a dozen cardboard packing cases stamped "apple juice" at the Sabena terminal in New York last night seem greatly agitated collecting them at the baggage carousel here. Since apple juice is obtainable everywhere and not worth its weight as hand luggage, one wonders what the boxes really contain. Nerve gas? Another mystery: the black gabardines remain perfectly pressed after the long flight, the locks neatly curled, the hats sportily tilted.

What does Belgium mean to me, my son asks, and I write down what comes first to mind:

> "*L'Esprit Belge*" (Baudelaire). Waterloo. Walloon. Wimpled nuns. Waffles with whipped cream. *Pain au chocolat* and Godiva. Sprouts, endives, *filet de boeuf flamande*. Kermesse. Two hundred and fifty days of rainfall. Fifteen hundred brands of beer and a brewery museum: "Beer-transporters" were a major craft guild in the 1400s, along with "fullers, cordwainers, metal-founders, and retailers of second-hand clothes (*oudekleerkopers*)." Lace. Tapestries, Jan van Tieghem's most famously, woven for the Gonzagas in Mantua. Bike races and walking races. Simenon. Hercule Poirot. Jacques Brel.

Emily and Charlotte Brontë and the *devoirs* they wrote at the Pensionnat Heger. Charlotte's infatuation with Constantin Heger. Verlaine shooting Rimbaud in the Hôtel Liégois. The Van Eycks, Memling, Petrus Christus, Rogier van der Weyden, Bosch, Brueghel, Rubens, Van Dyck, Félicien Rops, Ensor, Art Nouveau (the Stoclet Palace), Surrealism (Magritte, Delvaux, the imaginary mountains of Joachim Patinir's Meuse Valley). Mies van der Rohe. The mystic Jan Ruysbroeck. Jansenism. Josquin Desprez. Dufay. Cipriano da Rore, Adriaan Willaert. Grétry. César Franck. Albert Giraud (*Pierrot Lunaire*). Maeterlinck. Verhaeren. Yourcenar. Henri Michaux. Tenth-century Antwerp. Brabant (*Lohengrin*). The St. Cyprian concentration camp. Paul de Man. Gerardus Mercator.

Brussels taxis accept credit cards, as they would have to do after 10 P.M., from which hour huge supplementary tariffs are extorted, a ten-dollar fare for a ride of less than a mile, and several times that for the supplement.

In the streets around the Hôtel de Ville, restaurants reeking of *pommes frites* are three to four a block. We eat at the Royal Windsor, where the Stanford (California) Alumni Association, class of *c.*1940, is reunioning. The members and their spouses scarcely talk to each other, having long since run out of things to say.

More than one store window here displays toy soldiers, brightly colored in the case of eighteenth-century and Napoleonic uniforms (Bonaparte himself is absurdly tall), olive drab in that of the Waffen SS, sets of which are captioned "Normandy 1944, Repelling The Invaders." Do Belgians think of Americans as their World War II enemies?

Belgians were and still are a musical people. In 1506 the Venetian ambassador, Vincenzo Quirini, wrote that "marvelous tapestries from Brabant, and music, which is undeniably perfect, are the two principal exports of the low countries." Passing the church of St. Nicolas at vesper hour and seeing the door open, we enter as a priest and female acolyte are intoning a chant in parallel-sixth harmony, to which the congregation's responses are remarkably in-tune and rhythmically together. The building, in the *quartier toléré* (red-light district), dates from the tenth century, its Gothic apse from 1381. Nicolas was a patron of merchants.

24. Tonight's *Rake's Progress,* in the red-plush Théâtre Royale de la Monnaie, is a revival of the Hockney-Cox staging sung by a poor-to-competent cast in American English. Dragging tempos and long scene-changing pauses frustrate any sense of momentum, but the stilted language and music of the opening fifteen minutes ground the opus anyway. How could Stravinsky and Auden, admirers of the *in medias res* beginnings of *Figaro, Don Giovanni,* and the *Flute,* offer a preview of the plot as a first scene? "A year and a day hence," indeed.

The Act Two trio is a beautiful piece not quite ruined by Baba's intrusions, but why does Rakewell so feelingly identify Baba to Anne as "My wife"? (The strictly in-tempo and businesslike, but also moving exchange between Tom and Anne at this climactic moment strains the neoclassic aesthetic, but one thinks of the shrieks and carryings-on that a less original composer might have provided.) With the trio, the opera's passionate interval becomes the upward fourth: "O promise the heart" and its imitation in the horn; "Venus, mount thy throne"; "Forgive, forgive Adonis"; "The sun in the west is going to rest." Was Anne Trulove suggested by Dick Tracy's Tess Truehart? What on earth is meant by the line "Let folly purr"?

After the opera we swallow oysters at the Restaurant Scheltema, where, in 1952, following the Royal Command performance of *Oedipus Rex* at the Monnaie, I dined with the Stravinskys and Artur Rubinstein.

25. Less than halfway to the belfries and gabled roofs of the brick city of Bruges, through a pleasant landscape of poplar-lined canals and meadows, the road signs change to Flemish only. Our driver explains that a neo-nationalist movement seeks to overthrow the bilingual tradition on grounds that French was imposed by the Revolution and Napoleon. In 1940, he says, the Occupation discriminated against French-speaking Belgians in favor of the Flemish, whom the Germans regarded as racially and linguistically related to themselves.

In exaggerated contrast to the forsaken streets, desolate canals, and stillness, violated only by "the carillon announcing the death of the hours," as Georges Rodenbach put it in *Bruges la Morte,* the traffic arteries and museums are packed with tourists. Scores of open boats, each with megaphoning guide and thirty or so camera-clicking passengers, follow one another through the waterways only yards apart. Perhaps hinting at the town pipers of the city's great musical past, a flutist on one of the bridges plays Bach's B-minor Sonata, and an older man, music-stand and chair set up on a crowded sidewalk, blows a bass trumpet in what sounds like part of an ancient hoquetus. Forty years ago, the Stravinskys and I were alone here with the Memlings, but that was another world, another life. (Memling's fame and popularity, the art historian Max Friedlander says, have "gained a universal currency almost banal in character, thereby provoking the protest of connoisseurs." Dear me!) The haunting *Virgin and Child* and portrait of the donor are behind glass but can at least be seen close up, unlike Michelangelo's *Madonna and Child,* roped off at an estranging distance and protected by guards and reverential quiet—"No talking," in several languages.

We stop at St. Bavon in Ghent to see the cleaned and restored Van Eycks, but they look too new.

Mallarmé and Huysmans overpraised Rodenbach's novel; the plot is a too simple contrivance, and the language is indigestibly precious ("surcease from sorrow," a sigh "like that of a bubble expiring within a water-flower"), but the author's fetishistic obsession with long female tresses is a curious coincidence, Maeterlinck's Mélisande having been conceived at the same time and in the same place.

Bayreuth

Since the age of twelve I had wanted to hear Wagner's operas in the theater he conceived for them. In 1974 a Venetian concierge managed to procure tickets, no doubt because performance standards had declined, the shortage of singers able to fill the big roles become acute. I was accompanied from Venice by Mrs. Stravinsky, but she endured only the first and shortest of the Ring *operas, and resolved never to go again.*

August 9-15, 1974. As Tchaikovsky learned at the first performance of *Der Ring des Niebelungen,* Nuremberg is the closest city to Bayreuth where rooms can be found. The logistics of time come to five round-trips at two hours each way to hear the *Ring* and *Tristan,* with all restaurants closed on the return to Nuremberg. Fortunately the drive in the beautiful Franconian hills, with their red-roofed villages and half-timbered farmhouses, is pleasant. Baedeker (*Southern Germany,* 1902) says that on entering Bayreuth, "the Wagner Theater and the lunatic asylum on the right are conspicuous." At the *Festspielhaus* the audience in evening clothes steps from its Mercedes limousines in the glare and sweltering heat of the mid-afternoon sun.

A Red Cross station faces the entrance, a warning that Wagner can be dangerous: the uncooled theater is stifling. A kiosk next to it sells scores, recordings, opera guidebooks, and the official programs. These last are stuffed with commentaries on symbolic significances in the *Ring* according to Jungian concepts of myths as universal dreams. Wagner's Valhalla, as distinguished from the one in the Skaldic poems, is said to be a "supramundane transfiguration... in which the divinely inspired aggressiveness of its warriors is revealed as paranoia." At the mundane level, Siegfried's slaughter of the dragon represents "the overcoming of material rule." At the submundane, the Nibelungen gold-mining becomes an ecological problem, their ring "a symbolic compulsion to concentration...which can produce...destructive ability, and, through egocentricity...lead to autistic inertia." But the oddest new twist is that Hagen, Siegfried's murderer, is less importantly an embodiment of evil than, as the son of Alberich, a victim of heredity; nothing is said about an extra "Y" chromosome. Hagen "feels rejected," and malice gives him "self-assurance."

The program books mention neither Max Muller, who concluded that "Myth is not a transformation of history into legend," nor Saussure, who concluded the opposite and amassed a body of notes on the Nibelungen texts to prove that people and events in the legends were based on actual Frankish and Burgundian historical personages and occurrences. Saussure's search for real names and antecedent facts touches on the crux of Wagner's artistic philosophy as set forth in his 1848 essay, "The Nibelungen: World History as Revealed in Saga," and in his early drama, *Friedrich Barbarossa,* which introduces a mythical element into the life of the historical figure. But Wagner's decision to base his musico-dramatic creations on poetic myth and not on historical incident can only be attributed to his realization of the insuperable power of myth, as well as his intuitive knowledge, in Kerenyi's phrase, that "The gods act according to their given characters and not to those invented by the poets."

Long before starting time, the faithful begin to file into the cramped and cushionless wooden pews where, in the absence of a center aisle, they remain standing in preference to bobbing up and down for later arrivals. This refusal to sit suggests a congregational act of reverence, memorial service rather than stage spectacle. Add to this the mausoleum-like appearance of the theater—black curtain, Corinthian columns, *Bogenlampen*—and the absence of any sign of an imminent performance. Like the Nibelungs, the orchestra is subterranean and its entrance invisible, an ideological concept as well as an acoustical one, Wagner's intention having been to strengthen, or at least not to detract from, the stage illusion. The excitement and the sense of participation in a live performance that ordinary pit orchestras provide in other opera houses have no place in Wagner's aesthetics.

Shortly before the long E flat, the doors are locked and latecomers turned away, a rule so strictly enforced that a party of New Zealanders, after crossing oceans and continents, could miss the whole of the intermissionless *Rheingold* by a few seconds. Regulations at Bayreuth are rigidly observed: "Tickets Deformed in Any Way," a sign warns—folding? crumpling? nibbling?—"Will Not Be Accepted." Minutes before the downbeat, a total blackout occurs and mass catatonia begins, unbroken for two and a half hours by the sound of a shift in position or a muffled cough, which would draw hateful scowls.

The acclaimed *Festspielhaus* acoustics are actually very different on the sides, center, front parterre, and in the loges. Furthermore, stage position affects the pitch and rhythmic coordination of the singers, suggesting that they are not always within easy earshot of the orchestra, and resulting in a separation between voices and instruments, though this is not noticeable in the recordings made in the theater. True, voices are never covered, but their supremacy is obtained at the price of reducing the orchestra to an accompanying role. The balance within the orchestra is consistently satisfying, the strings predominating and the brass kept at bay. Violin lines, scarcely heard in other opera houses, are prominent, partly because of the placement, partly as a result of the large number of players specified by Wagner but employed almost nowhere else.

In Wolfgang Wagner's staging, all four *Ring* dramas are enacted on the tilted disk introduced by his deceased brother Wieland. But whereas the final scene of *Das Rheingold* divertingly resembles a vast pizza with molten *mozzarella,* the disk becomes increasingly difficult to disguise as the cycle unfolds. During the later scene-changes, curiosity mounts as to how the repetition of previous camouflages will be avoided.

During most intermissions, Wolfgang stands near the bust of his grandfather in the middle-loge foyer, a dead-ringer for him except that the marble features are sharper than the living ones. Dowagers trying to look like Cosima are everywhere.

The vocal performers are never good enough, a different soprano being required to sing Brünnhilde in each opera, and their histrionics are stilted at best. Wotan and Loge in Nibelheim are made to look like Dante and Virgil in Hell. Siegmund and Sieglinde in Hunding's hut are seated most of the time, the cello singing the brother's thoughts, the oboe the sister's, one of Wagner's greatest inspirations, but the siblings would have sounded better on their feet. After Siegmund's strenuous invocations for assistance from his tribal ancestors *("Wälse, Wälse")* in extricating the sword from the tree, he drops it with a clatter that would have wakened Hunding despite the nembutal in his nightcap.

Wagner was right to insist that the *Ring* be performed cyclically only. What seems disproportionate in the operas individually disappears in the perspective of the entity. Thus Fafner's role in *Siegfried* seems unduly protracted when the opera is given by itself, but with *Das Rheingold* still vivid in the memory, and the importance of the Giants as the autochthonous earthlings with precedence over the Gods, this criticism is voided. The effectiveness of the cross-reference connecting links is also much greater when the operas are performed sequentially, as in the storm music at the beginning of *Die Walküre* following immediately upon Donner's motif at the end of *Das Rheingold.*

Above all, to hear the music chronologically is to be acutely aware of Wagner's incredible growth, each page displaying greater mastery than the one before. In *Die Walküre,* for instance, he explores new skills in avoiding the perfect-cadence dead-ends that occur in *Das Rheingold.* On the debit side, the ever-increasing powers of musical invention are not always paralleled in the dramaturgy, and since love is a more promising subject than dragons and giants, the First Act of *Die Walküre* remains the most affecting in the *Ring* until the final scene of *Siegfried.* This Siegfried gives a remarkable performance on the hammer, striking every blow of his anvil aria exactly as notated, and with a sense of rhythm so superior to his sense of pitch that his talents would have been more usefully employed in the orchestra's percussion section.

The greater music of *Götterdämmerung* overwhelms the absurdities of the drama and its staging. The Gibichungs, a primitive people, move in perfectly drilled platoon formation. When Brünnhilde blames Siegfried's failure to recognize her on *his* treachery instead of on an enemy's wiles, the suspension of disbelief is strained beyond the limit: as Wotan's daughter, only recently demoted from demi-godhood, and, given her awareness of Siegfried's natural innocence, surely she must recall something of her past. The absence of any suspicion in Siegfried about Brünnhilde's strange behavior on seeing him is less puzzling for the reason that by this time the audience is accustomed to his stupidity. The final scene, in which, when

I first saw the opera, Kirsten Flagstad exited on a live horse, is now realized entirely by cinematography.

August Everding's staging of *Tristan,* intelligently conducted by Carlos Kleiber, attempts to divert attention from the impuissance of the voices. "There is virtually nothing in the Second Act but music," Wagner remarked, in a letter that defines some of the distance between himself and other opera composers: "I have been criticized for failing to include a glittering ball during which lovers would hide themselves in the shrubbery, where their discovery would create a scandal." The voice of today's Isolde suits her youthful song, *"Das war ein Schatz,"* but is quite unequal to the wrath that otherwise seethes in her throughout all but the final minutes of Act I.

The sail on Tristan's ship separates male and female living quarters, as well as the two dramatic levels, but less effectively than the current version at the Met, which is superior as well in such other respects as the use of psychedelic lighting and, as the potion takes effect, the framing of the lovers' heads in an aureole of light. At the Metropolitan, too, but not here, King Mark leads a procession boarding the ship to greet his betrothed, as the libretto requires, thus identifying himself to the audience before surprising the pair at the end of Act II.

Does the King discover them *in flagrante delicto?* Elliott Zuckerman's *The First Hundred Years of Tristan* argues that the music represents a *coitus interruptus,* whereas Michael Tanner's *Wagner* intelligently observes that what is generally regarded as music's most explicit image of consummated love, the climax of the *Prelude,* is in fact only another, albeit the most powerful, repetition of the "desire" motive. But no matter. *Tristan,* all of it, transforms the language of music more drastically than any of its other great milestones, the C-sharp minor quartet, *Pierrot Lunaire, Le Sacre du printemps.* After rehearsing it in Paris in 1860, Wagner wrote to Mathilde Wesendonck: "It was so incomprehensibly new to the musicians that I had to lead them from note to note." What did those musicians make of a form that disregards the exact duplications, right angles, rhythmic patterning, perfect cadences, diatonicism, and rhetorical contrasts that had characterized the art until then? And did any of them experience the ecstasy that Wagner was referring to when he wrote, "Really good performances would drive people mad"?

What a relief are the human beings of *Tristan* after the Teutonic theology, the gods, dwarves, Valkyries, and other monsters of the *Ring,* that gargantuan autobiographical indulgence, *Das Rheingold* being an opera about Wagner's debts and the intransigence of bill collectors, *Die Walküre* an allegory about his sufferings from conventional morality and escape by elopement, and *Siegfried* and *Götterdämmerung* musical dramatizations of the fate of genius betrayed by the jealous and the small and ultimately stabbed in the back. And how much more haunting is the music of *Tristan!* "I have never done anything like it," Wagner wrote. "I am utterly absorbed in this music...I live in it eternally."

Prague

The reason for our trip to the Czech capital was simply to observe the condition humaine *in Vaclav Havel's new democracy. We also wished to see the Terezin transit concentration camp, northwest of Prague, and the Egon Schiele Center in Cesky Krenslov, his mother's birthplace and the reality of his most famous townscapes, the colorful houses below the castle on the Vltava River. But each of these trips was too time-consuming. We went instead to Konopiste Castle, closer to Prague, to see the human and horse armor of the composer Don Carlo Gesualdo, the Prince of Venosa. Alva was with me.*

May 31, 1994. During our Czech Airline flight from London to Prague we try to recall what little we know about the country: of political history, only Jan Hus, his translation into Czech of Wycliffe, and his burning at the stake; Wallenstein; the Thirty Years War; the defenestrations, old and comparatively recent (Masaryk); the Seven Years War; the Lidice massacre; the Embassy of Shirley Temple Black. Of scientific history, only the Rudolph II period of Tycho Brahe and Kepler, Gregor Mendel, and Einstein (who was in the same room with Kafka in 1911 or 1912 at one of Berta Fanta's famous salons). Of musical history, Mozart and the first *Don Giovanni,* Smetana,

Dvorak, Mahler conducting the premiere of his Seventh Symphony, Janácek, the premiere of *Erwartung*. The only native-born artist I can think of is Alphons Mucha, whose fame rests primarily on his having shared a Paris studio with Gauguin. And of literature, only Kafka, Milan Kundera, *Good Soldier Schweik,* and the *Forty Days of Musa Dagh*. Not a single frame of the film *Last Year in Marienbad* was shot here. From the seventeenth century, we recall John Comenius, who was invited to become president of Harvard, but did not, and from the twentieth, Ivan Lendl, the "blank Czech."

To judge from the adverts en route from the airport, Prague is an up-to-the-minute Japanese-American city. Every room in the enlarging, renovating, and therefore noisy Inter-Continental is equipped with Canon fax and Mitsubishi TV, turned on to startle the arriving guest: "Hello, Mr. Craft." The roof restaurant offers vistas of floodlit Hradcany Castle and St. Vitus Cathedral, high above the west bank of the Moldau, and, on this side, of a forest of Gothic and Baroque spires; but the food is terrible and the red wines, including rare vintage Lafites, are refrigerated. In the evening we resist the lure of discos, casinos, rock groups, and the burritos and burgers of "Jo's Bar."

June 1. The Old New Synagogue is the center of Prague and has been for 700 years. The layer-upon-layer graveyard to depths of three-score and more feet conjures thoughts of a morbid archeology. The walls of the nearby Pinahas Synagogue are carved with 77,000 names of death camp victims.

Our Czech escorts are annoyed with the Clintons of Little Rock for having commandeered Prague's newest and best hotel, which is on the outskirts, for bringing a staff of 800 with them, and for staying only one day.

One of the new buildings defacing Wenceslaus Square is a McDonald's. The government licensed it because its toilets are free to non-customers, whereas the city's few public comfort stations charge admission "according to the user's purposes" (?). Most of the people here are long-haired-and-bearded backpackers, hikers, bicyclers, wearing frazzled denim shorts, white jogging sneakers with untied laces, and T-shirts that say "Orgasm" and "Franz Kafka." Whores and junkies are everywhere.

The Church of St. Nicolas is said to have the largest frescoed ceiling in Europe, but no matter: without a telescope, its pictorializations cannot be made out. Mozart supposedly played the organ here, and the memorial service for him that definitely did take place was a sellout. To describe the building as Baroque would be a litotes. The worst of it is the sculpture.

2. Konopiste Castle, south of Prague in a wooded park with gardens and lakes, is a Gothic fortress—moat, high walls, cylindrical towers—stuffed with stuffed animals. Before the assassination at Sarajevo, it was the main hangout of the Archduke Franz Ferdinand and his morganatic wife, Sophia Chotek, who had been snubbed by the Vienna Court. The Habsburg heir apparent, evidently trying to exterminate wildlife in Bohemia all by himself, kept a *Schuss Liste* of the 171,537 animals he had murdered up to 1906 alone. The castle's rooms and corridors bristle with antlers and groan with mounted heads of deer, bear, and boar. Among the trophies of his hunting exploits in Africa and India are lion and tiger skins and severed trunks of elephants. Harold Nicolson's *Peacemaking in 1919* notes that "the Czechs are trying to filch Konopisht from Franz Ferdinand's children."

The hour-long visit to the armory can only be undertaken in the company of busloads of school children and a bullying custodian who unlocks each room before us and relocks it after, making escape impossible. Ferdinand, an Este descendant, had inherited the family's Modena collection of weaponry, a depressing display of wasted craftsmanship and materials, of carved muskets and sword hilts inlaid with gold, silver, and ivory, of crossbows painted with biblical scenes, of etched, chased, and gilded halberds, spontoons, pikes, chassepots, culverins, poignards, shields, bullet pouches, gunpowder cases.

The tournament armor of Gesualdo of Venosa and his steed, if actually tailored to them, indicates that he was very small, his mount no bigger than a carousel pony. Made in 1594 in the shop of Pompeo della Cesa in Milan—the

Milanese, particularly of the school of Filippo Negroli, were the great artist armorers of the *cinquecento*—it must have been intended as a stage-property for the Este court in Ferrara, perhaps in enacting scenes from *Gerusalemma liberata;* the date accords with Gesualdo's stay there, but could he have jousted at that late period? The great musician's helmet has an orange plume. In 1607, his son Emanuele married the Contessa Maria Colissena of Bohemia, which explains the presence of the armor in this remote place.

The castle's other curiosity is the "smokers' lounge" and its adjoining seraglio, kept for the pasha-style post-prandial entertainment of Ferdinand's friends. Its existence had been a secret until 1989. Like all brothels, reputedly, it contains many washbasins and mirrors.

Prague's New (1890s) Jewish Cemetery is sunless, and its tall, close-together, dark-green trees, and unseen warbling birds, are jungle-like. "Dr. Franz Kafka," the stone says, a ridiculously inappropriate academic honorific for the great explorer of paranoia, claustrophobia, and unfathomable bureaucracy in the first quarter of the century. The grave is the only one not overgrown with ivy, no doubt because relatives and friends do not survive to look after the others. The names and dates of Kafka's parents, on the same stone with his, show that they outlived him, and an adjoining plaque gives the dates of birth, but not of death, of the three sisters who perished in the Holocaust. A sapling pine sprouts from the white gravel spread over the site. Next to it is a flower bouquet with a ribbon from the senders, *"Spoletnost Franze Kafky"* (the Franz Kafka Society). The stone is slender and light in color, in contrast to the many black marble monoliths behind it, some of them inscribed with tabernacles. The graves themselves are above-ground mounds, suggesting that families—parents, spouses, and children—are buried in tiers as they are in the Old Cemetery in the ghetto, where the area could only be expanded downward, sometimes to nine levels; some of the tombstones there record the occupation of the deceased, a pair of scissors denoting a tailor, a scientific instrument a doctor.

Following the Jewish custom, I leave a stone on the rim of the writer's grave. (Stones, as shown in the final scene of *Schindler's List,* are placed on graves to symbolize the anchoring of the shroud to protect the body from vultures in the desert.) A plaque in the south wall remembering "Maxe Broda" faces Kafka's stone.

Our new Czech acquaintances refer to Kafka and Rilke as if they had betrayed the culture by writing in German, and no matter that Rilke's *Two Stories of Prague* are more critical of the fin-de-siècle German minority than of the Czech majority, or that after the creation of the Republic at Versailles, he regarded himself as a Czech national. But the linguistic dichotomy is only part of the cultural confusion. Not for nothing did the medieval Rabbi Levi's's concept of the Golem, and the playwright Karel Capek's coinage of the English word "robot," originate in Prague. And this overlooks the splits in religion: the city has both a Catholic and an Orthodox archbishop, but the Old Synagogue, in which the hands of the clock turn to the left, seems to me its true focus of belief. The title of the Czech national anthem is "Where Is My Home?"

Czechs neglect their greatest native sons, Freud, Mahler, Rilke, because they emigrated and wrote in German. Freud is not respected and rarely even mentioned, even though his childhood experiences here—his seduction by the family maidservant, and his discovery of the Oedipal relationship in the precocious recognition that his half-brother was probably the father of his younger sister—are part of the foundations of his work. Still, the country's greatest associations are with foreigners, Mozart in Prague, Chopin in Marienbad (for his tuberculosis), Bach, Beethoven, Goethe, Wagner, and Stravinsky in Carlsbad (where Diaghilev commissioned *Le Sacre du printemps*).

Mozart stayed more than once in the Bertramka Villa, and composed the *Don Giovanni* Overture there during the night before the first performance. He had met Casanova at a party there. Partly because the famous Venetian lover, who was writing his memoirs in Count Waldstein's castle at Dux (Duchek), and the great composer were Freemasons, as well as Knights of the Papal Order of the Golden Spur, they became friends. In the absence of Lorenzo da Ponte, Mozart's librettist, who had been recalled to Vienna by Joseph II, Casanova wrote two drafts for Act II, Scene 10, of *Don*

Giovanni. Discovered at Dux after his death, these have suggested that Mozart may have been in some doubt about Leporello's contrition scene. Whatever the truth, Casanova's conception of the Don's servant is not that of the sniveling, disloyal coward of the opera as we know it, but of an apologist who blames his master's philandering on the female sex for having bewitched him.

The Villa, now called the Mozart Museum, contains nothing definitely connected to him. The posters and programs are copies of originals in Salzburg, the musical instruments are merely of the period, and the light brown hair in the glass locket is without provenance and could be anyone's.

Among the Art Nouveau sculptures in the studio of Frantisek Bilek, whom Kafka admired, is a striking image of the Virgin Mary as an old woman.

The "Blue Duck" restaurant, said to be Vaclav Havel's favorite, on the west bank near the Cathedral of St. Lawrence, has only seven tables, and tonight the conversation at all of them is in Japanese or English.

Au revoir to the Crushed Velvet Revolution.

Vienna

The intent of the first of the three Viennese sojourns described hereunder was to show something of the city and its art to my sixteen-year-old son. I took him to see the tiny room in which Schubert was born, to Freud's home, and more than once to the Kunsthistorisches Museum. The second visit was planned to acquaint Alva with the city and its environs, and the third was at the request of The New York Review of Books *to report on exhibitions and performances commemorating the bicentennial of Mozart's death. (This was duly published and reprinted in my book* The Moment of Existence.*)*

October 17, 1988. I take Alexander to the Zentralfriedhof graves of Gluck, Beethoven, Schubert, Brahms, Schoenberg, and Salieri (Schubert's teacher), then back by way of the St. Marx Cemetery where—somewhere—Mozart was interred. In the adjoining church of that name, the Empress Maria Theresa heard the twelve-year-old conduct his first Mass.

From Wee-enna, as the driver says, we go to Auden's grave in Kirchstetten. A photograph of him is encased in the gateway to the small church and surrounding cemetery, where his tombstone, shoed-in between two other plots, seems sadly out of place, and, with layers of faded flowers dumped on it, as unkempt as he was himself. An iron marker identifies him as, in part, a "Man of Letters," which would have appalled him. The "Audenhaus," at the end of Audengasse, is undergoing repairs that will turn it into a museum. To picture him in this melancholy village of shrines and crossroad crucifixes is difficult, whereas the debaucheries and the gramophone blaring Wagner in Audenhaus are easily imagined. At nearby Melk, where the Mozart family stayed en route to Vienna in September 1767, and returning to Salzburg in December 1768, the many steep staircases leave me pale and panting.

Returning on the Danube road, along terraced slopes of yellowed vine-yards and Baroque-ized hilltop abbeys, we stop at Durnstein Castle, Richard Lion-Heart's donjon in 1192-93, and, back in Vienna, Beethoven's Heiligenstadt house, which possesses no genuine relics but only facsimiles and such irrelevancies as a portrait of Napoleon.

18. The "Emilie Flöge and Gustav Klimt" exhibition at the Hermesvilla, the former Imperial Palace of the Empress Elisabeth in the suburb of Lainz, entails a two-mile hike through the Tiergarten, on a path through the red and gold Vienna woods shared with loden-mantled art lovers.

In addition to some of Klimt's best pictures, the Hermesvilla presents contextual displays of Art Nouveau clothes, jewelry, tableware, boudoir and other furniture, together with a large representation from the newly opened Estate of Emilie Flöge. As a creator of *haute couture* in the Casa Piccola salon that she and her two sisters directed in Mariahilfer Strasse, Fräulein Flöge exercised considerable influence on the painter, whose 1902 portrait of her marks the beginning of his heavily ornamented style.

As seen at the Hermesvilla, the Flöge sisters replaced the bustle, high-bosom, and tight-waisted Empire-style of the in-other-ways comfortable classes, with one-piece, figure-concealing, floor-length, and trailing gowns.

Sleeves were ample at the elbow and long enough to cover wrists, and collars were tall, as if to support the bouffant coiffures. The most striking example here of Emilie's own wardrobe, seen in a 1907 profile photo of her by Klimt, conceals the contours of the body but sets in motion a flow of folds from back to sides. Klimt himself wore a blue smock with surplice neckline, long and sufficiently loose to hide the hooves, for something about his head, as well as a great deal about his art and his bachelor life, suggests that he was part satyr: after his death, fourteen illegitimate children—a fifteenth had died—made claims on their omnifutuant father's estate. Priapus be praised!

The products of the Wiener Werkstätte at the Hermesvilla are of an elegance unsurpassed in the Western Europe and America of the period, such distinguished enemies of ornament as Karl Kraus, Adolf Loos, and Hermann Broch notwithstanding. To judge from this presentation, Josef Hoffmann is the artist who consistently achieved the most satisfying forms in, for example, a silver étui and square silver-backed hand mirror. The furniture is no less attractive, especially the late Mondrian-like monochrome panels of the Flöge salon's trying-on rooms and the Charles Rennie Mackintosh chairs, one of them from Klimt's last studio.

The photographs here of Emilie Flöge enable us to see how Klimt's portrait glamorizes her attractive but somewhat heavy face, rounding it, enlarging the eyes, increasing the fullness of the lips, refining the nose, rouging the skin. Similarly, photos of the Flöge model Frederike Beer, compared with the paintings of her by both Schiele and Klimt, show that the artists slenderized the body and remodeled the face. Klimt cosmeticized the women in all his portraits.

19. Back in Vienna and still on the Klimt trail, we go to the Belvedere to see the permanent collection on the top floor. The landscapes here are unlike any others by any other painter, and about a fourth of all Klimt's oils *are* landscapes, a large proportion, considering that he began to paint them relatively late in life (*c.* 1898), and that the primary world of his art at the beginning of this period was the remote one of allegory. He did not make sketches for the landscapes, as compared to the three hundred or so for a single painting of another kind, but, in *Poppy Field,* the underlying charcoal outlines are so transparent that they catch the eye even before the impasto clouds. Moreover, he continued to paint landscapes to the end of his life with no variation of approach, in contrast to the stylistic diversities and fusions in his other work, and with only one major submission to new influence, that of Van Gogh after the 1906 Vienna exhibition of his work, most overtly in the solitary *Sunflower,* drooping and sunless in Klimt's case, and in *Avenue of Trees in the Park at Schloss Kammer.*

The viewer is always *in* a Klimt landscape, *in* the meadow, forest, garden (in which, botanically speaking, the genus of a flower may not be identifiable and is less important than its color), *under* the pear tree, *out* on the lake with no shore in sight: like Monet, Klimt painted in a boat. This feeling of being *in* the picture is created in part by the absence of a natural frame: the picture seems to be a detail of a larger one. Klimt evidently used binoculars and a square view-finder to choose the patch of landscape he wished to paint. The whole of the woods or the field is never shown, and limbs and blossoms are arbitrarily cut off at the end of the quadrilateral picture space. The horizon, too, with few exceptions, is reduced to the smallest chinks of sky, thereby giving the picture an upward, bottom-to-top slant, a claustrophobic effect intensified by the blurring of perspectival boundaries. If the picture is not wholly flattened into two dimensions, the viewer must look very closely for the third. This calculated geometrical confusion is exploited to extremes in pictures of lakeside buildings; the relationship between the two turrets in the 1908 *Schloss Kammer on the Attersee* is deliberately off-kilter, and background mountains seem closer than foregrounds, as well as about to topple into them. Klimt's scheme of dislocation also depends on light that does not come from a particular direction, the whole picture being lighted equally. As a rule, less is shown of objects themselves—shrubbery, houses, an island—than of their shadows or reflections in water.

Klimt's landscapes are terrestrial, as opposed to celestial, in the sense that sun, moon, and stars are absent. This is in accord with what might be deduced about his cosmology in other regards, his only Biblical picture being of Adam and Eve in the prelapsarian state, and his only uses of Christian symbols are the black crosses on the robe of the skeleton in *Death and Life,* and the crucifix, clearly no more than a part of the scenery, in *Country Garden* (1911-12). But Klimt's world of Nature is also empty of human beings, a haunted emptiness in which blank windows stare, woods are all-seeing (tree barks with eyes), and the silence of ever-growing vegetal life deafens.

Gustav Klimt Women, the title of a new book, is redundant in that a monograph on Klimt's men is unthinkable. After the academic portraits of the mid-1890s, his only men are Franz Schubert in profile—the painting was destroyed in a fire, emblematically, it seems—the comic-strip hero of the *Beethoven Frieze,* and a few faceless and partly faceless lovers. Women, no one could deny, are Klimt's subject, and he is at his greatest in his oil portraits of dressed-up ones, and in the drawings of the undressed.

The women of the paintings are associated with symbols, the female principle and flowing water, brilliant colors and gold (the intercrural jackpot in *Danae*). In contrast, the women in the drawings are free of symbols and even of settings. They are private, intimate, simple, classical in the ductility of line, natural, unornamented. Klimt drew them for himself, and one of his friends reported that during the exhibition of *Goldfish,* the painter took the canvas home each night "to fantasize a bit more on it." No doubt this painter-Pygmalion "fantasized" as well on his drawings of nudes. (When did he find time to refocillate?) A substantial number of them, though only three are on view at the Hermesvilla, are clearly intended to stimulate. Most are faceless, or virtually so, until the late years, when he endows them with psychological animation. The drawings, some 3,000 of them, are the little-known category of Klimt's art. In them women are often presented as purely sexual objects, nude, semi-nude, fully dressed, and each one is the whole of her picture.

In the domain of the erotic, no discussion of either Klimt or Schiele manages to avoid comparisons with the other, though their birthdates are three decades apart and their temperaments antithetical. The teenage

Klimt's academic work confirms that his erotic sensibilities were developed no less precociously than Schiele's. Both artists feature pairs of female lovers; both reveal a predilection for pubic hair; both are attracted by semi-nudity, raised or lowered clothing, stockings rolled just above the knee, the half-opened blouse; and both exploit the same spread legs and writhing postures, the head resting on raised arms, parted lips, and heavy-lidded, half-closed eyes. Klimt is the originator, though not the more original artist, and his line is less powerful. Schiele is the follower, not only in the erotic but in numerous particulars in the paintings: compare Klimt's *The Kiss* and Schiele's *Self-Portrait with Black Vase,* which borrows from Klimt's *Portrait of Fritza Riedler,* and which was derived in turn from the arc of color behind the head of Velázquez's Infanta Maria Theresa. Like all of Schiele's self-portraits, the two middle fingers of the hand are held together and the forefinger and little finger splayed. The essential difference in the erotica of the two artists is that Klimt is the voyeur, Schiele the participant.

20. We go to the Sezession Building, the "Assyrian W.C.," as the Viennese call the temple-like structure, to see Klimt's Beethoven Frieze, his most ambitious, largest-scale creation, 145 lengthwise feet of painted surface. Removed from public view after the artist's death in 1918, it was returned to the Sezession only two years ago, after restoration, and not to its original position, but to a lower level of basement. Meanwhile, the building itself, also known to the Viennese as "the Golden Cabbage" because of its open gilded bronze cupola, had been restored as well.

At the fourteenth Sezession exhibition, in 1902, the center of the room was occupied by Max Klinger's life-size statue of Beethoven enthroned, while Klimt's allegorical mural was in an anteroom. (The occasion included a performance of an arrangement for wind instruments of part of the Finale of Beethoven's Ninth Symphony conducted by Mahler.) Klinger's Beethoven, once more on view, is a white marble nude, young, handsome, slender, smooth-skinned. Bent slightly forward, with legs crossed and feet encased in white sandals, the lower body is draped with a pleated garment rendered in polished gold. The composer's left foot rests on a slab of rock shared with a crouching, awestruck eagle. Lost in thought, the "hero, martyr, and redeemer of mankind," as Wagner called him, is unaware of the feathered biped. The back of the throne, in bronze relief, juxtaposes a Birth of Venus and a crucifixion, the confrontation of the Classical and Christian worlds that Klinger had introduced in his *Christ in Olympus.* The sculptor is said to have been inspired by the idea of Phidias's legendary chryselephantine statue of Zeus, but the result, which is kitsch, belongs in the Campo Santo in Genoa.

Without the statue, removed to the Gewandhaus in Leipzig after the exhibition, Klimt's frescoes lacked a raison d'être, and without the printed program of the Sezession, horribly poetical as it is, no one could have suspected any link between Beethoven's Ninth and the painter's parallel symbolic pictorializations. Even the two-dimensionality of the frescoes must be understood as a contrasting response to the spatial volume of Klinger's sculpture.

Professor Bouillon of the University of Clermont-Ferrand, an authority on the Frieze, resists only a few of the countless opportunities that the murals provide for exegeses. In the main he follows Wagner's 1846 program notes for *his* revival of the Ninth and his 1870 commentary, which disregards Schiller's *Ode to Joy* and discovers Beethoven's meaning exclusively in the music—a "struggle of the soul fighting for happiness against the oppression of the hostile powers." The Blake-like figures that float above the frescoes are meant to be understood as Klimt's translation of Wagner's phrase, "the tireless instinct which drives us with the energy of despair." In Wagner's peroration, the third movement represents love and hope, the last movement, "the cry of universal human love."

Is the Frieze Klimt's magnum opus? Its most perceptive critic, Alessandra Comini, justly remarks that Klimt's pictorial response to the Symphony "was essentially one of fantasy," not philosophy, and that his imagination was excited above all by "the depiction of the Hostile Powers." Perhaps we do look longer at this part of the Frieze, the Gorgons, the

Beardsley parody-figure "Excess," and the Giant Tryphon (whose opaline-glass eye must have been intended as the *oculus mundi*), than at any other part of the epic. Unfortunately, the pallid-to-grisaille conclusion of the narrative, the triumph of art and poetry, is its weakest episode. Its most successful aspect is in its embodiment of the musical principles of rhythm, movement, linearity, progression.

Climbing the staircase back to street level at Alexander's pace, I am afflicted by sharp chest pains, dizziness, and shortness of breath. We push on, nevertheless, to the abodes of the great. Whereas most of the pilgrims to Schubert's birthplace and Beethoven's Pasqualati house are Japanese, the only addresses in the guestbook at Freud's residence are from New York. After my birthday dinner at the Imperial Hotel, we tour a neighborhood in the Gurtel where the prostitutes in uniforms of leather mini-minis, white stockings, red blouses, and white umbrellas might be a chorus from a Broadway musical.

21. Waiting for our flight to Copenhagen, I read Jean Clair's *Le Nu et la norme* on Klimt and Picasso. Clair fatuously contends that Klimt's portrait of Adele Bloch-Bauer (1907) "is one of the most beautiful pictures that Occidental art has ever produced," and attributes a parallel importance to it and to Picasso's *Demoiselles d'Avignon*. According to Clair, the similarities between the pictures, which at first, second, and further sight, hardly seem to come from the same planet, are in the representation of women with erotic connotations essential to the meaning. He emphasizes the appearance of both works at a time of crisis in the public careers and private lives of their creators, in Klimt's case the University of Vienna's rejection of his allegories, his resignation from the Sezession, his change in style to flat, two-dimensional paintings with abstract decorative motives inspired by the mosaics of Ravenna, and his new, abundant use of gold to accentuate the iconic qualities of his portraits.

What Clair overlooks is that *Adele* was an end, the *Demoiselles* a beginning, that Klimt's art depends on style and abstraction, both of which

Picasso vehemently opposed (*"Le style c'est quand on est mort"*), and that Klimt's women, unlike Picasso's, are sexually desirable in the here and now. The *Adele* consists entirely of abstract decoration, featuring the sexual symbol of cloven almond shapes enclosed in squares, surrounding and covering a body petrified by gold and precious stones.

October 8, 1990. To Mayerling and Baden, stopping at Liechtenstein Castle and the subterranean lake near Hinterbrühl, a gypsum mine until 1944 when the Nazis drained and converted it to the factory that produced the first jet airplane. We also visit the mill of Schubert's *Schöne Müllerin* and the Cistercian monastery in Heiligenkreuz, where in June 1828 Schubert played the two organ fugues he had composed the day before. At Augustinhütte a marker identifies Beethoven's favorite Wienerwald footpath.

Only one detached tower of the Royal Hunting Lodge remains at Mayerling, the Emperor having demolished the building and erected a Carmelite convent on the site. Monarchists still maintain that the Crown Prince was killed in a brawl with Mary Vetsera's uncles, but a conference of historians and psychiatrists a few months ago decided that a murder and suicide pact must have been carried out. Just as the Emperor tried to suppress the scandal to the extent of having Vetsera's uncles spirit her dead body away sitting upright in a coach between them, so today the Habsburg heirs have prevented the exhumation that would determine whether she was shot through the left temple. We visit her grave, in a secluded cemetery nearby. Meanwhile, Brigitte Hamann's book, *Rudolph, Crown Prince and Rebel,* argues that Rudolph, emotionally stable and not in the least dissipated, was a liberal at odds with his autocratic father. The Mayerling legend is flourishing, in any case; during our visit seven busloads of American tourists arrive and depart.

The partly reconstructed second-century Roman aqueduct at Baden still stands, but the smell of sulfur is asphyxiating. Was it as strong when Beethoven spent his summers here, and when Mozart came to see his wife while she was taking the cure? Their biographers do not say. In the park below Joseph II's castle, the chestnut trees are yellow, the vines deep red.

At nearby Gumpoldskirchen, vine-leaves have been attached over the lintels of every tavern to indicate that the *Heuringen* has begun. Traffic is slowed on the road to Beethoven's—and Schoenberg's—Mödling, by a caravan of trucks hauling wine presses and barrels.

Richard Strauss's *Josefslegende,* at the State Opera, has good moments between banal quarter-hours, but the ballet is more pantomime than dance. No matter, though, since the title character's totally unclothed *derrière* is obviously meant to be the main attraction.

9. The Egon Schiele Museum in the painter's home town of Tulln is close to the Danube and a hundred or so yards west of a Roman tower erected in A.D. 80. Once a river port of the Romans, and, in the *Nibelungenlied,* the meeting place of Attila and Kriemhild, Tulln is surrounded by fields of the blackened sunflowers familiar from Schiele's autumn landscapes. It is also famed in the history of ethology for Konrad Lorenz's work here. A plaque at the Museum entrance boasts that the native son's pictures, a disgrace and embarrassment locally when he was alive, have brought the city world renown. We return to Vienna via Klosterneuburg and the sanatorium in Kierling where Franz Kafka died.

In the *Elektra* at the State Opera, the curtain rises on a mammoth decapitated black statue, its booted foot resting on a globe. Hildegard Behrens kvetches in great voice.

June 14, 1991. Drive to Carnuntum, the Roman capital of Pannonia, near the Czech and Hungarian borders. Established by Augustus Caesar on the site of a Celtic *oppidum,* it was a garrison city of 5,000 with 70,000 civilians, when Vindobona (Vienna) was still a tiny settlement. As the headquarters of Tiberius and Claudius, and as the walls, still in good condition, attest, the fortress covered a vast area, only portions of which have been disinterred. Marcus Aurelius wrote the second volume of his *Greek Meditations* here, and it was here that Diocletian called a summit of the leaders of the Empire. But Carnuntum disappoints; only a few columns and a large stadium remain. Besides, it is raining. In nearby Rohrau we seek refuge in the house where Joseph Haydn was born, now more notable for its modern W.C. than for a few artifacts associated with the composer. The museum in nearby Harrach Castle displays Monsù Desiderio's *St. George and the Dragon,* reproduced on the cover of Maria Nappi's new monograph, *François de Nomé and Didier Barra, the Two Painters Corporately Comprising Monsù Desiderio.*

Dinner in Vienna's Majestät: lake fish with a Wachau white. The urinal in the men's room has a personalized automatic flusher, or, at any rate, one that does not go off at regular intervals. The sign next to the cord in the hotel bathroom tub, "SOS: Pull in case of Emergency," suggests a catastrophe on the scale of the *Titanic.*

15. At midnight we go to the wine tavern in the courtyard of the Beethovenhaus in Heiligenstadt. Taxis being difficult to find in the small hours in this neighborhood, we ask the driver to wait and invite him to join us. A Palestinian Arab, born in Amman, he says that seven of his sisters live in Kuwait, the eighth in Los Angeles, and that he himself spent five years in Rhode Island before moving to Vienna, where he is working for his baccalaureate at the University. Knowing we are from New York, he will vouchsafe no opinions about the Gulf War; nor, of course, will he touch the open white wine. When I ask the *hübsch* blonde waitress the exact location of Beethoven's rooms, she says: "How should I know? That was a long time ago."

Cities of Castile

For the cover of my recording of Stravinsky's The Flood *(1998), I had wanted to use the picture of Noah's Ark from the* Beatus Apocalypse, *executed in the late eighth century at Liébana in Asturias. Meyer Schapiro describes this treasure as "one of the great achievements of medieval art," a work of "extraordinary power of color and expression." Of the twenty-two copies made between 900 and 1200, the most complete and best preserved is in Spain's Gerona Cathedral. I was determined to see it, and an opportunity arose when Alva's son, Ted, a young painter on his way to the 400th Anniversary Velázquez Exhibition at the Prado, invited us to join him. We had heard reports of endless queues, and since the museum already owns more than half of the artist's work, thought we could go another time. Finally in Madrid, the concierge at the Ritz said that he could not arrange accreditation for us to see the* Apocalypse. *As an alternative, he proposed that we fly to Bilbao and take in the new Guggenheim Museum. We elected to stay in Castile.*

Since prehistoric artifacts have been discovered near Madrid, as well as many Roman sites, why, one wonders, was the city no more than an outpost of Toledo until the eleventh century, and why, after that, did it not vie in importance with Seville, Cordoba, Granada, and Valladolid until the seventeenth. One explanation is its setting in a "hideous, grassless, treeless, colorless, calcined desert." Then in 1605, Cervantes published *Don Quixote* there, and soon after Lope de Vega, Calderón, and Velázquez were all living and working in the city.

On the way from the airport, I do not find the old Madrid of pompous monuments (the Dos de Mayo with its eternal flame), triumphal arches (the eighteenth-century Puerta de Alcalá), parks (the El Retiro) much changed, apart from the incursion of ill-assorted, everywhere-in-the-world office buildings. What delights me is to see that since my last visit the principal boulevards have been named for Manuel de Falla, Miguel de Unamuno, Antonio Machado, Garcia Lorca, and José Ortega y Gasset, all of them victims of Franco.

Reaching the Ritz Hotel, I am assailed by memories of Ortega in 1955. I picture him walking down the corridor of an upper floor with the tall, young, and beautiful Marquesa de Slauzol on his arm; Ortega was surprisingly short, about Stravinsky's height. The next four hours were among the most stimulating of my life. Stravinsky opened with questions about their mutual friend Victoria Ocampo in Buenos Aires, to which Ortega had fled during World War II. Had Victoria introduced him to Jorge Luis Borges, who had translated *Perséphone* for Stravinsky's performance of it there in 1936, and who wrote for her review *Sur?* (Ortega did not remember, but Borges's fame was yet to come.) And had he seen Manuel de Falla? (No, the reclusive composer lived too far from the city to expect visitors.) Ortega said nothing about his humiliating life in present-day "invertebrate Spain," where he was not published and lived virtually under house arrest. Stravinsky told him that he had been struck by his comments on the role of *Petrushka* in the *"Dehumanization of Art,"* and was flattered to hear that Ortega had attended his 1951 concert of *Orpheus* and *Oedipus Rex* at the *Ars Viva* in Munich. (A little acid here from Stravinsky about Cocteau.) Ortega was the most vivid, spontaneous man I had ever met and his death only six months later was a deeply saddening event. (Was he aware of an illness that night?) When he proudly took from his wallet a photograph of himself with Gary Cooper in Aspen in 1949, he mentioned that Albert Schweitzer was there at the same time (a larger spritz of acid from Stravinsky) and that the mythic charisma seemed to be true: deer did come out of the woods to him. (I wonder if Ortega took any notes about our meeting.)

The Ritz has modernized its bathrooms and acquired new furniture, but its style of service is as rigid and formal as it was forty-five years ago. A notice on our night-tables instructs us to call the concierge if we wish to play tennis and are attired for it, in which case we, our unsightly arms and legs, would be escorted out of the building by a private exit, thus maintaining the front lobby's standards of dignity and rectitude. The service in the restaurant, which opens at 10:30 P.M., is as courteous and reserved as I remember it.

In the morning Ted reports that the Prado queue lasts only fifteen minutes. We stroll with him in the attractive red Plaza del Arrabal, then decide to tackle the masterpieces. After all, the Prado has almost no French paintings, only one English, and except for Dürer's powerful *Christ,* no German. The great Italians are there (and an interesting Francesco Furini: *Lot and His Daughters*) only because Titian had lured Habsburg taste away from the Low Countries. We go directly to Velázquez, who was not pro- lific—not quite a hundred paintings—being more interested in his career as courtier than taking up his easel, which he did, for the most part, at the request of his friend the King.

Our traipse-through raises questions. How could a painter of supreme genius aspire to be a mere gentleman, a *cortesano,* a Knight of Santiago? And what about his subject-matter, apart from the sixty official portraits, of mostly Royals and grandees? Dwarves, duennas, dogs, rearing horses, *bode-gónes.* And why, in an age when most artists painted more religious pictures than any other kind, did he produce so few of them, all somewhat odd? The subject of *Christ after the Flagellation* is unknown everywhere except in Spain, and even there has only two or three precedents. To me, the kneeling child, said to symbolize the commiserating "Christian Soul," and the point- ing angel, seem insipid, both as concept and expression. The *Presentation of Joseph's Bloodied Coat to Jacob* is lacking in strong emotion of any kind; the dissimulators are unconvincing, as they are meant to be, but Jacob's face is blurred, and the King Charles spaniel barking in the foreground trivializes the scene. The *Landscape With St. Anthony* looks like a Joachim Patinir. And as for the *Christ on the Cross,* one of only two religious pictures done in the last three decades of the artist's life, I cannot agree with Jonathan Brown's *Velázquez: Painter and Courtier* that

> The exquisite draftsmanship of the body, the beautiful motif of the
> hair falling over the right half of the face, the subdued glow of the

halo around the head [where else?] impart elegance and dignity to the subject...Velázquez has captured the redemptive power of Christ's martyrdom, the benefits of which are offered to the faithful through the ineffable beauty and perfection of His body.

But "elegance" and the Crucifixion do not go together, and the "benefits," nothing less than the salvation of all humanity, are hardly attributable to "the ineffable beauty" of the body which, in fact, is too perfect, the legs too posed, the loincloth too artfully arranged. Moreover, the curtain of hair draping the right side of the face is coy, since the curls on the other side of the head are in place.

Velázquez also avoids mythology, or presents it eccentrically. His seated *Mars* seems puzzled and weary, in what I can make out of his face in the darkness. The god is naked except for a helmet and a cloth covering the waist—to show the deep abdominal wrinkles and the virtually hairless body, a handlebar mustache excepted. But I am forgetting that Velázquez did not like scenes of action—the *Surrender of Breda* shows no movement on the battlefield, and no signs, apart from background smoke, of any disturbance. The *Feast of Bacchus* is also peculiarly static, the god surprisingly young.

Of the many portraits of the thick-lipped King, I prefer the *Philip IV at Fraga* in the Frick Collection, if only for its technical mastery, the rose-colored baldric, the silver braid and sleeves, and, yes, even the head. But the most arresting picture for me today is the *Innocent X* enthroned. Velázquez seems to evade eyes that are not windows of the soul, but here, through them, he captures the Pope's laser-like intelligence and only slightly concealed malice. *Las Meninas* has been too much explained in recent years.

Ortega calls Velázquez the "disdainful genius," partly for his independence of the subject, partly because of his progress from painting objects to painting "the experience of seeing." The feat of the painter's resolve "to fix the one point of view," he says, is comparable to the revolution of Hume and Kant. Before Velázquez, the painter's eye had ptolemaically revolved around each object, following a servile orbit. In an early Italian or Flemish painting, "the smallest figure, there in the distance, is as complete, spherical, and detached as the most important." The painter "seems to have gone to the distant spot where they are and from near at hand to have painted them as distant." In Velázquez "the point of view has been retracted, has placed itself farther from the object, and we have passed from proximate to distant vision. Proximate vision dislocates, analyzes, distinguishes—it is feudal. Distant vision synthesizes, combines, throws together—it is democratic. Velázquez despotically resolves to fix the one point of view."

Modern highways have replaced the narrow and bumpy roads that I remember from our excursions to Toledo and El Escorial, and the once deserted countryside is now filled with rows of brown, balconied houses, shopping malls, gasoline stations. On a hillside to the left, about twenty miles out, is the immensely tall granite cross erected by El Caudillo. Behind it, tunneled into the mountain, is his tapestried crypt, said to equal in length the nave of St. Peter's in Rome, the result of ten years' work by thousands of laborers, a reminder of the First Ch'in Emperor's tomb in Xi'an. But the Castilian landscape has not been entirely spoiled. The ilexes, elms, and oaks are still there, the pinewoods at the lower levels of the snow-covered mountains, the stony fields, the parched, dun-colored land.

After we cross the snow-covered Navacerrado, and the last bridge before Segovia, the Roman aqueduct comes into view, its huge two-storey ashlar arches like a strut in the lee between the sides of the valley. The gray stone bisecting the colorful city that has grown up higgledy-piggledy around it seems alien to the churches, the plazas, and the other buildings, and one wonders what this most imposing of Roman ruins is doing in a city hardly mentioned in ancient history, and why it was built at all, since the water supply from the Eresma and the Clamores Rivers must have been adequate. The river it conveys from the nearby Riofrio Mountains is subterranean until it reaches the aqueduct. Built in the period of the Spanish Emperors Hadrian and Trajan, the mammoth stone blocks with which the 167 arches and 128 pillars are constructed had to be cut to fit together, chamfered and hoisted into place, since mortar was not used. It is now feared that vibrations from recent motor traffic may be loosening the smaller stones in the voussoirs, which, if dislodged, could topple the construction.

The walk through the city is all downhill. Historians agree that Christians, Moors, and Jews lived here in perfect amity in the fourteenth and fifteenth centuries. Nothing Moorish remains, except for Mudéjar elements in the city's twenty or so Romanesque churches, and for the churches themselves, the Moors being skilled stonemasons. The Jews—the mythology of the city claims that it was founded by a great-grandson of Noah about 1076 B.C., which is several millennia too late—have left a cemetery and a famous name, Abraham Seneor, who was the last Court-rabbi, as well as a renowned financier. A legend of consequence in Segovian history surrounds a young Jewish woman, Esther, who had been unjustly condemned to be flung to her death from the parapets of the city. At the last minute, calling to "the Virgin of the Christians" for help, she was duly saved, converted, and eventually enshrined as Maria del Salto ("of the jump"). The miracle is venerated in a splendid Baroque arch that spans the main highway.

The Cathedral is too big, too rich, too ornamented, and too Gothic for me, and the Baroque organs, and lectern with an open music-book manuscript, that we wish to see, are on the other side of the locked choir grille. The spire is part mahogany from America and gold-covered lead. We prefer the small, simple San Millán, with its three semicircular apses, side atriums, and the Mozarabic towers that characterize the Spanish Romanesque. The twelve-sided Church of La Vera Cruz, outside the walls, is another mixture of Moorish and Romanesque, with beautiful modillions (moldings). We visit the Dominican Convent, whose prior was once the terrifying Torquemada, and the sumptuous mausoleum of St. John of the Cross, which would have appalled the self-mortifying mystic who wrote the beautiful strophe

…night which joins
The lover to the beloved,
The beloved into the lover transformed.

The humble dwelling of the writer Antonio Machado has been conserved by the University of Segovia. The twelve years he spent here teaching French, 1919-31, were his most productive as a poet, as well as his most active in political and social affairs. His *ars poetica* of that time should be better known, even in translation:

> Slowly now, nice neat letters:
> The point is to do things well,
> not just to do them.

> A state of feeling [*sentimiento*] is sensibly created by the individual subject out of materials from the outer world made over in one's heart.

The Segovia Alcázar is everyone's idea of "castles in Spain." In 1412 Queen Catalina of Lancaster lived here, and in 1474, at the time of her coronation as Queen of Castile, Isabel the Catholic. In 1570 Philip II celebrated his marriage to Anne of Austria in the Alcázar, and Charles of England, later Charles the First, ate trout here in 1623. Wellington conquered it during the Peninsular War.

Seen from a distance, the freshly restored and new-looking walls of Avila are "like the walls of an old city in a book of hours," or so Somerset Maugham wrote, and he goes on to give poor marks to the city itself: "there is nothing much to do there and little to see.... The cathedral has not much to offer you but an effect of sombreness...A silent city...The men are soberly dressed and the women wear deep mourning..." Today the quiet is shattered by busloads of pilgrims and tourists streaming in and out of the countless shops selling *bondieuserie*. The Convent commemorating Saint Teresa's birthplace (1515), which was in the Jewish quarter—in spite of her family's claims to *limpieza* (purity), she is now thought to have been of Jewish origin—is as drab as she would have wanted. Eleven thousand Jews, about half of the total population, were expelled from the city in 1492, but the space within the walls does not seem nearly large enough to contain a population of that size.

Of Teresa herself, I know only what I have read in Victoria Sackville-West's *The Eagle and the Dove,* and Crashaw's poem from which this title was taken; it has been estimated that one-third of Crashaw's work is indebted to the contumacious, hysterical, and well-intentioned saint. In my youth, and milieu, the commingling of pain and joy—Teresa writes of one of her seizures that "so surprising was the sweetness of this excessive pain that I could not wish to be rid of it"—was an illness treated by psychiatry. Adolescents then were regaled by the Président de Brosses's witticism on seeing Bernini's marble sculpture of Teresa in ecstasy: *"Si c'est l'amour divin, je le connais."*

Avila should also be known, but is not, as the birthplace of Tomás Luis de Victoria, the greatest Spanish composer of the Renaissance, and as the sometime home of his near contemporary, Antonio de Cabezón, Spain's greatest composer of keyboard music, though blind from early childhood. Cabezón was as close to Charles V and Philip II as Velázquez was to Philip IV, and in some respects his *tientos* and *glossas* are far in advance of any other music of the period.

Hannibal captured Salamanca from the Romans in 217 B.C., a year before he defeated their largest army at Cannae. The city became Roman again after the Second Punic War, then Visigothic, and, for three hundred years, Moorish. It is chiefly famous for its buildings, its Plateresque and Churriguerresque architecture, and its University, which, with Paris, Bologna, and Oxford, is one of the four oldest in Europe. Its forty colleges were larger than Oxford and Cambridge put together. Moreover, the Copernican system was openly taught here before anywhere else in the world. Columbus studied astronomy at Salamanca, and we have come to see his copy of Dante, inscribed by him, in the library, as well as to see the collection of musical instruments, which includes the oldest European organ (1380) and a set of shawms. But we are too late. Our driver has misinformed us about the distance and the necessary time to cover it. The golden-brown city's narrow streets project an architecture of shadows, and in the old city, the traffic is either one-way or exclusively pedestrian. Worse still, our driver deposits us on a corner not far from a college we wish to visit and promises to fetch us in the same place in a half-hour. The street is the place of the confrontation, October 12, 1936, of the Falangist General Millán Astray and Miguel de Unamuno, who had been Rector of the University for fourteen years and taught Greek there before that. *"Viva la muerte"* and *"Mueran los intellectuales,"* the General shouted at the writer, who soon after lost his reason. Unamuno, in despair because of the Civil War, died at the end of the year.

When we see no more of our driver for an hour and a half, Alva and Ted go to a hotel, luckily find a girl who speaks English, and persuade her to telephone the Ritz in Madrid to find the driver's agency. At long last the concierge reaches him on his cellular phone and provides directions to find us. When he finally arrives, we learn that not only had he been hopelessly lost but that he had never been in Salamanca before. We regain the Ritz at 11 P.M., the proper dinner hour in Madrid.

Ifriquiya

Carthage (Kairouan, Dougga)

The 1987 Carthage exhibition at the American Museum of Natural History in New York was at the root of my desire to see Tunisia. Carthage was a disappointment, but Dougga and Bardo exceeded my expectations, and I felt euphoric in the climate, as would any sufferer from sinusitis. Alexander and Alva were with me.

May 25, 1990. Rome, the Bernini Hotel. The beauty of the city is not conducive to reading, which partly accounts for my slow progress through Flaubert's *Salammbo*. But the novel has impediments of its own, including a negligible plot, mannequin characters—Salammbo herself becomes a statue all but literally when her pet python is wound around her naked body—and story-stalling digressions about Hannibal's father. However finely enameled in French, the style is exasperatingly archaic in the Modern Library's English ("dost thou?" "mayhap thee"), and so is the inverted word-order: "a fountain, where swam fish," and no ordinary fish, either, but "descendants of the primordial eel-pout" with precious stones attached to their gills. "Where think you that you are now?" Salammbo asks at one point, and I, for one, would have to backtrack many pages to find the answer. Flaubert even forgets that he is not writing history, referring to an aqueduct having been "enlarged later by the Romans." Where he excels is in recreating antique exotica—the feast of jujube wine, snails in cumin, asafetida, bread dipped in oil and malabathrum, garum sauce—marinated, or putrefied, fish guts, the recipes for which in Pliny, Martial, and Apicius (who feasted on broiled ostrich meat) seem to indicate that it was not known in Flaubert's pre-Roman Carthage. The swashbuckling adventures, however, might have been written with a Spielberg movie in mind, Harrison Ford and Sean

Connery, as Matho and Spendius, breaching the wall of Carthage at night to steal the *zaimph,* the veil of Tanit the moon goddess.

27. Positano, the Hotel Le Sirenuse. After a harrowing dream in which I narrowly escape my pursuers by hang-gliding, I decide to leave this cliff-dwelling, stair-climbing city and go earlier to Carthage. In Naples, however, we mistakenly board a local train, arrive too late at Rome airport, and end up at the Hassler Hotel for another night of reading, this time Sallust's *Jugurthine War* (it was one of the texts in my paternal grandmother's Latin class in Poughkeepsie, New York, in the 1880s); the Sallust obelisk dominates the Piazza Trinità Dei Monti next to the hotel. "To Carthage then I came," Augustine wrote, unknowingly providing a line for *The Waste Land,* but unlike him—and being neither historian nor classical scholar—I travel with bags full of books that include Lucan's *On the Civil War* and Renan's *Studies in Punic Epigraphy.*

28. In contrast to Flaubert, Sallust is terse, and his rhetoric, in the reconstruction of the probable reasoning of long-dead generals, and aphoristic style ("the timid man looks ahead, the bold man tends to be rash") are not serious encumbrances. Moreover, he balances a bias against Jugurtha, the "cunning Numidian king," by an appreciation of his intellectual and other qualities as a young man when he fought for Rome. Sallust wrote some sixty years after Jugurtha's war against Rome, in the first century B.C., Flaubert, one of whose principal sources was Sallust, more than two millennia after the War of the Carthaginian Mercenaries, 241-237 B.C., the subject of *Salammbo.* Both describe the positioning of slingers and archers, the operation of mantlets, siege towers, javelin-discharging machines, and javelin-throwing thongs, the construction of contravallations, the deployment of elephants. Sallust is our contemporary, both as political analyst—"the elections were due shortly, and he was anxious to bring hostilities to an end before that"—and provider of logistic information, viz. a delegation escaping through Jugurtha's lines near Carthage made its way to Rome "in the course of a few days."

29. Half of the short flight to Ifriquiya is taken up with crash instructions in Italian, French, English, and Arabic, and down-the-aisle sales of duty-free cigarettes, perfumes, and whiskey, from which we learn that Tunisian money is not accepted abroad or even on the plane. Two of the passengers are Berbers, the man wearing a black caftan and chechia—the small red-felt hat—the woman a blue robe with silver agrafe at the shoulders, a red head shawl, and a silver anklet, the kholkal, a symbol of fidelity since the Carthaginian period. Approaching the Barbary Coast over the Cape Bon mountains and the aquamarine Gulf, we land on the Carthage promontory and are boxed to the terminal in a stifling bus. At the carousel, the female Berber collects and carries the male's baggage. In the lobby, women in blue snoods, black smocks and pants empty the disposal cans and mop the floors.

After strepitous, choking, exhaust-filled Rome, with its beeping Fiats and roaring Vespas, the traffic seems noiseless, the air like ozone. Tunis is a city of gleaming white apartment buildings, dark green cypresses, palm-shaded boulevards, flat roofs with TV antennas, square, obelisk-like minarets. Our driver gives us large jasmine buds that supposedly exfoliate in an hour (but do not), and offers his services for the entire day tomorrow at the same price, twenty-six dinars, as today's ride from airport to hotel. Will the weather be good? I ask. "If God wills it," he says, reminding us that we are in a culture of final causes, though he would probably argue that immediate causes such as meteorological activity are determined the same way.

In spite of the preponderance of French tourists, no one on the hotel staff speaks the language with any fluency, and the waiters know barely a dozen words, not including mine complaining that the couscous is too bland. The Carthage *vin ordinaire* is potable, but vintages do not exist, nor any imports, and the only white is as sweet, *mutatis mutandis*, as Yquem. In the Roman period the littoral was covered with vineyards—Bacchus is the most popular god in Tunisian mosaics—and the commercial rivalry with Italy provoked a wine-war. The piped dinner music is from *West Side Story.*

Impatient for a glimpse of Carthage, in the late evening we taxi there by way of the shuttered beach houses of La Marsa and La Goulette, where Cervantes was imprisoned after his capture at Lepanto. We gawk for a few minutes at the remains of the deserted ancient city from behind a modern barrier wall, then are approached by police who motion us to return to our taxi. The driver explains that the Presidential Palace is on the other side of the ruins, and that because of recent political disturbances, a curfew might be in effect. Even under a starry sky and within earshot of the softly lapping surf, Carthage lacks romantic appeal. Astarte does not come to mind, or Dido, or Salammbo, or Sophonisba, Massinissa's noble queen, but only Cato's curse. The all-male and teetotalist open-air cafés in the modern quarter seem almost as joyless.

30. Returning to Carthage in the morning, we try to bear in mind that, centuries older than Rome, it was once the center of half the known world, a capital of 200,000 by the fourth century B.C., with a fleet, larger than Rome's, capable of transporting 150 elephants to Sicily. Razed by Republican Rome—*Carthago delenda est*—it was rebuilt by Caesar Augustus and stood for 700 more years before it became an Arab stone quarry. Of the culture of Roman Carthage, however, little seems to be known after Augustine and Marcianus Capella, author of *Satyricon* and the texts edited by Hugo Grotius. Gibbon tells us that by the sixteenth century it had dwindled to "a mosque, a college without students, twenty-five or thirty shops, and the huts of five hundred peasants." Compared to 1858, when Flaubert was here and before extensive excavation, the present area of the ruins is vast, and the truncated square towers on Byrsa Hill form a forest of chimneys. But the remains are the deadest, most derelict imaginable; and the cleanest-picked: nothing is left for the maggot-like tour groups deposited by the buses that clog the streets around. As if in keeping with this, the main attractions are the necropolis and the urns containing the ashes of infants ritually burned alive by their well-to-do parents to appease Moloch.

On a secluded terrace just inside the entrance to the rubbled city, an old man kneels at his prayers (*Zuhr*), shoes by his side, touching his head to the ground again and again. On the beach immediately below the walls, girls wear one-piece and far from splashy swim-suits that nevertheless offer liberal exposures of lower dorsal flesh, the more surprising in that only a few blocks from here the hegab headdress and the all-enveloping chador attest to the modesty of most older women. One wonders about a connection between those hair-hiding hoods and body-hiding shrouds and the high incidence of adultery, the most common crime in Tunisia, according to Ali, our new driver-cicerone, who adds that "*women* are harshly punished" for it (not men), though not as harshly as prescribed by the Sharia, the savage Islamic code. Muslims are allowed to have four wives, he says, and as many concubines as they can afford.

The amphitheater, including all the upper tiers, has been restored and is used for dance performances, plays, concerts. As we enter, a troupe of French actors, musicians, and singers—in a plaintive, early-Renaissance motet—is rehearsing for a pageant. The perfect acoustics waft the lovely sound toward us.

Phoenician, Punic in Latin, was a living language throughout the Roman period, or so one deduces from Augustine's letter to the Pope advising him that clergymen sent to Carthage should be able to speak it as well as Latin; the latter, to judge from the two exemplarily simple sermons by Augustine recently identified in a manuscript in Mainz, could not have been highly developed. One of the jokes in Plautus's *The Carthaginian* (the *Poenulus*) is that the vocabulary of Hanno, the Punic-speaking hero, is comically sesquipedalian —as are such English examples as floccinaucinihilipilification—which seems to have inspired Plautus to invent amusing names of fourteen or so syllables for people in his other plays. I browse through some of these, in Duckworth's translations, and learn that such prototype roles in European theater as the young lover (*adulescentes*) and the courtesan (*meretrices*), as well as the play of mistaken identity, the play of randy masters and conniving maid-servants, and the play, nearly two millennia before Beaumarchais, of the servant who outwits his master, were firmly established in Roman comedy.

The neighborhood bordering Tunis's Belvedere Park is distinguished by mansions, Mercedes-Benzes, and a branch of Citibank, in contrast to most of the city, where young men, part of the unemployed 25 percent of the work-force, bide their time at sidewalk cafés. Their only hope is in finding jobs overseas, Ali says, adding that he himself found one for a time in Roskilde, Denmark. His disgruntlement with President Zine al-Abadine Ben Ali's Constitutional Democratic Assembly, a "one-party dictatorship," he says, stems from its interdiction against the fundamentalist En Nahda, which has the support of nearly half the voters and, paradoxically, as he no doubt thinks *we* think, is "the true progressive party." It was responsible for the nation-wide pro-democracy demonstrations not long ago, and advocates a free market to replace the failed planned economy of Ben Ali. Not being Islamic fundamentalist, it does not seek to get women back into the veil and return to a seventh-century dispensation of the law. And, anyway, since Tunisia is the most Westernized of the Arab countries and tourism its main industry, fun-damentalist blue laws—closing the hotel bar, replacing the Gideon in the bedroom with the Qur'an—could not be enforced. "But," he adds, "Fundamentalism is unstoppable." Knowing that we are from New York, he declines to answer questions about the Palestinian and Algerian situations.

Seeing me clutch my wallet-pocket as we pass the panhandling urchins at the entrance to the casbah, Ali assures us that we are not prey to pick-pockets here "because of the severity of the laws"; not the Sharia, he adds, seeing me shudder. The souk's alleys and warren-like tunnels are only inter-mittently paved, and then unevenly. Cobblers and metal toolers, scribes and notaries work in small street-side shops and offices, while merchants sell clothing, slippers, leather cushions, tobacco, hookahs, hook-shaped Berber daggers, and food: grains, dates, pomegranates, collops of mutton, squares of baklava. The street vendors, less tenacious than at Carthage, sell "Roman" coins and other tourist junk.

31. Of all the great museums that I have seen, the Bardo, the former Beylical palace, with large galleries, painted-wood ceilings, tiled walls, broad staircases, is the most beautiful building. In the mid-seventeenth century, the Beys of Tunis moved out of the casbah and into this *"zone verte"*— *"Barde"* means *"froid"* in Moorish (*i.e., "Ces lieux sont frais"*). The *"Barde,"* including the harem apartments, became a museum under a treaty by the French Protectorate in 1881. Its contents were greatly enriched after 1907, when a sponge diver found a trove of Grecian sculptures in the half-buried hulk of a Roman galley three miles off the port city of Mahdia. Since then, the Bardo has been the principal repository of excavated art from all over the country. Of the ninety-seven objects in the 1987 American Museum of Natural History's Carthage exhibition, eighty were on loan from the Bardo, whose collections include most of the mosaics, attached to the walls by iron tenons, recovered from the country's Roman villas and temples. The Bardo is the world's largest mosaic picture gallery.

In 1846, when Alexandre Dumas, driven from Tunis in a cabriolet during a sandstorm, was a guest at this *"résidence de fantasie,"* it was walled and further surrounded by a village of providers, now a tour-bus parking lot. The Bardo's most interesting exhibits are the eighth-century B.C. Punic stelae; the wooden sarcophagi, still with dust and bones; the terracottas from the tophets, the child crematoria; and the underwater Mahdia marbles, gnawed by limestone-hungry shellfish. The treasure of the Mahdia rooms is a winged Agon in bronze with coiled, calamistral hair. Claude Poinssot and other scholars believe that some of the vases here are replicas of the "Borghese vase" in the Louvre, excavated in Rome in the sixteenth century in what were once the Gardens of Sallust.

The principal subjects of the mosaics are hunting and fishing (a paradisal profusion of birds, animals, marine life); agriculture and domestic life (a woman with distaff, women playing pan-pipes, lutes, castanets); the games of the public baths (pugilists wearing cestuses); the blood sports of the arena, condemned by Augustine as "criminal bouts"; and scenes from mythology. Whereas the names of popular gladiators, champion race horses, and the poet Virgil are inscribed next to their portraits, deities are identified by their accouterments and symbols: Neptune with trident and sea-horse chariot, Venus with a mirror, Diana with a bow, Theseus with minotaur. Fabulous beasts and half-beasts, chimeras and sea monsters, satyrs and centaurs are favorite subjects, as are unicorns, wyverns, griffins in European art. In the mosaic portrait of Virgil seated between two muses, the poet holds a scroll in his lap, a text from the *Aeneid* inscribed upside down from the viewer's perspective, and legible to him or her only by reading it that way.

In the most memorable mosaic, thirty-two spectators are intensely concentrated on an arena. All except a graying and balding older man display the same hair style and thin rim of beard semi-circling the face close to the ears and under and back from the chin; and the same complexions: the colors are restricted to black, and reddish and whitish-brown. Their noses are long, their mouths small and tightly pursed, and their deeply reflecting eyes wide open. Each face expresses the same dread, yet each is differentiated. However barbarous the entertainment in the arena, the universality of the human emotion conveyed in this close-up is the work of a consummate artist.

June 1. Hadrian's aqueduct, on the way to Kairouan, seems much taller, and is far better preserved, than the aqueducts on the mountain side of Rome. The sight of its arches vaulting across the plain is an awesome reminder of the ambition (*gloria*) of the empire. Sixty miles long, it carried thirty-two million liters of water a day to Carthage.

Kairouan, a tangle of bicycles and ancient, battered automobiles, is Tunisia's oldest Arab city, and, after Mecca, Medina, and Jerusalem, the holiest in Islam. As late as the early twentieth century infidels were not allowed to enter it. At the pinnacle of its power, in the year 800, Harun Ar-Rashid (*Arabian Nights*) founded a dynasty that two decades later conquered Sicily. On a visit in the spring of 1914, Paul Klee wrote that he was "penetrated by intoxicating aromas." Whether or not the same kinds, those that penetrate us today in the souk have no physical or mental affects in any agreeable sense. This labyrinth of narrow, crooked, unpaved streets seems less fake than the one in Tunis, and the purveyors—of amber necklaces, beaten brass and copper wares, leatherwork camel saddles, bird cages, embroidered robes, anti-scorpion amulets, colored yarns—are less importunate.

Kairouan is one of the carpet capitals of the world. Ali steers us to the main emporium for them with the justification that the building's upper balcony overlooks the courtyard of the Sidi Sahab Mosque, closed to us today. (Sahab means companion, in this case of the Prophet himself, from whose beard Sidi Sahab preserved three hairs, the Mosque's most venerated relics.) From the balcony we descend to a showroom where an array of woven (*kilim*) carpets is spread out for us. Cheaper than the knotted kind (*mergoums*), they are also brighter in color, with strictly geometric patterns. Moving to a smaller room, we are invited to drink mint tea and inspect government seals and American Express credentials. Priced according to the amount of labor, the most expensive carpets (*zerbia*) have been knotted 250,000 times per square meter over a period of from two to three years. The most popular design is of the lozenge on the lamp in the city's Great Mosque. Most are polychromatic, but one type is restricted to the colors of natural wool, black, white, brown, beige. Only colorless wool will hold a dye.

Once we have nibbled, indicating preferences and reacting to prices, thereby showing our hand for the appraisal of our pocketbooks, carpets are unfurled for us with increasing rapidity, no doubt in the belief that the more we see the greater our sense of obligation to buy. When our choices are narrowed to two, haggling begins and prices drop drastically. Less wily than anticipated, the sellers quickly retreat from $20,000 to $8,000, from which we mistakenly conclude that the bottom must be lower still and stick to a $7,000 bid. A vociferous conference in Arabic follows but no further reduction is forthcoming, and we leave empty-handed, regretting the decision for the rest of the day, since we want the carpet and it would cost ten times as much in New York. We tell ourselves that the size, the rich colors, and the intricacies of design would not have suited our room, but this is rationalizing. "Eight thousand was a bargain," Ali says, thereafter remaining sulkily silent all afternoon, obviously having lost a commission.

The Great Mosque, which is closed to us, was the repository of the most beautiful Qur'ans of the Abbasid period, and its minaret is the world's oldest. Circumcisions are still performed in it. Outside the Medina's north gate, Bab Djebli, the butchers' stalls display eviscerated organs, tongues, testicles, the heads of sheep and cattle. A sign advertises "Camel rides for tourists." One hundred thirty years ago, N. Davis, the British author of *Ruined Cities,* described "the piteous moanings and infuriated gargling of ten thousand camels" in a nearby encampment.

Kandinsky spent the year of 1904-05 in Tunisia. Klee, a decade later, remained for only a short time, but he left a fascinating account of an artistic epiphany experienced in Kairouan. Colors "possessed" him here, especially the pinks and violets of early evening, "as tender as they are clear." But he fled back to Europe. "What I had felt was too powerful; I had to leave to regain my senses." The shock of recognition in his case was the realization that individual colors can be beautiful in themselves (Kant's *Ding an sich*) and not only, as Proust maintained, "in their harmony." Both arguments are supported by Klee's abstract aquarelle *In the Style of Kairouan,* with its blocks of reds on one side, and of purples, browns, greens, blues, yellows, blacks, and oranges on the other. After Kairouan, his pictures feature deserts and palms, minarets and marabouts, Arab gardens and crenellated walls, donkeys and camels (the marvelous *Brown and Black Camel* of 1915), and, my favorite, the woman, eyes peering just above the rim of her veil, in *Arab Song.*

In Thapsus, in 46 B.C., Julius Caesar, with Sallust at his side, defeated the fifteen cohorts of Pompeii's army, as Lucan's *De Bello Civili* recounts. In tourist-thronged Sousse, or Süsa (the Roman Hadrumetum, the Vandal Hunericopolis, the Byzantine Justinianopolis), we explore the Ribat, a ninth-century Muslim fort and religious retreat for devout warriors. The lookout tower was part of a network that could relay beacon messages from Egypt to Morocco in a single night, but the tall stone steps are without railings and the heat is fierce. A loudspeaker blares the muezzin as we leave the Medina. Part of the road back to Tunis, which we enter from the east via Hammam-Lif and the massif, follows the white sandy shore.

2. André Gide's journals of the war in Tunisia and the deliverance of the capital in May 1943 express boundless admiration for the Germans: "very dignified…they showed endurance, discipline, courage and they yielded only to superiority in weapons and numbers." To read Alan Moorehead's account of the same month, in *The End in Africa,* side by side with Gide's is to cross and recross the German lines. Moorehead's eye-witness version of the fighting in the Medjerda Valley concludes with the capture of Tunis. Unaware that the enemy was even near, German soldiers in the city were sitting at sidewalk cafés when British tanks began to clank down the streets in front of them.

Moorehead's maps reveal that some World War II battlefields were the same as those of the Carthaginian and Roman periods, and for the same strategic reasons in both the ancient and the modern wars. In 241 B.C., Hamilcar forded the Medjerda with seventy elephants and 10,000 men, surprising Carthage's mutineering mercenaries from the rear and raising their blockade of the capital. About 130 years later, the first battle between the Romans and Jugurtha's Numidian army was also fought near the Medjerda, which, according to Scullard's *Scipio Africanus,* ran a significantly different course 2,000 years ago. Tunisia is a land of beaten paths.

Polybius tells us more than Sallust about elephants in battle, and the chroniclers of Alexander in India (via Peter Green's *Alexander of Macedon*) more still. At the battle of the Jhellum, Porus's elephants impaled Macedonian soldiers on their tusks, or, lifting them with their trunks, dashed them to the ground and trampled them underfoot. Jugurtha deployed elephants like tanks in front-line charges, scattering the Roman cavalry and mangling the infantry. Livy says that the Romans were slow to discover that elephants could be frightened off by fire.

Not much seems to be known about the introduction of the camel into northern Tunisia. Norman Douglas (*Fountains in the Sand*) deduces that the animal was unheard of in Julius Caesar's time and was not in general use until the fourth century, but a mosaic excavated in Thysdrus in 1960, showing a tipsy Silenus riding the animal, can be dated to before A.D. 238, the year that the Romans destroyed the city in reprisal for its murder of a tax-assessor.

On our way to the Punico-Roman city of Dougga, we stop only very briefly at Thuburbo Maius: the scrub-desert valley here shimmers with heat-haze and the wind is like a hair-dryer. The road thereafter is bordered by red poppies, yellow daisies, purple thistles, bougainvillea. Beyond this are wheat fields, olive groves, flocks of sheep, herds of pasturing goats, colts running loose in the grasslands, nomad bivouacs (*foundouks*) with reposing camels. In the villages, sides of lamb hang from hooks in front of butcher shops, watermelons are suspended in nets, and donkeys drink at ancient troughs. Remnants of Rome are everywhere, bits of broken arches, disintegrating monuments, walls incorporated into houses. Near Medjez-El-Bab a modern wall encloses the graves of 3,000 British soldiers killed in the winter of 1942-43.

Dougga—Tukka in Punic, Thugga in Latin—covers sixty-two acres of the plateau and sloping side of a djebel that on the steep side, at 2,000 feet, overlooks the Oued Khaled. Favored by a natural mountain-top defense— the gray-yellow limestone with which the city was built—a moderate climate, arable land, an abundance of natural springs, it also enjoyed good fortune in politics. As the seat of the Numidian king Massinissa, Jugurtha's grandfather, who supported Rome against Carthage in the Third Punic War, Dougga prospered throughout the Pax Romana, during which wealthy citizens could purchase honor and fame by donating public buildings and supporting good works (euergetism). After the fall of Rome in the fourth century it was occupied by the Vandals, then by the Byzantines, but the ruins were inhabited until the 1950s, when archeologists resettled them in the Medjerda Valley below. From the town of Teboursouk the road winds up the mountain until the Corinthian columns of the Temple of Saturn come into view on the skyline. At the entrance, the straw hats for sale against the powerful midday sun are exactly like the one worn by a fisherman with rod and line in a Dougga mosaic in the Bardo.

The Punic mausoleum and the amphitheater, which seats 3,500 people on its nineteen semicircular tiers, have been restored, but Thugga-Dougga generally is well preserved. Historians believe that classical Latin plays were not performed here—only a few in the audience would have understood the language—but in their stead, pantomimes, burlesques, acrobatics, duels, debates, prestidigitations, though the view from the cavea of the plain below gives sufficient pleasure. Unique of its kind, and oriental rather than Graeco-Roman, the 3rd-2nd century B.C. mausoleum of the Numidian Prince Ateban, outside and below the city, is a three-layered structure with a pyramidal roof. Thought to have been erected during the reign of Massinissa, its bi-lingual (Lybico-Punic) "Here Lies" inscription was pilfered by the British Consul in the 1840s and is now in the British Museum.

Poinssot (*Les Ruines de Dougga*) rates the Capitol "the most beautiful Roman monument in North Africa." Beautiful, too, are the vistas from its porch of the ruins immediately below, the olive slopes, the fertile valleys extending to distant hills. The temple of Juno, Minerva, and Jupiter, the city's most imposing structure, is dedicated to "the safety of Marcus Aurelius." Its Jupiter statue, to judge by the mutilated head in the Bardo, all that was found, must have been colossal. The bath of Cyclops, originally embellished by mosaics depicting giants wielding sledgehammers, still has a dozen toilets (for remarkably small people), and some mosaics are in place in floors and pavements. As befits an inland city, most Dougga mosaics in the Bardo picture maritime adventures—Ulysses, bound to the mast to prevent bewitchment by the Sirens—and scenes of fishermen hauling in nets, setting lobster pots, harpooning an octopus.

The temple of Caelestis (Juno?), Baal's consort, the equivalent of the goddess Tanit, and the triumphal arch of Septimus Severus stand to the west in a bucolic setting, and in a magical stillness measured by the distant braying of an unseen donkey. The only discernible features of the Hippodrome (A.D. 214) are the outlines of the oval track over which chariot races were run, and of the *spina,* the central barrier. The olive groves on the hills behind were planted by Andalusian Moors who settled here after Philip III expelled them from Spain in 1609.

The excavation of more than 700 funerary inscriptions in good condition reveals that Dougga's adult males—no records were kept of females—enjoyed an astonishing longevity. Whether or not this is related to the circumstance that the largest house in the city is the Trifolium brothel has not been determined. Sallust says that the indigenous populations of the region "rarely die of disease; most of them die of old age." In fact, 10 percent lived to the age of ninety and longer, 5 percent were centenarians, and one doyen died at 115.

South of the city, near the beginning of the desert, are the cave homes filmed in *Star Wars*.

The USSR

Mirgorod (Sorochintsi), Riga,
Leningrad

The British documentary film-maker Tony Palmer had engaged me in an advisory capacity to accompany him and his London Weekend Television crew to the principal Russian locations in Stravinsky's life. The high point of the tour for me was my meeting with Rimsky-Korsakov's granddaughter.

August 27, 1981. London, 12:30 A.M. At Paddington Station an all-night Fotomat regurgitates the wanted-dead-or-alive likeness required for my Soviet visa. Mr. Cattermole, the clerk, and the station itself, deserted except for memories of a departure for Lyme Regis with the Stravinskys in August 1957, would provide good raw material for a scene in a spy novel.

28. 8 A.M. To Heathrow with Palmer and his team, on the way to film a few Russian sites of significance in Stravinsky's life, to videotape rehearsals of his music with Soviet orchestras and choruses, and to interview on camera two people who had known him, however slightly, Tatiana Rimsky-Korsakov, the granddaughter of Nicolai Andreyevich, his teacher, and A.A. Yacovlev, widower of Stravinsky's niece, Xenia, now the custodian of the Stravinsky family archives in Leningrad.

Part of my feelings of isolation and apprehension at Shermet'yevo Airport are attributable to the disproportionately small number of aircraft in evidence for the capital of the world's second superpower. Inside the terminal, guns-at-the-ready soldiers check our identities while we wait behind a gate that locks after each admission. All other personnel, customs officials, collectors of currency declarations, ticket agents, are women. In the absence of porters, we drag our bags and the heavy film equipment to the Philips X-ray machines at the inspection counters. Why is the "Philips" sign, testifying to the USSR's technological self-*in*sufficiency, so prominently displayed?

Pavel Kurchagin, our government shepherd, greets us inside the customs area. Soft-spoken, about thirty-five, he wears a brown leather jacket and, like all Russians who can find them, jeans. Withdrawn but friendly and good-natured about our complaints, he is less wary of the British crew than of me. (Has he read my 1962 Russian Diary?) His head honcho, Soviet Minister of Culture Kuharsky, has been cooperative from the planning stage, to the extent of providing footage of Ustilug, which is out-of-bounds to us but vital to the film, Stravinsky having written *Zvezdoliki,* the Balmont songs, some of *Sacre,* two of the *Japanese Lyrics,* and the first act of *The Nightingale* there.

The increase in traffic since my last drive from the airport to the center of Moscow nineteen years ago is scarcely believable. Another surprise is that some road signs and advertisements are in English as well as Russian, not including quotations from Brezhnev on placards and overhead passes. The Kremlin seems less awesome than in 1962, perhaps because a coat of bright yellow paint makes it look too new.

The filthy airport waiting room for the flight to Kharkov reeks from the unwashed bodies of Cameroons asleep on every bench and most of the floor. Aloft, a stewardess built like an Olympics weightlifter carries trays of an ersatz fruit juice that must be gulped immediately to avoid a second go-around to collect the empties. The "emergency exit" and "no smoking" signs are in English as well as Russian.

Kharkov. 11:45 P.M. Rain. 50° Fahrenheit. We stow our gear and ourselves—ten of us, counting Pavel, the driver, and his guide—into a decrepit minibus. Not having eaten for twelve hours, I propose that we spend the night here but am overruled; our hotel in Mirgorod is supposedly no more than a two-hour drive away. But with its cargo of half a ton of cameras, sound equipment, tripods, and ten passengers, the bus can barely make the hills, and its maximum speed empty is only about thirty kilometers an hour. The seats are not cushioned, and the road is a mere topping over dirt. The driver stops near Poltava, examines the motor, shrugs his shoulders, but we push on through steady rain and, on treeless stretches, opaque fog. To judge from the picture-language road signs—Red Crosses, beds, arrows indicating directions to hospitals—as well as from a near-collision of our own and three on-target ones by others, accidents are frequent.

From about 4 A.M., between Poltava and Mirgorod, people emerge on the sides of the road like war refugees in old newsreels, but, like ourselves, going to Sorochintsi Fair. They carry suitcases, fardels, baskets, sacks, live geese and turkeys slung in shoulder nets, watermelons, trussed lambs, and one of them leads a nag by a rope. The Mirgorod Hotel is still dark at 6:30, but we manage to rouse a young woman—stainless-steel teeth—and a short, fat, bulbous-nosed old man with the first smiling face I have seen since London. The elevator being nonfunctional, we must carry our bags to our third-floor rooms. As cells go, these are small, but equipped with bathrooms of a sort and inoperative television. Since breakfast is in two hours, and our bus for Sorochintsi departs immediately thereafter, I go to bed in my clothes and overcoat as a cock crows under my window.

29. A statue of Gogol marks the turnoff to the fair, where the road abruptly worsens with bulges, craters, ruts. The country must have looked much the same in Gogol's day: wooden cottages with picket fences; windmills; poplar, willow, and chestnut trees; walled cemeteries with ornate crosses. The unrelievedly black garb of the peasants on the roadside, suits, blouses, skirts, sheepskin caps, kerchiefs, boots, does not prepare us for the colorful clothes at the fair. Here, as in the airports, the proportion of men in uniforms is remarkably high.

Three days of flooding rains have turned the fairgrounds into a sty of black mud. This presents no obstacle to the booted Ukrainians, but I slip and slide in my thin Italian shoes like a neophyte on a skating rink. Despite the cold, I decide to proceed barefoot, which might be compared to walking in chocolate ice cream. Duckboards are nonexistent, and the few patches of higher grassy ground are already occupied. At one place a tractor is hoisting a car sunk up to its hood.

In the dry clearings, itinerant fiddlers, reed-pipers, and accordionists attract dancers from among the onlookers, but except for a grunt produced by rubbing a piece of wood on the drumhead of a tambourine (an effect Stravinsky used to demonstrate for percussion players), the music is not of much interest. More Stravinskyan are the female choruses in which, recalling *Svadebka,* a high soprano wails above a chant-like rhythm in the other voices. Many of the songs begin with solo voices or duets, followed by choral responses. A melodic pattern stressing the leading tone, a feature of Stravinsky's music, is also evident. But what would have delighted him most are the suction noises of feet extruding from the ooze. At one point an overamplified rock band blares out, and one marvels that indigenous music survives at all.

A *Petrushka*-like goblin is displayed at one booth. On raised platforms elderly women demonstrate old-fashioned wheat-threshing by hand, and cloth-weaving on treadle looms. Lacquered bowls and spoons are for sale, and pottery made uglier by glazing. The swings, and the greased poles to be shinnied up and slid down into piles of sawdust, are the same as at American Midwest fairs, and so is the flavorsome watermelon: no wonder the Stravinskys craved it.

After four hours of slithering in the mud, carrying a heavy box of film, and providing a landing pad for small, light-green frogs, I retreat to the bus with the "London Weekend Television" placard in the window, in the mistaken expectation that the mire on my feet will dry, like plaster of Paris, and I will be able to remove it. Back in Mirgorod, as I walk to a department store to buy shoes, my bedroom slippers attract glares of disapproval. I consider myself lucky to find a pair that fit, but they are ten times heavier than my ruined ones, and the thick plastic soles feel as if they might be cothurni. The cashier, a heavily built figure, shifts some beads on her abacus and charges me 15 rubles and 80 kopecks, about twenty dollars.

Dinner in the hotel restaurant is frugal, a small dollop of poor quality caviar on brown bread, rice, a tomato salad. Vodka and the sugary Russian champagne are available only at room temperature, and ice cannot be made in less than three hours. At table Pavel talks about John Le Carré, telling us that cold-war samizdat spy stories are popular in the USSR. The word "defector" is used in this conversation, but Pavel claims not to have heard of Brodsky or any of the writers or musicians under political penumbras. When asked about Mandelstam, he says: "I have not read him because every new edition is sold out on publication." He clearly believes me to be a CIA mole.

In bed: visions of farmhouses with wood-lace window frames; of geese waddling on grass; of low carts drawn by horses with surcingles; of an old man with Taras Bulba mustache, boots, and caracul; of Uzbeks with white-beaded hats. What I do *not* feel is any *nostalgie de la boue.*

30. By daylight, from Mirgorod back to Kharkov, we see that most houses have asbestos shingles, which, besides being carcinogenic, must be noisy in the rain. The cornfields, sunflowers, and loam are reminders of our Midwest, as are the police cars with revolving lights, and the queue at the only gas station between Poltava and Kharkov. But the Ukraine is less flat than Kansas, its fields bounded by forests, the road, at times, by walls of trees. Large concrete public lavatories are found every few miles along the roadside, but why, in this sparsely populated country and with scarcely any highway traffic?

We do not see a single grain elevator, or silo, or any farm machinery, or even any farmers, but only three old women, each tending a single cow on a rope. The corn and wheat crops in two fields have been harvested but are rotting in the others, most of the apples in the endless orchards having already fallen to the ground. What has happened to the largest grain exporter in the pre-1917 world? Economists write about periodic crop failures, but the failure in front of our eyes is that of not reaping.

The Intourist Hotel in Kharkov (Lenin Avenue, a few blocks from Gagarin Avenue) has an elevator, but its double doors open in and out so awkwardly that we prefer the stairs; and while the bathrooms are an inevitable improvement on Mirgorod, the showers have been designed for pygmies. The restaurant is hot, foul-smelling, and loud, being partly a dance floor on which girls in tight jeans and Western hairstyles are doing the twist. About half of the customers are tall Africans wearing long striped robes and crown-like hats.

I lie in bed puzzling about the contrast between Stravinsky's hyperacute time-sense—the split-second calculations in his manuscripts, his stop-watches and electric metronomes, his impatience with unpunctuality—and the indifference to the clock of his present-day fellow-countrymen. Nothing takes place at the appointed hour, no one appears as scheduled, and every estimate by Pavel and our drivers is eons off. But then, Pavel is always con-ducting behind-the-scenes operations, disappearing to make telephone calls to higher-ups, which explains many of the delays and all the oscillations as to whether or not appointments will actually take place.

31. At breakfast in the hotel restaurant, Brian, our sound technician, who withholds no gripe, says that the "woodwork" is a laminated plastic on chipboard that would burn in a few seconds. Nick, our imperturbable cam-eraman, spends his nonfilming time reading *Lord of the Rings.* Max, his assistant, keeps a tiny phial containing a "stress remedy" so strong that a single drop can pull him back from the brink. As for Tony Palmer, he thinks and adapts quickly and works even harder than his coolies, editing tran-scripts of interviews on buses and airplanes, and persisting hour after hour for "yet another piece of the mosaic."

At the airport we wait in a dirty, fly-infested, stand-up snack bar, in which most of the customers are drinking glasses of sour cream. The adjoin-ing room is a barber shop with a line of small boys and their mothers stretch-ing to it from beyond the outside door. "Look at us Russians, we are always waiting," a character in Turgeniev remarks, but Russians wait less patiently in airports, and in fact scramble and shove when boarding buses and planes. During our flight to Riga the din of Russian Muzak never lets up. Since the wings lack flaps, the takeoff and landing are bumpy and abrupt, which reminds me of flying thirty years ago.

The two women who meet us at the cold, rainy Riga airport speak Lettish between themselves, Russian with Pavel, and good English with me. The wooden houses on the outskirts, with fences and windowsill flowers, are dark reds, blues, greens. The stone buildings in the center are Gothic, or, as in the case of the Latvian Theatre, neoclassical. The city is livelier and its people more brightly dressed than Kharkov and its citizens.

Our Hilton-style rooms have practical bed lamps, impractical telephones (a foreign call must be placed three weeks in advance), large-screen television, "disinfected" notices on the toilet, wash basin, and bath. Best of all, six elevators are working. In the lobby, the only clue that we are east of NATO is the limitation at the kiosk to Soviet-bloc newspapers.

Another innovation is the hard-currency bar, in which the money of most countries except the USSR can buy famous brands of liquor, real coffee, cigarettes. As if in further imitation of the United States, this room is overly air-conditioned. Possibly voicing a criticism of American customs, the bartender asks me: "Would you like too much ice, sir?" From the twenty-sixth floor, where we dine, Riga is a neon city, and with electrically moving signs.

September 1. We film the Latvian Choir in the organ loft of the thirteenth-century Domsky Sobor, a remarkably inappropriate name for this Gothic building, with its coats of arms of the Teutonic Knights, its quotations from Scripture in German, and its Baroque organ. The German-speaking curator, talking to me about her son in Seattle, claims that while Riga's Russian Orthodox and Protestant churches have been closed, its Catholic ones are open. Not this one, though, and is a cathedral stripped of its altar a church?

At Philharmonic Hall each of the eighty-five braided blondes in the bevy comprising the Dzintars Choir wears a headband like the Adolescents in *Sacre*. Their performance of Stravinsky's *Podblyudniye* is the most spirited I have ever heard. During the recording I am interviewed simultaneously by a reporter from *Tass* and the editor of a newspaper for Latvian refugees in the United States. After the session, the choir presents me with a large bouquet of freshly cut flowers. The director says that he heard me conduct in Leningrad in 1962, which makes me feel very old.

2. The waiting room in the Riga airport for the 6 A.M. flight to Leningrad is less dreary than the others, or so I think until I begin to read L.I. Brezhnev's *The Great October Revolution and Mankind's Progress,* described on the cover as a booklet for "progressive tourists." In Leningrad, Igor Bogdanov, another *Tass* correspondent, joins our party.

The disparity between the grandeur of St. Petersburg's buildings, parks, and perspectives and the misery of its inhabitants might be intended to prove the truth of Kierkegaard's "A revolutionary age which is at the same time reflective, leaves everything standing but cunningly empties it of significance." In contrast to the deserted sidewalks by the Hermitage and the Admiralty, the lobby of the Astoria Hotel is overpopulated with tourists. Here porters take our bags to spacious and well-furnished rooms with beds in curtained-off alcoves. But the refrigerators are purely ornamental: problems with the *elektrichestvo?*

In the Necropolis of the Great Masters we film the tombs of Dostoyevsky, Musorgsky, Rimsky-Korsakov (an elaborately carved Gaelic-style church stone), Borodin (themes from the Second Symphony and *Polovtsian Dances* in gold mosaic), and Tchaikovsky (an aggravated expression, no doubt because of the proximity of two female angels, one behind him with a cross, one in front with a book). The monument to Fyodor Stravinsky and his son Gury, the composer's celebrated basso father and younger brother, is superior as sculpture and in better taste than any of these. Across the canal, the pink, white, and gold Alexander Nevsky Monastery embodies some of the finest architecture in the city, as well as beautifully filigreed ironwork in gates and fences. In contrast to the hordes of sightseers at the graves of the masters, the monastery's inner cemetery, where the tombs of small children are shaped like cradles, is deserted. Pigeons perch on every sunny ledge.

In the huge and too-resonant Astoria restaurant, an overamplified rock band blasts out *"Bei mir bist du schön"* six times during a "dinner" that takes two hours to order and three to receive. Though the menu is several pages long, absolutely nothing on it is available, and a maddeningly apathetic waiter recites the two possibilities to us over and over. In contrast, service in both of the hotel's hard-currency bars is prompt, and business in them thriving. Are these bars a CIA stratagem? After all, Coca-Cola addiction might bring about the downfall of the USSR more rapidly than other forms of poison-chemical warfare.

3. Climbing the four flights of stairs to the Rimsky-Korsakov Museum, in the composer's former apartment, I feel as if I am literally following Stravinsky's footsteps. The ceilings are high and the double windows large. The furnishings, including three pictures of the first production of Rimsky's *Mozart and Salieri,* and the photograph of Igor and Catherine Stravinsky with Rimsky and daughter and son-in-law are much the same as at the time of the composer's death.

The apartment's lived-in feeling is attributable to such details as Rimsky's spectacles placed on a 1905 Moscow newspaper on his desk, and his fur hat and *shuba* on a coat rack. But it is Tatiana Vladimirovna, with her striking resemblance to her grandfather, who brings the surroundings to life. She tells me in genteel English, pointing to a divan, "This is a national monument, but I think we can sit on it."

After describing her encounter with Stravinsky in Moscow in 1962, she says: "As a pupil, Stravinsky was a notorious complainer about his lack of money. Once my father and aunt and uncle gave him twenty kopecks to arrange and play *God Save the Tsar* as a waltz. Stravinsky took the money and wrote a very witty piece." Of the chorus that he composed for Rimsky's sixtieth birthday, she says:

> It was prepared as a surprise. The singers, who were the Rimsky-Korsakov children and their friends, gathered in the music room

adjoining the one with the dinner table. The chorus, with Stravinsky at the piano, began to sing at the sound of popping champagne corks. My grandfather opened the doors and came in to listen and to congratulate the young composer and the performers. Later that night, my grandfather wrote in his diary: "Not a bad piece."

She adds:

I am not a musician, so I cannot speak about Stravinsky as a composer, but I think he has been a much misunderstood figure in this country. I was born in 1915 and did not know him, but I have always been told that he was virtually a member of our family, coming early in the morning and staying until late at night.

Two of the portraits on the walls are of Wagner, two are of Tolstoy, and one each is of Schumann, Chopin, Berlioz. Tchaikovsky is conspicuously absent. The showcases contain music notebooks very like Stravinsky's and the same size as his early, Rimsky-period songs. A telegram from Stravinsky himself: "How is the health of Nikolai Andreyevich please telegraph. Ustilug [May] 22, 1908," is exhibited.

The turquoise, white, and gold Nikolsky Sobor is now a consecrated church in better condition than most Leningrad buildings—it was closed when we were here in 1962—and the parquet floors, icons, votive lamps, and candle trays are remarkably well kept. The worshippers are not numerous—technology, not religion, is the opiate of the masses—but we witness two services at, respectively, the center and left side of the refulgent iconostasis. When the priest, a young man in blue vestments, raises the gospel to his and then our lips, Pavel flinches.

Like the second storey in other Russian churches, this one is twice as tall as the first. In the pinnacle of the ceiling, the Eye of Osiris watches from its pyramid, a Freemasonic emblem probably dating from the Alexander I period. The gold here and a gory, life-sized crucifix remind me of Mexican churches. The detached campanile, a hundred yards or so closer to the

Krukov Canal, is even more beautiful than the church. While we film it, two nefarious types approach, furtively unwrap an icon from a newspaper, and offer it for sale. Unlike their counterparts in capitalist countries, they do not wheedle and insist, but the speed with which they give up is depressing.

Only a few hundred yards separate the Nikolsky and the Maryinsky Theatre, which is no more than five hundred yards from the Stravinsky apartment, and the Conservatory, so important as a concert hall in the composer's youth, is just around the corner. Thus the musical, theatrical, and religious institutions that to some extent determined the forms of his life's work were within two blocks of his home. Yet no marker identifies his residence, whereas a plaque next door to it memorializes that of the very minor conductor E.F. Napravnik. Surely a little marble could have been spared for Stravinsky, even if it had to be quarried from the pedestal of one of the Lenin statues found at every factory, collective farm, public building, village, town, and city square.

Pavel has been shaken by his exposure to practicing Christianity. He tells me that he once "took a course in the history of religion, but no such instruction in the history of atheism and disbelief was available, and, if it had been, would not have been presented fairly."

At the Theatre Museum, which was apprised of our visit months ago as well as yesterday and this morning, nothing has been prepared for us, the curators are hopelessly inept, and we wait an hour in a gallery of photographs of actors playing Lenin before the Stravinsky memorabilia are brought in. These consist of Vasily Shukhayev's portrait of him, painted in Paris in 1933; three unidentified Diaghilev-period stage designs by Sudeykin; Golovin's costume designs for the May 1918 Maryinsky *Nightingale;* some Benois sketches for *Petrushka;* and, best of all, Bakst's costume design for Anna Pavlova as the Firebird. The treasure of the lot is Fyodor Stravinsky's notebook containing 183 of his drawings for costumes in his sixty-six roles at the Maryinsky. (Balanchine gave me a complete copy of these photographs procured during his 1972 Russian tour.) Four of Fyodor's other drawings are of Ustilug, three of them dated ("July 1889,"

"June 19-July 16, 1889," and "1890"). A fifth page, "Summer 1896, Bad Homburg," contains his caricatures of an Englishman (Sherlockian pipe and fore-and-aft cap) and of the Kursaal piano player. "Drawing by daddy," the fourteen-year-old Igor wrote at the bottom of the paper, and no doubt "daddy" did it to amuse his son.

4. After trying for two days to obtain information about flights from Leningrad to London through Copenhagen, I have been instructed to appear at 8 this morning in the Aeroflot building on Nevsky Prospect. Knowing that the ticket will not be issued unless I present my passport and visa, I knock long before that time at the door of the Astoria office in which passports are kept. A girl holds up five fingers, but since five minutes means at least an hour, I return to the hard-currency bar and drink espresso, fearing that I will need the *ticket* in order to get the *passport.* When the office finally opens, the clerk insists that she is not allowed to separate my documents from those of the British television crew. Fortunately, she soon goes off duty and her successor is unaware of this probably non-existent rule.

Long lines extend from every ticket window at Aeroflot, but the side room for international flights is empty. An hour passes before the ticket is issued, despite the involvement of seven girls in my simple transaction, one to calculate the currency exchange, another to take my money, the third to fill out forms, the fourth to write the ticket, and the fifth, sixth, and seventh to pool their English. Can the bureaucracy mocked by Gogol and Dostoyevsky have been as inefficient as this? What worries me now is that my Paddington Station visa photograph, compared with the present reality, may prevent me from getting through, experiences such as this one having changed my hairline and in other ways drastically altered my appearance.

The restaurant tonight reverberates with the shouts and laughter of inebriated Finns. Pavel says that they come to Leningrad in order to drink themselves into stupors less expensively here than they can do at home.

After accomplishing this, they are literally piled into their returning buses. The puritanical Soviets tolerate this behavior for the hard currency it brings in.

5. On my last day we arrive at what should have been the starting place on the Stravinsky trail, the apartment of A.A. Yacovlev. Here is the huge diary kept by Fyodor until the last months of his life, at which time his wife made the final entries for him. In this immaculate record, every event of every day is described in detail, including the expenditure of each kopeck, tabulated in the right column. The birth of Igor is framed in red ink as carefully as if he had done it himself. "3 rubles for Karpovitch," the midwife, Fyodor has written, "75 kopecks for the acting midwife, before Karpovitch," and "1 ruble for the bath to wash the newborn." The book is a history of Igor's first twenty years, as well as evidence of the continuation of the orderly habits and meticulousness of the father by the son.

The collection of photographs from the 1890s to 1912 shows that Igor was a dandy even in adolescence. Whether or not in compensation for his small stature, his clothing and the way he wore it made him stand out in any group. But why would a man in his early twenties choose to wear wing-collars and dress ties in provincial Ustilug, where they must have looked as absurd and felt as uncomfortable as the evening dress of the British in India? Whatever the answer, the fact of his abundant wardrobe complicates the dating of the photographs, for the reason that ties, scarves, suits, and hats rarely appear more than once.

The most interesting of these pictures are of Igor with Andrey and Vladimir Rimsky-Korsakov; Andrey, wearing the same kind of spectacles as his father, resembles him to a confusing degree. Snapshots of Igor with Nadiezhda Nikolayevitch Rimsky-Korsakov in Berlin in 1902, at the time of Fyodor's Roentgen treatments there, raise a question about the relationship of the young couple in the years before their respective marriages, since, to judge from these glimpses, they seem to be devoted to each other. Also worth noting is that while Fyodor stands in distant corners and looks away from the camera in group portraits, Igor invariably places himself in the middle of the front row and becomes the focus of the composition. Stravinsky junior, moreover, always looks directly into the camera, where the action is. Most conspicuous among the ancestral portraits is the large oil of Fyodor Ivanovich Engel (1779-1837), whose considerable wealth was inherited by his step-granddaughter, Igor's maternal grandmother. The most interesting art in the apartment is in Dimitri Stelletsky's illuminated letters to, and in a few cartoons of, his composer classmate.

"Transporting explosive matters is prohibited," an airport sign reads. Poems as well as bombs? My fellow passengers on the Aeroflot to Helsinki are hung-over and still-drunk Finns, some carrying huge teddy-bear souvenirs. We land at a frightening speed, but the bamboozled Finns applaud the pilot. In the airport restaurant, I devour herring and boiled potatoes, overtipping the waiter for his efficiency, celerity, and affability, qualities totally absent in the acedia of socialism. Then as I try to read an interview with myself on the front page of today's *Pravda,* a man at the next table is emboldened to address me in Russian. Understanding that he wishes to borrow the paper, I tell him, with my smattering of the language, that he is welcome to it. "Thank you," he says in Oxonian, adding, "I am so sorry that you are not one of my fellow countrymen." Thanks, but *I* am not sorry. I melt into Finnair for a flight to London.

Asia

Nepal

The inspiration for this trip was New York's Asia House exhibition, "Nepal: Where the Gods Are Young," and, in particular, the fifteenth-century silver image of embracing tantric gods, described below. This sculpture, reproduced on the cover of the catalog of the show, was the property of Doris Wiener, the Madison Avenue gallery owner and collector and an expert on Kangra paintings, from whom, in the 1970s, Vera Stravinsky acquired most of her wall of Indian miniatures. Alva and Alexander traveled with me. The culture shock and the impact of Himalayan landscapes changed the life of the latter. Denmark is flat and not very exotic.

January 19, 1990. Leaving Paris, our Air India flight shows a film on basic bathroom behavior: how toilets are flushed, how hot and cold water can be conjured from a faucet, how to use a wash basin, how hands and faces are dried with towels.

20. The New Delhi airport is stultifying, soul-corroding. Older men squat on their haunches next to the walls, while young ones in ill-fitting red denims go through motions of sweeping the floor. During the seven-hour wait for a constantly delayed Royal Nepal plane, we can do little in the dim light except watch the ebb and flow of arriving and departing human herds. "Patience, patience," a ticket agent says, joining his palms together (the *namaste*) as if to pray. Most of the people in the boarding-area "lounge" have Mongoloid features, but turbaned Sikhs are here, too, Hindu women in saris clutching strings of "rosary" beads, and American flower-power counterculture types, with backpacks and trekking gear. An alluring young woman, long braid, bangle bracelets, suckles her baby while squatting on the floor in lotus position. When we finally board she carries the infant in a papoose.

Launchings of new Nepali airplanes are accompanied by the ritual sac-rifice of animals. Mercifully not further detained for such ceremonies, our Caravelle rises steeply over sprawling tenements and parched and rutted land intersected by irrigation ditches. The stewardesses—violet saris, flowers in their hair, the vermilion tikka on their foreheads and collyrium on their eyelids—remind us to advance our watches fifteen minutes, an odd, Through-the-Looking-Glass differentiation symbolizing independence from India. In the Nepali calendar, today is the seventh in the month of Magh in the year 2046.

Suddenly the Himalayas burst into view, the white top of the world, plumes of snow blowing eastward from the peaks. In reddish late afternoon light we descend over green hills, terraced rice paddies, and—surprisingly, since Katmandu is southeast, not north, of Delhi, but also appropriately, since the architectural form originated here—a pagoda. Tribhuvan terminal is new, but the brown filigreed woodwork is in traditional Nepalese style. We buy rupees and surrender our bags at Customs, where they are ransacked, a consequence of yesterday's interception of a cache of heroin from Hong Kong. Five rapacious porters, one per bag and two dollars each, push their way toward a small taxi, leaving us to scrimmage against a wall of outstretched hands, like those of tantric gods with a superhuman multiplicity of arms.

Traffic is to the left, theoretically, but the road is indivisibly narrow. The city streets are unpaved, dust-clouded, choked with people and animals—sacred cows (given wide berth), goats, pigs, chickens, dogs (but no cats: they embody evil spirits)—through which Hondas honk and bicycles weave like figure skaters. In the absence of street lights, the driver takes bearings from cooking fires and the candles of the small shrines and temples that are on every block. At the Yak and Yeti Hotel the doorman's fondness for saluting brings Gunga Din to mind.

The furnishings in our teak-paneled rooms are Japanese: mini-bar, tele-phones, TV—one channel, but with a news program in English. The windows are permanently locked against entomological activity—fly whisks are a fixture in Nepalese genre painting, even in depictions of life in heaven—and the outside sills are beds of nails, not for fakirs but against the noisy pigeons that nevertheless roost there during the night. In the coziest of the hotel's three restaurants, five booths surrounding an open wood fire with brass funnel chimney, we drink Pol Roget and eat Boris's beetless borscht; Boris Nikolayevich Lissanevich (d. 1985) was a White Russian (his life is recounted in Michel Peissel's *Tigers for Breakfast*) who danced in Diaghilev's Ballets Russes before emigrating to Nepal and founding its tourist industry, persuading the government to issue visas and to create international hotels. The waiters wear white livery with red sashes and Nehru-type *topis,* the national headgear for men.

By ten o'clock the streets are totally dark, and, except for a taxi-stand of three-wheeled bicycle rickshaws, deserted—a curfew, perhaps, because of political tensions. In the hotel garden we stroll among small statues of Ganesh, the elephant-headed son of Shiva and Parvati and the god of "auspiciousness," whatever that means.

We go to bed in a state of high expectancy. Ever since the New York exhibition, ancient Nepali statuette sculpture, figurines representing deities in the image of man, has seemed to me the most perfect in the representation of human form. Venerated as icons, they are not primarily works of art at all, nor do they merely "represent," since the actual spirit of the living god is believed to reside in the image. I am thinking above all of a numinous ninth-century Bodhisattava Maitreya (the future Buddha) and, from the same period, an incomparably graceful Parvati with "blossoming breasts" (in a word, *abhinavayauvanodbhinnakuchabhara*), both in gilt-copper; an exquisitely modeled twelfth-century Indra with jeweled diadem; and a silver image of embracing tantric gods: locked in each other's eyes, arms, and legs and locking out all thought of the separation of mind and matter, of "I" and "Thou," subject and object: their bodies melt together in an eidolon of nonduality.

I am also elated to be in the land of the birthplace of Siddhartha Gautama—at Lumbini, in the West, in elephant and tiger country. "Here the Buddha Sakyamuni was born" is the inscription on a column from the third century B.C., excavated in 1896. (Or should it be "Buddhas," in view of the succession of his rebirths? The fact of his predecessors reminds us of the Essene role model, and the description, "the god who has appeared on earth and undergone the fate of man," sounds Christian.) Here in Nepal he may already have begun to dispute with the subtle Brahmin sages about the irrelevance, in a world of human suffering, of preachments on the origins and meanings of the Universe, of how the Infinite could produce the Finite. Here he may have put forth his belief that "within this mortal body, conscious and endowed with a mind, is the world and its origins, and its passing away."

I am curious, too, about the phallocentric culture—including techniques of *imsaak,* seminal retention, and tantric erotic practices, stamped out in India by the Raj but living on here—the social institutions, and the ingrown mores of a landlocked, high, remote state that isolated itself still further in fear of annexation by British India and closed its borders from 1816 to 1950 (only 153 Europeans were allowed to enter the country between 1881 and 1923). Left entirely to its own resources, Nepal has understandably developed an eccentric and grotesque character:

> …the wildest dreams of Kew
> Are the facts of Kathmandu.

And I am not a little frightened of a country in which men still volunteer to have their tongues pierced with a steel spike to ensure direct ascent to heaven when they die; and of a country in which animals are slaughtered on feast days to propitiate gods. In the annual celebration of the Durga deity's victory over the buffalo demon, Mahasisura, 1,008 buffaloes are beheaded with the *kharga* sword in a temple courtyard, the executioners standing ankle-deep in blood. And what of a country whose king must receive yearly permission to continue his rule from the four-year-old Kumari, "living goddess"of chastity, born Rashmila Shakya in a lower-caste family (the Shakyas are artisans). More Lewis Carroll fantastication.

21. By mid-morning the fog has burned off and the mountains and skyline of spires and tridents (Shiva's weapon) begin to emerge. Katmandu's only entirely paved, reasonably smooth, comparatively negotiable road extends from the Royal Palace along Durbah Marg (Palace Way), which has sidewalks, shops with plate-glass windows, and even street lights. Here, as everywhere else, buses and trucks emit smoke-screens of chemical-warfare density. Here, too, traffic is regulated by impertinent *flaneurs*, the untouchable ruminants who stroll into the center of the road and often settle there for a nap. Road signs are in English, as are billboards, store-front advertisements, and the bizarre slogans proclaimed on posters, such as "Mother and Motherhood are Greater than Heaven."

Patan, thought to be the oldest Buddhist city in the world, is a peerless aggregation of palace, pagoda, and temple architecture, a museum of the art of carving in stone, teak, and tusk, as well as a medieval world of indescribable misery and squalor. The Archeological Garden possesses many steles with limestone reliefs and some detached wood sculpture, but no example of the jeweled silver and gold figurines exhibited in New York. Even so, some of the craftsmanship of those ancient image makers survives, no matter how debased the art. A few families in the Bincha Bahal neighborhood still carve the life of Buddha in ivory, and Newari men, descendants of the oldest inhabitants, still cast bronzes that Newari women file smooth.

A nineteenth-century engraving of Patan's Durbah Square reveals only minor differences with the same perspective today. All but one of the eight temples crowded together here are in the Indian steeple style, but the exception, Krishna Mandir, in the Mogul tradition and constructed entirely of stone, is more memorable, partly because of the pillar in front of it topped by a gilded statue of Garuda, the bird-god and Vishnu's means of aerial conveyance, here in human form and kneeling. This, and another pillar surmounted by an enthroned king with the hovering hood of a cobra as panoply, stand in about the same relation as the St. Theodore and Lion of St. Mark's columns in the Piazzetta in Venice—the only Orient-Occident parallel that makes any sense to me so far.

In the food market, dried fish, betel leaves, oranges, giant cauliflower, radishes, and leeks are stacked on the ground, while salt crystals, chilies, grain, ginger, turmeric, cardamom, and buckets of curds are piled on tables. Goats, sacred monkeys, and cows mingle with a teeming humanity of mostly barefoot children, many of them young girls with still younger brothers and sisters strapped to their backs; Katmandu valley is one of the most densely populated regions in the world. The women, dark eyes outlined in black kohl, are remarkably beautiful. Many of them carry head loads, which accounts for their erect, regal bearing.

The center of the seventeenth-century Sundari Chowk (courtyard) is the Malla king Siddhi Narsingh's octagonal bath, Tusha Hiti, celebrated for its ornately carved stone walls depicting Nagas (sacred serpents), rain goddesses, and Asta Matrikas (mother-earth goddesses), and its sculptures of fish and aquatic animals—turtles, crocodiles. Only the conch-shaped basin, a yoni symbol, has escaped mutilation, or perhaps been restored. On the walls of the adjoining temple of Degu Talle, the personal deity of the Malla dynasty (1350-1769), first traced by Giuseppe Tucci (*Alla Scoperta dei Malla,* 1960), nature has gnawed away some of the decorative intricacies of the wooden struts.

While we try to imagine the place as it must have been, a small boy asks in good English where we come from. When I confess, he responds with "Albany is the capital," after which we become more interested in him than in the history he begins to relate. Handsome, shining with intelligence, this fourteen-year-old is fluent in English, French, Italian, German, and Japanese. (He has lived in Japan, but can he have learned his usages of the other languages from tourists?) Nor is he simply reciting factual information by rote, since he answers questions unrelated to his work as a guide, provides reasoned explanations, and sustains conversations. He brings to mind the untutored Florentine mathematical prodigy in Aldous Huxley's "Young Archimedes," who draws Pythagoras's theorem in squares and triangles with the charcoal end of stick.

This young guide, Rahne Patne, takes us to the eleventh-century Buddhist monastery, Uku Bakal, and to the Temple of the Thousand

Buddhas, expounding the while on the significances of symbols. Of these, the ubiquitous lingam-and-yoni looks like a juicer, a dome in a circular strainer with a spout to drain the liquid, and it was used in a similar way: liquids were poured over it in ritual bathing. Unlike these Hindu phalluses, some Buddhist images are erotic to contemporary sensibilities—"admirably formed for amorous dalliance," in Boswell's phrase—above all the dancing damsels carved in wooden temple struts who shake trees to shower the Buddha's pathway with scented petals.

Patan's side-by-side Hindu and Buddhist temples serve the devotees of both, a natural syncretism. Shrines of Shiva as Bhairava, his most fearsome form, include both the Shiva lingam and toylike images of Buddhist shrines (stupas). In painting and manuscript illumination stylistic differentiations between the art of the two religions are often indiscernible. Yet the same god is identified by Buddhists as the bodhisattva of compassion and by Hindus as the lord of death.

The glossy, glamorizing photographs in travel brochures are no preparation for the wretchedness of the human condition in Patan. Plumbing seems to be unheard of, though it existed in the drainage systems of the temples centuries ago, and even latrine ditches are apparently non-existent. Human as well as animal feces litter the streets and alleys (the Durga goddess decreed that only a man found defecating in the direction of the sun could kill the buffalo demon), and the whole city is an open toilet reeking of excrement and urine. A hill of garbage on which pigs are feasting and children scavenging rises directly behind a row of primitive dwellings in the middle of the city. An old stone bath near it, the size of Tusha Hiti, has become a cesspool in which, despite the filth and slime, a young girl wades to her knees trying to find a clean patch of water in which to wash.

On the path to the sacred Bagmati River, a tributary of the Ganges (Varnasi, the former Benares, is less than a hundred miles away), bicycles, motorcycles, and men and women balancing bamboo shoulder-poles force their way through the ragged populace, stirring the dust-filled air; no wonder most people are coughing, expectorating, blowing noses onto the ground. Many faces are vacant—only someone unaware of population statistics and living conditions could doubt that inbreeding must be common —and no one can have escaped prenatal and all-other-age malnutrition. Medical and dental care is totally unknown, and whatever the ratio of doctors to population in Patan, it is reputedly one per 300,000 in the provinces.

At the river bank, cremation fires are stoked high on two of the ghats— funeral-pyre platforms—and the air is laden with the stomach-turning stench of burning human flesh. Across the river, women in bright saris labor in minutely segmented fields, as their Iron Age ancestors must have done and with similar implements.

At Swayambhunath (the primordial Buddha), now a Tibetan refugee center, we climb the 330 steps to the top of the mountain where, among the monkeys and pines, Siddhartha Guatama is thought to have preached. On a terrace near the top, guarded by a mythic leonine creature, is the statue of a thunderbolt (symbol of the Absolute, a male instrument), not Jovian-jagged but in the shape of a dagger. The 2,000-year-old white-domed shrine at the summit is famous for its painted pairs of lotus-shaped eyes and inverted-question-mark noses, representing dharma, virtue, a device peculiar to Nepal and the country's best-known landmark, what the Eiffel Tower is to Paris.

Above the all-seeing eyes, surveying the world from the four cardinal directions, the stupa is crowned by thirteen upward-tapering coils, somewhat like the Guggenheim Museum's ramps, for the thirteen stages to Enlightenment. Shaven-headed and saffron-robed monks circumambulate the stupa clockwise, chanting the mantra *"om mani padme hum"* and spinning prayer wheels in eternal supplication of heaven. In an adjoining shrine, priests with *topis* like tea cozies are reverently placing the evening meal in front of a golden Buddha with curly hair, bow-shaped brows, and elongated ear lobes. Outside, monkeys scamper over the dome and swing from vines and trees, while ten-foot horns groan a Tibetan version of "Taps." TV antennas sprout from two smaller buildings not far below the temple compound, and at the foot of the mountain women worshippers inch their way around its perimeter on their stomachs.

Back in the Yak and Yeti, I forego the Nepalese version of *Sesame Street* on TV and finish Siegfried Lienhard's *Songs of Nepal,* an anthology of verse in Newari, the state language of Nepal before the Gurkha conquest in the eighteenth century. Much of the subject matter, and all of it from the five centuries of the medieval period, derives from Sanskrit literature, but a general history of Newari chronicles (*Puranas*), late Buddhist sutras, manuals on dharma, stotras, dramas, epics (the *Mahabharata,* the *Ramayana*) has yet to be written. If I understand Lienhard, the chief difference between classical and modern Newari is the alternation produced by apocope, the contraction of the last two syllables of most words. What *Songs of Nepal* lacks, verse being sound primarily, is a table of pronunciation comparable to that in Garma Chang's edition of *The Hundred Thousand Songs of Milarepa.*

The love poetry is more engaging than the religious, at least in English prose. I learn from it that in sexual union between deities (Yab-Yum), the goddess sits astride and facing the god (in the lap of the gods), what Dr. Alex Comfort's *The Joy of Sex* calls the pompoir position. "He crossed his legs and I sat in his lap," Gopi tattles on Krishna, and in the poem "Krishna and Sudamen," the line, "One embraces one's wife on one's lap," is a refrain. (As represented in art, mortals, like most mammals, practice the rear entry.) I also learn that a wife who wishes to show deep affection for her spouse sleeps with her head adjacent to his feet, the reverse of Leopold, vis-à-vis Molly, Bloom. Not necessarily from affection but according to Hindu law a bride must wash her husband's feet and then drink the water. In both Newari and Hindi poetry the body of the beloved is described from toe to top, her heels compared to eggshells, hips to pillows, vulva to an oil-lamp, breasts to the water outlets in a fountain, hair-knot to a spinning spool.

Lienhard includes songs in music type transcribed by ethnomusicologist Inge Skog. When both the vocal and the instrumental versions of a piece are given, the differences between them outnumber the resemblances. While the rhythms are primitive, especially of the cymbal and drum "tabla" (a drum shaped like an hourglass is common in Nepalese genre painting), the microtonal inflections and the embellishments—as in Nepalese wood carving—are complex beyond the resources of European musical notation. (The bamboo flutes touted and tooted in Katmandu streets sound the simple pentatonic scale.) But if I have been unable to form an appreciation of the totally foreign reality of Nepali music, I must declare an even greater barrier with regard to pre-eighteenth-century Nepali painting. Without knowing the stories in what is essentially an art of pictorial narrative, I am lost in a jungle of symbols. Moreover, the disregard of perspective and the laws of gravity makes me dizzy.

The Rising Nepal's front page is largely devoted to the activities of the royal family. King Birendra Bir Bikram Shah Dev is both the world's unique Hindu monarch and a reincarnation of Vishnu, therefore a ruler by divine right, a god-king quite literally. But in Nepal, where Hindu theological texts mention three million deities, *everything* is religion-related. The recent coming of age of Crown Prince Dipendra Bir Bikram Shah Dev was observed by a procession from temple to temple, the heir-apparent riding in a carriage accompanied by Gurkha foot guards armed with *kukri* knives and wearing Scottish-style tartan-draped uniforms.

Each September the king must call on the Royal Kumari ("virgin," and the name is that of Shiva's daughter-in-law) to receive the red *bindi* on his forehead from this four- or five-year-old, and with it her permission to continue his reign. The Kumari is chosen in part by the Royal Astrologer, who consults the stars to see which child's horoscope best matches the king's, and in part by priests from the Taleju Temple, the child being regarded as an embodiment of the Hindu goddess Taleju. The child is brought up by custodial substitute parents in Kumari Ghar, an eighteenth-century three-storey red brick house near the Royal Palace that encloses a courtyard where supplicants gather, hoping for a glimpse of her in an upstairs window. Like Mozart's Pamina, she must undergo tests for bravery, in the child's case by showing no fear in a dark room in which demons howl and the still-bleeding severed heads of sacrificial animals are displayed. The Kumari is allowed outside only to attend one or more of thirteen annual festivals, on which occasions she is borne through the city in a palankeen placed on a chariot. At the first sign of menarche, she becomes an ex-deity and is returned to ordinary life.

The Rising Nepal extols the glories and virtues of the monarchy, and a feature of each issue is the king's own "thought for the day." Item: "All of us should concentrate our energies on the task of national construction and economic development, steering clear of useless political polemics." But the first benefits of the national economic development, referred to locally as 75 percent tourism and 25 percent drugs, have been channeled to the construction of a vast new royal palace and the purchase for it of new royal Mercedes limousines, whose passage halts all street traffic, including ambulation. Every room, shop wall, lobby in Katmandu displays a portrait of the king and queen, who do not remove their dark glasses on their thrones.

Today's feature article claims that Mahendra, the present king's father and the son, though only fourteen years younger, of King Tribhuvan, "far-sightedly banned the party system in order to safeguard national identity. It is under the institution of the Crown that the Nepalese are enjoying democratic rights and justice." One can only say that the widespread enjoyment of Mahendra's democratic rights is far from apparent. The phrase "partyless democratic system of the panchayats" (district legislative organizations) is so mindlessly repeated that one begins to overlook the contradiction in terms. In actuality, when the social democratic party won a substantial majority in the 1959 national election, Mahendra jailed the prime minister and the cabinet and announced his own direct rule. His most notable building project was the erection of an obelisk at the Buddha's birthplace in Lumbini inscribed with a list of his own achievements.

Succeeding his father in 1972, Birendra blamed the government's failure to improve living standards on the corruption of the panchayats. When violence erupted in 1979, he agreed to hold a referendum on a democratic system, but the results were overturned the following year in a rigged election. While royal proclamations were granting more freedom, in actuality every vestige of representative government disappeared.

Birendra has the reputation of being remote and wholly unconcerned with public relations. After a high-toll earthquake two years ago, he put off visiting the area for two months. Last year, he purchased anti-aircraft weapons from China, thereby provoking an economic blockade from India. Student demonstrators soon appeared in Katmandu's streets, not, however, to protest Birendra's highhandedness, but to condemn India's action. Birendra was so out of touch with his subjects that he mistook the movement as a rebellion, shut down the universities, and jailed the students. Today, Birendra is the absolute monarch of an unreconstructed feudal society, and one of the richest men in the world. So much for an Eton education, and a year at Harvard reading political science, not to mention the lessons that might have been learned back home in Nepal from, if any, the gods of compassion.

With a yearly per capita average income of $150, Nepal ranks as the fourth poorest country in the world. Until recently only 4 percent of the population was literate, and, even now, only 100,000 in a country of 21,000,000 are able to read the "wall newspaper" distributed monthly to some seventy districts. Jeremy Bernstein's humane and intelligent *In the Himalayas* says that two out of three children in rural Nepal do not survive infancy, while the life expectancy of those who do is only twenty-six years. Not only the gods are young in Nepal: the lives of most mortals are cruelly, though in some circumstances perhaps mercifully, abbreviated. According to artistic convention, old age and death are never portrayed, but only serenity and youthful charm. Today's *Rising Nepal* announces that "an effort is being made to provide hospitals with modern equipment including X-ray machines." According to Penguin's *Travels in Nepal,* a TB hospital, set up at the town of Jiri by the Swiss Association for Technical Assistance, had only two patients in 1989 because none of the personnel had had any medical training, and because the only X-ray machine had long since broken down.

In Durbah Square, Bhaktapur, one of the mammoth sculptures of toothy lions with long, well-groomed manes is a Narasimba, the angry man-lion incarnation of Vishnu. For some reason the bellicose deities are more corpulent than the benign. Less mysteriously, the god of wealth is pot-bellied. Due to the devastating 1934 earthquake, the Square is much wider and more open than the one in Patan, and, thanks to German aid, the result of a visit by Helmut Kohl in 1987, the brick-paved streets and drains are in comparatively good condition. Furthermore, the inhabitants appear to be less indigent and more industrious. Potters are at their huge wheels—the potter caste is the city's largest—weavers are at their looms, wood carvers ply their jigsaws, stone carvers their hammers and chisels, and one man pedals a foot-powered sewing machine in the middle of the street.

The three-story Cyasilian Mandap, or Pavilion of Eight Corners, is being restored by the Viennese architect Götz Hagmuller from a nineteenth-century photograph. Of the eighteenth-century original, only a few carved panels remain.

The vendors display yak-hide boots, yak-tail whisks; the life-size Nava Durga puppets (bulging black eyes like those in eighth-century heads of Bhairava); and the *saranghi,* a kind of rebec or vielle that emits a faint squeak. A stele in the Patan Archeological Garden depicts Naranda, lord of heavenly musicians, portrayed as an emaciated, every-rib-showing penitent, playing a four-stringed instrument similar to but larger than this one and plucked rather than bowed; a larger member of the same string family appears in an eighteenth century cloth painting in the Bhaktapur Art Gallery, an apparition of music-making in heaven.

Having shown interest in the *saranghi,* I cannot escape its salesman. "Two hundred dollars." "Too much." "Fifty dollars." "Too much." "Ten dollars." I do not purchase it only because my bags are already bursting, but feel guilty: the man is not offering a fake antique but a product of an artisan tradition. Moreover, musicians should help each other; Stravinsky never refused a street fiddler.

Nyatapola, the five-tier wooden pagoda temple, is the tallest in Nepal. Its outside, Palenque-style staircase, is guarded by stone sculptures in flanking pairs. At the lowest level are muscled and mustachioed wrestlers (*malla* means wrestler), ten times as strong as an ordinary man. Above them are two elephants, ten times stronger than they, and above them two lions (without ruffs in Nepal), ten times, etc. Next above are two dragons and, on top, two goddesses, each species ten times as powerful as the one below. According to legend, Devi, the temple's resident deity, can be seen only at night and only by Brahman priests, but supposedly the door has not been opened since the temple was consecrated in 1702.

The Peacock Window, in a nearby alley, a masterpiece of carved wood-work exposed to the elements, will not survive much longer unless placed behind glass and protected by climate controls, as the Getty-supported Katmandu Valley Preservation Trust is no doubt aware. The guidebooks, which copy each other, fatuously compare the golden gate, a treasure of gilded-metal sculpture, to Ghiberti's baptistery panels. Bhaktapur, a largely fourteenth- and fifteenth-century city, boasts one of the country's sacred sixty-four lingams, as well as its largest, an eighty-foot pole erected in a stone yoni and adorned with greenery and banners.

Bhaktapur worships Vishnu in his manifestation as Ganesh, god of wisdom and prudence, in human form with elephant head. But Hindu human-animal composites, the grafting of human thoughts and feelings onto partly animal-shaped stand-ins, repels me, the human body with a boar's head (a reminder of ass-headed Bottom) even more than men with elephants' trunks and pendulous ears. Nor do I care for gods with more than the normal quota of heads and arms, though the reason for it, in the Eleventh Discourse of the *Bhagavad-Gita,* when Krishna reveals himself to Arjuna, is obvious: the many limbs symbolize the cosmos. Of living animals, goats are the most common here, some of them tethered in upstairs rooms and balconies. Non-Hindus are not allowed inside the Teleju Temple, and a soldier stops us from photographing the outside, waving us away with his rifle. Why are soldiers, everywhere conspicuous in Nepal, guarding places of worship?

Pashupatinath is 2,500 years old. Shiva as Pashupati is Nepal's national god, and for Shiva worshippers it is one of the three most important pilgrim-age sites in Asia. For Westerners with no experience of India, it could register a ten on the Richter scale of cultural shock. Buddhists were expelled long ago from this Hindu holy ground, and the temples are open only to Hindus. Much longer ago still, when the gods inhabited the earth, Shiva, a deity of deed rather than of thought, took the form of a gazelle for an amorous frolic, thereby incurring the wrath of higher-up gods, who broke off one of the animal's horns. This lingam, as it became, was lost in the forest until a wandering cow indicated its whereabouts by miraculously gushing milk on the sacred place. Duly excavated, the lingam was installed as Nepal's top icon behind silver doors in a golden pagoda. Outside the doors is a larger-than-life image of Nandi, Shiva's bull, eyes made of diamonds, tail of solid gold, hooves of solid silver. Hindu holy men touch its testicles, then walk around the temple chanting *om nama shivaya* ("I bow to Shiva"). The lingam itself (*vajra*), a three-foot black stone set in a red yoni (*Padma,* lotus), can be touched only by an India-born Brahman priest. The daily ritual of this phallic-fetish worship, 4 A.M. to 8 P.M., includes the lustral bathing of the lingam, priestly hymn-singing to it, exposing it to mirrors for self-contemplation, dressing it in golden cloth, serving a rice-with-chutney lunch to it.

Unlike the metamorphosed gazelle horn, many of Pashupatinath's sculptured lingams are remarkably lifelike. In one temple, barren women try to induce fertility by rubbing their vulvas against the phallus of a Shiva-Bhairava. In the erotic unification with the deity, "consciousness of what is outward or what is inward" dissolves, as the Upanishad says, and so it might during *mahasuka* (orgasm), which even the comparatively puritanical Buddhists, with their celibate clergy, equate with nirvana.

Pashupatinath is Nepal's holiest cremation site. Over and above it hangs an aura of death, even beyond the sickening smell of burning bodies. The ghats on the west bank of the Bagmati are launching pads for the journey, or transmigration, of the soul (*atman*) to a better life. Death, for the Hindu, does not mean liberation from the bondage of rebirth, the tyranny of the Karmic cycle, "the weary wheel of endless becoming." As the funeral chant begins, "You go to your god and so do not have to come to this life again." While we walk across the river on an ancient stone bridge, five young men, bare to the waist and wearing white cotton pajamas against the pollution brought by a death in the family, fan a fire on a ghat directly below.

The sinister aspect of Pashupatinath is the treatment of the moribund. Brought here from all over Nepal, they are carried to the river and their feet are dipped into the water, thus ensuring the peaceful afterlife of the spirit. After this baptism of death, they are placed in a house adjoining the ghats, from which their cries and moans are gruesomely audible. The corpses are taken to the river, washed, and a piece of camphor is lighted in the mouth. Flowers are placed on the forehead and a yellow shroud is spread over the upper body, which is then lifted to the pyre of burning logs. Unless the cremation is performed by a son—female relatives are not allowed to witness it—the spirit is condemned to wander eternally. What Hinduism most cruelly lacks, it seems to me, is a god of merciful oblivion.

A hundred yards or so downstream from the scattering of the ashes, children play in the shallow water and women wash clothes. At other times expiating ablutions take place here. On the transpontine side, where a stone staircase mounts a steep, wooded hill, we encounter a yogi, legs crossed behind his head, body raised and balanced on his hands—the "peacock" *asana* position (*Mayurasana*), I think—but the contortion looks more spider- than bird-like. Sadhus, Hindu ascetics, are here, too, naked except for wooden chastity belts, with, for extra mortification, a weight attached to the penis. They have smeared the white ash of cow dung on their bodies, painted their foreheads, and, to symbolize the chaos of the world, tousled their long, greased hair. Their eyes turn inward as, seemingly, in the *samadhi* trance, but however that may be, their state of consciousness is not normal, and one expects them to froth at the mouth.

Monkeys cavort around the ghats and shrines, while flocks of vultures perch on the temple roofs. The dung of the sacred cows is scooped up by hand, still steaming, molded into patties, and placed in the sun to dry. The mendicants here are more tenacious than in Katmandu and Patan, and to escape them, as well as the specter of the Hindu holies and the odors of the unwashed living as well as the burning dead, we depart, swooning. Pashupatinath is only two miles from Katmandu's jet airport.

The more I read in the two recondite tomes of Benjamin Walker's *Hindu World,* the less I understand of Hindu Reality (Brahman), which is inexpressible, has no qualities, cannot be defined, yet is experienced as concretely as pain. The faculty of reason, at the same time, is as precious in the scheme of Hindu intellectualism as it is in that of humanistic Buddhism.

23. The great white stupa at Bodhanath, built in the same hemispherical form as Swayambhunath, and with the same four pairs of peering eyes and the quizzical noses, is the largest Buddhist shrine in Asia. Bright-colored pennant-like streamers flutter around the stupa, suspended from the top. At its base, Tibetan pilgrims turn the 108 prayer wheels with great fervor. An arcade of shops, with carved-woodwork door and window frames, surrounds the shrine, some of them with signs: "VIP Furniture," "Hollywood Tailors," "West Point English," "Siddhartha Pharmacy." But the throng of souvenir sellers of brass Buddhas, daggers, turquoise, coins, Indian annas and piçe is so dense that we have to fight our way out.

A Sherman tank would be the best means of conveyance for the three miles of gullies and loose stone that make up the road from Katmandu to Kirtipur, and the city itself, on the summits of twin mountains, is so cratered and rubble-strewn that our automobile cannot enter it. The nearly deserted streets are lined by dilapidated three- and four-storied brick houses with overhanging roofs, carved wooden balconies and window frames. The triple-tiered Bhairava temple, used by Hindus and Buddhists alike, is in even more decrepit condition. People of low caste live outside and beneath the fortifications of the ancient citadel, but the only inhabitants that we see of this tumbledown town are beggars and ragged, barefoot children. "Michael Jackson," the children say, over and over, like a mantra.

From Kirtipur we take the Arnika Highway—the map rates it as a highway, at any rate—to a viewing point for Mount Everest and a road to Tibet. The sporadic and rudimentary paving soon deteriorates still further, and we bump along as if we had lost not only our tires but also the fellies and are riding on the spokes. In a region marked with brick kilns, an in-construction apartment building has glass windows, most uncommon even in Katmandu. The hillside houses, thereafter, are mud-masonry huts with thatched roofs. In one village, the women's winnowing trays, here called *nanglos,* are about the same size and shape as the one in Courbet's *Wheat Sifters*. Farm machinery is non-existent.

After two hours on the steepest, most vertiginous incline I have ever experienced, a narrow dirt ledge with only a few brambles between our sputtering, oxygen-starved car and the bottom of a ravine, we reach a dry stream-bed and manage to turn around in it. Not hiding his disappointment in me, the driver says that we are at an altitude of 12,000 feet and not many miles from the Tibetan border. But I am short of breath in the attenuated air—as Father Greuber, the German Jesuit who walked from Beijing to Katmandu in 1661, described it—and unable to bring myself to look out of the window. In a few moments, and although the last visible habitation was at least a mile below, several half-clothed urchins appear, and a man, carry-ing what looks like a cudgel, comes running down the road ahead begging for rupees. The descent is even more giddying.

Back in Katmandu, our driver urges us to attend the festival of Basanta Panchami and see the sacrifice of 108 bulls, now in full butchery, a thrilling spectacle, he says, not to be missed. But since I have never forgotten two Mexican *corridas* attended long ago, and became a vegetarian (temporarily) after seeing the hecatombs and the slaughter-house sequences in Fassbinder's *In a Year with 13 Moons,* I do not want to know more about the celebration.

After packing clothes and books (the good ones are Tucci's, Bernstein's, Joshi's and Rose's *Democratic Innovations in Nepal,* and Ernst Waldschmidt's catalog for the 1967 Essen exhibition of Nepali art), I lie in bed thinking that while cremation may be the best way, inhumation gave us the art of Egypt, Greece, Etruria, and so many other cultures; and that the number of people before and after Nietzsche who realized that God is dead is infinitesimal compared to the number of people who have not.

24. A few minutes after take-off, Everest— Chomolungma, the Goddess of the Snows—is in view.

February 20. New York. The news from Katmandu: the "Movement to Restore Democracy and Human Rights" launched a protest two days ago, Nepal's "Democracy Day," was met by guns and clubs. The government's sanitized report says that seventeen were killed, scores injured, and hundreds jailed, meaning that a carnage took place, unarmed people shot down in the street.

March 21. An editorial in today's *Christian Science Monitor* by the anthropologist Barbara Nimri Aziz, who spent twenty years in Nepal, tells the horrifying story of a Nepali girl who had demonstrated at a provincial university and been raped by the police. The Queen, Aishwarya Rajya Laximi Davi Shah, came to visit her in a hospital but was greeted by the girl's shouts of hatred for the regime and a spit of contempt, whereupon the Queen ordered her execution. "Off with their heads," but this time in the realm of the Reverend Dodgson, not of Lewis Carroll.

April 3. The coming revolution in Nepal has reached page two of the *Times,* and *The Washington Post* prints an action photo. Fifteen protest marchers were killed on April 1, the government says, though the dissidents put the figure at more than double that. A crowd of 4,000 near Tribhuvan University and uncounted others in downtown Katmandu, some of them barefoot people in rags, faced guns and tear gas supplied to the brutal regime by the United States.

8. The news from Shangri-La is that the king has capitulated and is offering a multi-party electoral system, a resile, it appears. One wishes that the palace had been stormed, the king bundled off to Estoril or St. Moritz. As is, will his concessions go far enough, and will he be able to adjust to a lower level of venality, let alone to being a constitutional figurehead?

Alexander visited us in New York in June, and, still excited by Nepal, we went to the Asia Society exhibition of art from the dzongs, the monastery-fortresses, of Bhutan, "The Land of the Thunder Dragon." The installation of the altar in the innermost room was accomplished with the help of the Karma Triyana Dharmachakra community in Woodstock, New York, where one of the regents of the Karma Kagyu lineage had promised to grant local Tibetans the empowerment of Shi Tro, the introduction to death. We learned this from a booklet that said absolutely nothing about the contents of the show, nor did its preface, by Bhutan's Buddhist King, Jigme Singye Wangchuck, who is married to four sisters, attempt to reconcile this overt advertisement for tourist dollars with his publicized vow to keep the country even more tightly closed than it already is. On admission, tourists must pay a $250-a-day tax.[1]

In the foyer, two closely sheared Bhutanese boys, sitting cross-legged with a woodblock between them, were printing prayer flags, one of them brushing the surface of the block with thick, black, retchingly smelly ink, the other pressing broadsheets of thin cotton cloth on it. One of the drawings in the center of the flag depicts the Horse of the Wind carrying a wish-fulfilling jewel. The text describes a combat between gods and demi-gods that the former were losing until the ur-god Indra appealed to the Buddha for help.

Videos in two of the exhibition rooms showed masked dancing and the Tsok celebration of Rinpoche, the eighth-century guru who converted the country to Buddhism. An enthroned lama officiated at the Tsok ceremony, in which a three-note unison chant was repeated over and over, accompanied by a drum, a pair of cymbals (to mark time), and two long Tibetan horns—*two* of them so that the players can take turns breathing and the sound never stops. The music, vocal and instrumental, has great majesty. The horns in display cases, including a pair made of conch shells fitted with metal mouthpieces and metal-flange amplifiers, are sounded from the roofs of monasteries to call people to prayer. Another pair was made of human

1. In 1998 a fire totally destroyed the country's most famous monastery, the Taktsang, and its sacred silk hangings with their changka figures.

thigh-bones, the organic, once-living material symbolizing the triumph over the fear of death. According to a caption, "music is part of every aspect of the spiritual practices of Vajrayana Buddhism."

The most intriguing object in the show was a *tashigomang,* a portable shrine resembling a large doll house. Every surface of the structure, which is carried from village to village by itinerant monks, consists of doors opening on inner doors to expose small doll-like figures in scenes illustrating Buddhist teachings. The faces here, and in the Bhutanese paintings exhibited, were Chinese, with wispy chin-beards. Peacock feathers adorn many of the objects.

July 20. Letter from my niece in Ahmednagar, Maharashtra, India, where she teaches English to young children and assists in a medical clinic:

> It's early morning, and I have awakened again with the birds, whose songs are so exotic I am tempted to tape them. Soon will come the sounds of India waking up, the wheels of bullock carts creaking by on the path, bicycle bells, and farmers flicking their whips and calling out in Marathi. At 5:45 the night watchman walks by our rooms ringing a bell so sweet it would only wake those intended to hear it. The children are from Arangaon, a tiny and poor (whatever that means in India, where 250,000,000 are below the poverty line) farm village in the middle of Maharashtra on the Deccan plateau. Only their huge brown eyes are visible over the desk tops. The first time I entered, they shrieked and hid under the desks, never having seen such a pale person up close before, since they don't have TV or movies or tourism. The initial horror has worn off, and we're getting on splendidly now. The middle-aged women shrug, giggle and invent answers to our silly questions, which seem utterly irrelevant to them, such as "How old are you?"... The Hindus just celebrated "Polo," in which farm animals are honored by being given the day off and painted all colors of the rainbow. Now punk-pink goats can be seen wandering around in the streets.

Korea

My German concert agent Ruth Übel had arranged for me to conduct several times in Seoul, but I suspected that I would not want to stay there for more than one event, and in any case could not spare the time. The concert was my first since Mrs. Stravinsky's death in September 1982. The orchestra was good, the players were cooperative, the accommodations were comfortable, and the cachet was beyond any I could have earned in the United States at that date.

August 17, 1983. No sooner does midnight flight 007 take off for Seoul than the stewardesses change from military uniforms and New York-style indifference to flower-patterned kimonos and oriental manners: quick, short bows at every contact. A "heavy snack" is served: hors d'oeuvres (ginseng root), a "starch" course ("France fried potatoes"), *bulgogi* (marinated beef), and *kimchi* (fermented pickle of cabbage). The menu reproduces a Yi-dynasty (1392) embroidery of the mythical bird Bong Hwang, which "luckily foresaw coming catastrophe of the country." The pilot's English and Korean are indistinguishable, but the all-night TV advertising of duty-free products is mercifully silent.

The seven-hour lap to Anchorage ends with a shocking—it is 2:00 A.M. local time—outburst of rock music. When we are airborne again, a midnight-blue dawn begins to break over the shimmering lights of the city and harbor, but we plunge into darkness for the remaining eight and a half hours. The approach to Seoul at sunrise replicates a Chinese painting: morning mist, glittering wet land in the low tide along the shores of the Yellow Sea, sinuous rivers, humped mountains with terraced rice-paddy slopes. The green of the valleys, parceled by irrigation ditches, is far richer and deeper than the summer landscape of the upper New York State I have just left. As I deplane, a bowing stewardess thanks me for flying with them

In the dense traffic from Kimpo Airport to the center of the city, mammoth trucks threaten to crush my tiny taxi. The road signs, on the south bank of the Han River, are in Korean and English, and the ubiquitous *"dong"* (as in the one with the luminous nose), meaning street or area, is probably all the Korean I am likely to learn. The buildings, new high-rise monstrosities, and the poetic willow trees lining most of the road, could hardly be more incongruous. The only reminders of an earlier time are an old man pushing a cart, a woman with a load strapped to her back, and another, younger one, carrying a basket on her head. The Han is wide but shallow, as the sandbars and dredging machinery indicate. Crossing the last of several low bridges, we begin the steep ascent to the Sheraton Walker Hill, where the desk clerk says that I was expected yesterday, a confusion attributed to the crossing of the International Date Line, and have been written off as a no-show. While waiting for a room, I window-shop in the basement among the watered silks, lacquer wares, bamboo trays and mats, lavishly costumed dolls.

Fixtures and furniture are scaled to the small Korean body, which makes for awkwardness in the bathroom. My sixteenth-floor window looks toward the Han in the center, to a large new section of the city on the right side, and wooded and farm lands extending to the Chinese-shaped mountains on the left. Immediately below is an Olympic-size swimming pool and a large red balloon trailing a Coca-Cola advertisement.

19. The headline story in the English-language *Korea Herald* is devoted to a U.S. General's announcement that "GIs in Japan are ready for Korean action, the North being capable of invading the South, and the United States committed to defend the Republic of Korea." The General "sincerely hopes" that "no situation will develop on the Korean peninsula that will require the use of nuclear weapons," which is another way of saying that they are already here. A sheet inserted in the *Herald,* "Aid to Current English," lists as today's word assignments "orchestrate" (nothing to do with music), "break," and "broke." The examples for the last two are: "Can you break a bill of 10,000 *won*" (pronounced wawn), "Give me a break,"

"The company went broke," and "Someone broke wind." The Korean versions of the first three of these sentences are the same length as the English originals, while that of the indecorous last one is twelve lines long. "Dear Abby" is the feature of the other English-language newspaper, the *Korean Times,* which also has an article attributing AIDS transmission to "homosexuals, hemophiliacs, and Haitians"; several letters to the editor protesting the false picture of Korea in *MASH;* and a report from Japan on the replacement of workers by robots, a process the Japanese Labor Ministry justifies not as economy but as part of "the search for higher precision and quality."

The Romanization of the Korean language follows two radically different systems, with the result that the Ministry of Education's maps and those published according to the international McCune-Reischauer method do not conform. The M.O.E. replaces *k* by *s, p* by *b, ch* by *j, r* by *l, n* by *r,* and adds the silent English *e* to *o,* as in "Seoul."

20. Walter Gillessen, the German resident music director of the Korea Philharmonic, whose 255th subscription concert I am to conduct, talks to me about his recent trip in the south. The country is an armed garrison on wartime alert, he says. This does not surprise me: early this morning I watched a long convoy of open trucks rattling beneath my window, transporting soldiers in camouflage uniforms. Moreover, a blackout has been announced for 9:30 P.M. tomorrow, and a midnight curfew is always in effect, foreigners and hotel nightclubs exempted. All newspapers are censored, which is to say that Rim Young Sam, who advocates democracy, is never mentioned in them, while every word of the dictator President Chun is reverently reported.

Gillessen says that while only a year ago the orchestra's principal players were European, the personnel is now entirely Korean. He advises me to stay away from local inns unless I have a strong sense of adventure: the floor beds and pillows are too hard for sleeping, and cockroaches are abundant.

21. To Inchon, returning by way of Chilbo Temple and Suwon. Since tomorrow's rehearsal has been canceled, I try to cancel the driver who was to have taken me, but he says, "I wasn't coming anyway because tomorrow is my day off." Willows border both sides of the Seoul-Inchon expressway, but they do not conceal the "industrial miracle" of faceless factories and apartment houses behind. The man in the tollbooth bows to me as my driver pays the token.

Unlike the people of Seoul, many Inchonians are dressed in the style of an earlier period, the men in loose white blouses and pants fastened at the ankles, the women in long skirts and turbans, carrying their children on their backs. The harbor is said to be the largest in the world in tonnage as well as area, but it has few docks, all short; large ships are anchored offshore, where smaller ones load and unload them. The waterfront is a long row of restaurants whose street levels are aquariums of squid, eel, crab, lobster, and fish of every size, stripe, design, color. When the customer points to his choice, the proprietor scoops it out of the water with a net, serving it, cooked or raw, in second-story dining rooms.

We climb a steep hill that affords a stunning panorama of the harbor and, except for an absurdly heroic statue of General MacArthur, an attractive esplanade. Concrete fortifications and artillery and radar installations are only half hidden by thick shrubbery and blankets of flowers. On the edge of the lookout is an eleven-story wooden dovecote built more than a century ago. The entrance to each apartment is a different shade of red, blue, green, and yellow, only slightly faded, and the center panel displays the Buddhist vortex, a pinwheel of colors.

In the wine-growing region near Chilbo, the roofs of most houses are blue and pagoda-shaped, and the vines are garlanded, woven together to screen the wind. The turnoff to the temple is a dirt track with a 90° slope. Halfway to the top is a Christian cemetery with mound graves very like the Korean royal tombs. Below Chilbo Temple, red peppers are drying on tables outside a farmhouse, presumably the home of the ranking Buddhist priest. On a hill above the Temple stands a statue of Miruk. White except for a stylized black pompadour, a tiny green mustache, chin beard, and reddened lips, he wears an academic's mortarboard, but with eight tassels instead of one, and with the four corners of the eaves upturned in the Chinese style.

Every outer surface of the temple is painted with poppies, gammadions, and flute-playing Krishnas. Inside, the ceiling is covered with paper lotuses, each with prayer attached, indicating that the gold image of a god seated on the altar must be Padmapani, the lotus-born. A huge bell and a mallet occupy one corner of the room, an old scroll, cups, kettles, silver candlesticks, prayer mats fill another. Every panel is painted or hung with scrolls depicting scenes from the life of Siddhartha Gautama. Driving back to the main road, I encounter four old men, pilgrims who wander from temple to temple with all their worldly possessions on their backs.

The eighteenth-century wall at Suwon has been preserved, which helps me to imagine the gates of the old castles.

22. Silluk-sa Temple, south of Seoul, is one of the great monuments of the Silla dynasty (50 B.C.-A.D. 935). Bicycles, some carrying crated chickens on the handlebars, are numerous on the road, as are pedestrians bent from loads on their backs tied to what look like stepladders, but the only motor traffic is that of U.S. military trucks on the way to army camps.

In contrast to Chilbo, Silluk-sa is a large compound of temples and bowers, of fenced-off stupas and steles. The approach is a long avenue of booths selling tawdry souvenirs, as well as computers and transistors. Tourists, who arrive here in droves, are confronted by placards containing historical information in both Korean and a kind of Chaucerian English: "Priest Naong droue a fling dragon away with a mistrious briddle." A flying, fire-breathing dragon is suspended from the ceiling in one of the pavilions, but whatever the meaning of "briddle," why does this creature have fish fins, and why does it face a huge drum and a bell six feet high and almost as wide?

The treasure of the temple is a stupa enshrining the bones of Ranong, whose epitaph, composed by a Confucian scholar in 1379, has been inscribed in marble. One house contains twenty life-size gypsum statues of priests and ogres. Another, the monastery's living quarters, is closed to visitors, but a glimpse within reveals such incongruities as an electric coffee percolator on a shelf next to a dozen bowls with chopsticks, and, on the wall, a Westminster clock.

The colors in the newly painted main temple are blinding, the perfect preservation of the ornaments there indicating the monks' skilled artisanship. Two birds are suspended from the Buddha's betel-shaped altar like doves of the Holy Spirit, but his smile does not express *"anatta."* Climbing to a rock promontory above the Han River, I inadvertently intrude on a man delousing a woman's hair.

23. The streets around the Korean Broadcasting flagship station, where my rehearsals take place, are lined with bulletin boards pinned with notices and votive pictures begging for clues and information about relatives missing since the 1950 war. Some 3,000 families, out of the hundreds of thousands who were separated, have been reunited since June, thanks to television appearances, which may be the medium's most constructive, humane, and redeeming achievement.

Language is the main impediment in my rehearsals. Only one member of the orchestra speaks English, a Kansas-born Korean-American cellist, though *he* does not speak Korean. The *Fidelio* Overture and Prokofiev's Second Piano Concerto are comparatively easy for the players, but *Sacre* is as new to them as it must have been to Monteux's musicians in 1913. Between rehearsals, Dr. Kang-Sook Lee, general director of the Korea Philharmonic Orchestra and an eminent ethnomusicologist, tries to enlighten me on the heterophony and the elastic, non-metrical rhythms of Korean classical music.

26. My concert begins with the Korean national anthem, sixteen measures of Western-sounding melody and harmony in which the downbeat feels like the upbeat. Tumultuous applause.

Postscript. One week to the day after my return to New York on flight 007 the same airplane, off-course, was shot down by a Russian MIG. There were no survivors. When I heard the news, Baudelaire's line swooped down on me like a black crow: "I felt the shadow of the wing ... pass over me."

Thailand

May 22, 1985. Tokyo, the Okura Hotel. Girls in kimonos and obis stand by the elevators on each floor to greet arriving and departing guests, with a great deal of bowing. After unpacking soiled clothes, I anxiously fill out a list stamped with the warning: "Garments badly worn out will be returned unlaundered." Ergo, my frayed shirts and frazzled underwear will probably be rejected. The room-maids trot, rather than walk, and they bow low both before and after turning down the bed.

June 1. The drive to Kunitachi Hall, in Tsuyama, takes two and a half hours on streets even more clogged with Toyotas, Isuzus, Hondas than Manhattan's. The average age of the players in the Kunitachi Orchestra is only twenty. But they are lightning learners, good-looking, well-dressed, polite, and harder-working than American and European orchestra musicians would be able even to imagine: we rehearse for four hours without intermission or break. More than half of the personnel is female, young women scarcely larger than their cellos and horns and considerably smaller than their basses and tam-tam, for the percussion section is entirely "manned" by girls. With little experience of shifting-meter music, and after only a few rehearsals, the orchestra performs the *Sacre* almost perfectly and without apparent effort, but so robot-like that the music is stripped of its power.

Herr Renicke, the orchestra's permanent conductor, and his Japanese singer-wife come to the Okura for dinner. He has been invited to the United States to give an *Amadeus* program, meaning a Salieri overture followed by two of the Mozart pieces fractured in the film. "Should this gimmick be taken seriously?" he asks, and I answer that a concert organization in London has programmed a Salieri sinfonia next to Mozart's *Jupiter,* an unkindness that even the movie villain does not deserve.

2. Most of the other passengers on my Thai Air flight to Bangkok are hippies ultimately headed for Katmandu. After five hours, we turn inland and cruise over Vietnam, Laos, Kampuchea, the Mekong River—in pampered luxury, served by seductive girls in moiré sarongs, as if all memory of what happened and is still happening below had been erased. "Welcome to the Kingdom of Thailand," the sign reads at Don Muang airport. The taxi fare to the city, 300 bahts, $12, must be paid in advance and a contract signed in duplicate with the driver.

Traffic is left-side, English-style, and directions are in English as well as Thai. Why does "Keep Left" require about eighty-five letters and diacritical marks in the native language? Near the airport are a few stilt-style Le Corbusier apartment houses, then miles of slums only partly hidden by advertisements for Mitsubishi, IBM, Dairy Queen, and Dunkin' Donuts. The largest sign, in the center of the city and in Times Square neon, is intended to protect a homegrown industry: *"V.D. INTERNATIONAL CLINIC FREE CHECK-UP."* As Paul Theroux wrote, this "city of temples and brothels smells of sex as Calcutta smells of death."

Tonight marks the conclusion of Visakha Puja, the festival of the Buddha's birth, enlightenment, passage into Nirvana, all—and it seems the best way—in one day. We pass a festooned enclosure in which the faithful, like Russians at Easter midnight, circle a temple carrying lighted candles and joss sticks.

The porters and lift boys at the Oriental Hotel are dolled up in the white tunics and ballooning black plus-fours of the Royal Guard. Assistant manager Pornthem Hantrakarnpong (not a name to drop) escorts me to the fifteenth floor and the large "Jim Thompson" apartment overlooking the Chao Phraya. One wall is inlaid with glass shelves containing jewel-encrusted gold jars. Another displays a silk-screen picture and a mural of nineteenth-century Siam, framed in red with gold borders. A statue of a courtier, smaller-than-life, carved in Thai teak and richly robed, stands spookily at the far end of the room. The rattan tables are heaped with orchids and fruit: mangoes, papayas, lichees, pomelos, pineapples. A note is attached to the last: "Thais eat pineapple with salt." A sign in the bar asks the guest to "Fill out the honesty check," and another above the bidet advises that "Massages are available from a professionally trained staff."

The bedroom is gory with red-lacquer tables and chairs, wardrobe, desk—where my name is embossed on the writing paper—and a bed with matching silk curtains, pleated headrest, filigreed canopy. Handles are gold, as are the legs and feet of the furniture—claws, rather, for they are dragon-shaped. The bed linen is the softest silk.

The balconies, doors, and windows are locked against scorpions, giant roaches, spiders, lizards, and rats, all revoltingly pictured on a card. I plump like a potentate on the pile of pillows in the living room and study Thai grammar. In principle this could hardly be simpler, each word being employable as noun, verb, adverb, adjective. Word-order tends to follow the pattern: subject, verb, object, modifier, but in practice any word can be placed after any other. Genders, articles, conjunctions, conjugations of verbs, plurals, prefixes and suffixes, and tenses can be ignored. But communicable pronunciation is impossible owing to the lack of equivalent English vowel sounds, and the letters to spell the tones and inflections by which the meanings of identical words are differentiated.

3. At 6 A.M., the Chao Phraya, muddy, thick with palm fronds and clumps of matted vines drifting downstream, is already teeming with sampans, bamboo rafts, pirogues, houseboats with rounded tin roofs, ferries shaped like Mississippi steamboats, passenger boats—sharp-pronged and so narrow that their roofs provide no shelter—and low-in-the-water barges, both singly and linked together like railroad cars. The landscape beyond the huts on the opposite shore is lush with poincianas now in orange flame.

Today's *Bangkok Post* features a photo of the float on which a Buddha relic was taken yesterday to Sanam Luang for veneration. Other photos are of barefoot and ragged children from the north who have been subsisting on dried lizards. The front-page story is about monkeys pickpocketing tourists and snapping television antennae in the vicinity of the summer palace of King Rama IV (Yul Brynner). It seems that an attempt was made to entice the marauders into banana-baited cages, but the ruse failed when a long-tailed macaque successfully ejected a clump of bananas before the trap had sprung. A parliament of monkeys was then convened on the palace roof, after which none of them approached the cages again.

Mr. Niloubel, who comes for me at 8 A.M., spends most of my temple-visiting time praying. The solid five-and-a-half-ton Golden Buddha sits in stifling heat, humidity, and incense at the top of steep staircases, the saffron scarf of peace draped over the left shoulder. At its feet are offerings of elephant tusks, wilting flowers, and spoiled food. (This reminds me that Caligula built a temple that contained a solid gold statue to himself that priests fed every day with grouse and peacock meat.) Outside and below, in the monastery compound, saffron-robed monks shamble vacantly about, their heads so closely cropped that shearing must be a daily ritual.

The grounds of Wat Pho, with the temple of the recumbent Buddha, cover an immense area. I begin to reel on unshaded paths, and, envious of the Thai pilgrims sensibly traipsing through under large parasols, am fearful of sunstroke. The peeling gold-leaf skins of the 108 nearly identical Buddha statues lining the inner walls flicker in the breeze as if on fire. Farther inside, tin figures depict yoga positions. Still farther are ninety-nine Eiffel-shaped spires (*chedis,* stupas) containing relics and royal ashes and encrusted with bits of colored glass and blue and green Chinese porcelain. The Chinese stone sculptures here include camels, horses, dragon-tailed lions, Marco Polo with nineteenth-century European-style stovepipe hat, and more than one Confucius. But what is *he* doing here? Great sages are desirable anywhere, of course, but isn't Master K'ung's pragmatic humanism in conflict with *sannyasa,* the elimination of self?

The sides of Wat Pho's sloping roof are in the form of mythical serpents whose jeweled coils represent steps to heaven. The temple fits its giant reclining Buddha (160 feet long, 45 feet high) as snugly as a coffin, head almost touching one end, feet—soles inlaid with mother-of-pearl pictures of the 108 reincarnations—the other. Except that the deity's eyes are open and his head is propped on his right arm, he could be in a grave—or warehouse junk room, for he needs regilding. Numerous diminutive Buddhas line the periphery of the mammoth one, some holding the palms of their hands outward to pacify the seas and at the same time assure the annual return of the rains. They bring to mind an illustration of Gulliver bound by Lilliputians. In an adjoining temple, a smaller bronze Buddha has been fitted with branches newly cut from a Bo tree and made to look like wings.

At midnight I go to an outdoor shrine of Vishnu (why is the solar god worshipped at night?), whose image is enthroned on a dais piled high all around with flowers. "Very scared ground," Mr. Niloubel says, pronouncing the typographical error for "sacred." From each corner of the enclosure, small girls in skin-tight, heavily gilt costumes slink forward, perform slow dance movements, and, it could be claimed, sing. They are barefoot, but bedizened from ankles to *chados,* the Thai crown with the spiked, Prussian-helmet superstructure. A small orchestra plays between the dances. Before starting, the musicians bow over their instruments—bamboo flute, wood xylophones, drums, cymbals, a high-pitched double-reed—and pray to the spirits of their teachers. Tuning up is another ritual, but the equidistant system sounds excruciatingly "off." Half threnody, half concert for cobras, the music is low in volume and only fleetingly audible above the street noise. Swooning from the candle smoke, incense, odors of flowers, decaying food, and perspiration, I retreat.

Greatly overestimating the erotic effect of the dancers on me, Mr. Niloubel tries to steer me to one of the massage parlors on Patpong Road, "very private house, very nice lady, good friend of me." Bangkok guides, it seems, are pimps primarily, sex being the lower backbone of the economy. The chapter "Bangkok at Night," in the latest *Thailand Insight Guide,* is both comprehensive, what with paragraphs on price ranges (120 baht per hour depending on "how elaborate a massage you require") and explicit: the editors boast that their "menu of vices," which includes the services of transvestites (*Kra-toeys*), "is not couched in innuendoes." What *Insight* and Mr. Niloubel do not say is that today's sex traffic includes chartered flights from London and New York and is based on child prostitution. We watch as a bus pulls up in front of a brothel and about thirty middle-aged Americans step from one form of transport into the promise of others.

4. Some attractive old wooden buildings survive in Chinatown (Yaowaraj), most of them owned by gem-cutting and money-changing establishments. I go next to the zoo to see the white elephants. The mother of Buddha having dreamed of one during her pregnancy, these off-pink albinos are regarded as holy and are the property of the king. Mr. Niloubel assures me that most of the reptiles in the zoo can also be encountered in the city's parks and canals. Near the entrance is a pet shop advertising "Newly-Whelped Tigers."

For me the main attractions of the Emerald Buddha and the Dusit Palace are the electric fans. The emerald-and-jade idol is small and at a squinting elevation, while the decor of the palace's royal audience room will make little impression on anyone who has seen the Oriental Hotel first. But this is niggling: the gold statues of mythical man-animals, of warriors with roosters' tails, and the music of golden bells windblown under temple eaves are dazzling.

We drive to Nakorn Pathom province to watch elephants lifting teak logs, much as steel cranes hoist girders in New York. Though still found in the northern jungles in herds of two to three hundred, and given priority on Thai roads, the elephant is an endangered species, largely because the bulls easily mistake tuskless males for females, and trappers have learned to use the edentate males as decoys. The mahouts, young boys in black turbans and loincloths, mount the elephants while they salaam, riding them either standing on their backs or seated on the lowered tusks, like chauffeurs in the open front seats of ancient roadsters. Droppings are quickly scooped up, still steaming, like precious lava.

On the return, through rice paddies, banana plantations, watery fields of lotus, I try to engage Mr. Niloubel on the subject of the Pathet Lao and the refugees now crossing the border only 150 miles away. All he will say is that Thais were embarrassed by the "exaggerations" in *The Killing Fields,* meaning either that he prefers the Khmer Rouge to the Vietnamese, or that, following the official U.S. line, he thinks I do. But why should this believer in the supreme desirability of ultimate extinction bother with the come and go of politics? He talks instead about cholera, still the main killer in Thailand, and the shortage of crematoria. He says that many corpses have to be left on the charnal ground under trees until the bones have been cleaned by birds and animals. "The Buddhist body must wait seven days for cremation, by which time is not smelling good."

The airport at midnight is in a turmoil over the arrival of Jimmy, Rosalind, and Amy Carter en route to a refugee camp. My non-stop flight over Burma, India, Afghanistan, and the USSR to Copenhagen, is the longest in my experience.

January 25, 1990. After six years, Bangkok is scarcely recognizable, transformed into a banal winter resort. Where fewer than a hundred visitors could be counted in the Emerald Buddha compound in 1985, tourists are now queued up by the thousands.

Following Joseph Conrad, Somerset Maugham, Noel Coward, Graham Greene, and John Le Carré, Gore Vidal has been received into the Oriental Hotel's literary pantheon with a suite named for him. What the Oriental's publicity magazine does *not* divulge is that Maugham (*The Gentleman in the Parlour*) found the city's temples "garish," their "fantastic ornaments" full of "malaise," and that he spent most of his time here in bed recuperating from malaria.

By the River Kwai bridge, in the infamous POW labor camp, stands the Jeath Museum, on the site of the original long bamboo hut on which it is modelled. The museum is stuffed with Japanese war relics, uniforms, swords, guns, unexploded bombs, photos of every stage in the construction of the Death Railway to Burma, as well as photos and drawings of tortures. One of these last shows the hands of a prisoner caught stealing food being hammered to pulp. The pictures survive because the guards expected Japan to win the war. Sixteen thousand captured British, Australian, American, and Dutch soldiers died here of disease, malnutrition, and overwork. Yet Japanese visitors far outnumber Caucasians. The economy of the old city of Kanchanaburi, near the bridge, is entirely dependent on selling souvenirs related to the movie, which was filmed in Sri Lanka.

On the way back to Bangkok, competing for road space against trucks piled high with the sugar-cane harvest, we stop to see a performance by the Samphron elephants. The language of the loudspeaker is English, though the audience consists of perhaps 3,000 Thais and thirty Americans. The grand entrance of the lumbering beasts is accompanied by an overamplified recording of Musorgsky's "Great Gate of Kiev."

28. At midnight, waiting in Don Muang terminal for our flight to Rome, we watch Japanese tour groups open their hand luggage and change from summer to winter wear. The Singapore Air stewardesses are slinky mannequins in tight-fitting floor-length gowns.

Bali and Borobudur

Colin McPhee's Music in Bali, *which transcribes the cipher system of notation into the European, and more recent books, such as R.A. Sutton's* Traditions of Gamelan Music in Java, *contributed to my decision to visit these Indonesian islands. My enjoyment of gamelan music being rather limited, the most persuasive factor was the 1991 exhibition at the Metropolitan Museum in New York of "The Sculpture of Indonesia."*

December 2, 1996. Singapore. Changi airport is spacious, roaring with flight announcements, exotically landscaped with plants and flowers, and helpfully equipped with Mitsubishi "travellators," moving walks whose gradually sloping ascents and descents eliminate the steep steps of escalators. Taxis are not large enough to hold both ourselves and our baggage, and we are compelled to go separately. The road to the city is divided, multi-laned, shaded by trees on both sides and in the middle, and bordered by bougainvillea all the way. The skyscrapers and freighter-filled harbor come into view suddenly.

The restored Raffles Hotel is faithful to the original to the extent that creaks in the floorboards have been retained, but the air-conditioning is so new that the bathroom, bedroom, and breakfast-nook temperatures are comfortably different. Our balcony overlooks a garden of frangipani, poinsettias, hibiscus (that "boisterous plant," as Harold Nicolson calls it in *Journey to Java*), and umbellate palms, whose large fronds spread like peacocks' tails.

Christmas decorations throughout the city remain in place for seven weeks, inappropriate though they seem in the sweltering heat, especially the snowmen with top hats and carrot noses and the different sizes of Santa Claus with sleighs and reindeer. Wreaths and festoons of lights and tinsel are everywhere, and the glittering tree across the street from the Raffles is nearly as large as the one in Rockefeller Center. At the entrance to a shopping mall, a Dutch windmill, a London Bridge with larger-than-life-size Beefeaters, a Tour Eiffel, and a too-tilted Tower of Pisa are outlined in colored lights, There is, of course, no crèche. Mammon is the undisputed god here.

The maitre d'hotel in the Raffles "fine dining" restaurant is from France with a year en route in Mauritius. He has not yet recovered from the visitation here last week of Michael Jackson and entourage, and tells us how windows had to be kept open in one of his suites for him to wave to his hysterical fans. Most of the diners are sunburned Americans returned from cruises, or pale-faced ones about to embark on them, Singapore being a stopover city. All are excitedly exchanging the names of their home towns, and their American voices grate. In bed, after fourteen airborne hours, we feel that we have not yet landed.

3. Singapore is a giant department store, and all the expensive name brands, Tiffany, Cartier, Bulgari, Georg Jensen, Gucci, Dior, Versace, Vuitton, own a piece of it. But the prosperity, cleanliness, and orderliness have made it dull. A driver from the hotel—"I show you interesting places"—shows us the little that remains of old Chinatown, the narrow streets and small, attractive houses that Joseph Conrad would have recognized. The "interesting places" on the way to the Jurong Bird Park are a Mercedes factory, country clubs, and a golf course.

The aviary's scarlet ibises, sulphur-crested cockatoos, Mollucan cockatoos—orange crests raised when alarmed—Malay fish owls, and New Guinea double-wattled cassowaries are wonders of nature, but the most gorgeously colored of all is the New Guinea bird of paradise. Penguins live in air-conditioned comfort and with ice-water pools. We learn from our visit to the world's only breeding pair of kiwis that some feathers are composed of filaments held together by as many as a million interlocking barbules. A few cages are empty, the tenants presumably having flown the coop, and to judge from the fixed positions of the screeching macaws, they have been foot-cuffed to their tree branches to prevent them from doing the same.

A ten-minute ride on a panorail costs $26 and forty-five minutes in queue. The departure of the little train is accompanied by a recording of the *Russlan* Overture, followed by one of an English-speaking guide, whose facetious commentaries seem to puzzle the passengers. When we come to a lake with swans, the music switches to Tchaikovsky's ballet. Our driver explains that the panorail is new ("before don't have"). When we tell him that we saw three boys on it chewing gum—against the law in Singapore— he is convinced that the criminals must have been Japanese.

The contents of the War Museum, built on the site of the infamous Mount Crescent World War II prison, are limited to photographs documenting the bombing and sinking of the two British battleships in December 1941, General Yamashita's triumphant entry into the city, the pedaling of the Japanese bicycle army down the peninsula in February 1942, and the departure, on foot through the jungle, of British and Australian prisoners-of-war to build the River Kwai railroad.

4. Throughout our afternoon flight to Denpasar, Singapore Air hostesses in contour-tight, floor-length but slit, leg-revealing gowns serve *blanc-de-blanc*. We spend the two and a half hours reading Urs Ramseyer's *The Art and Culture of Bali,* but progress only as far as his explanation of the two-calendar system, the Javanese-Balinese 210-day year of thirty weeks, and the Indian year of twelve new-moon-to-new-moon months, corrected to the solar calendar every thirty months by the addition of an intercalary one. Bali's coastline and low-lying rain clouds are visible shortly before the brief equatorial sunset. Immigration processing and luggage delivery in Ngurah Rai terminal are immeasurably less efficient than in Singapore.

Our hotel, actually seven enclaves of thatched-roof villas, each in a walled compound, occupies a terraced hillside on the Bukit Peninsula, across Jimbaran Bay from the airport. The reception desk, concierge, lobby, and restaurant are open at the sides to the elements, as well as, no doubt, to bats and aerial creatures that sting and bite and grounded ones that crawl and slither. As we register, a girl brings sickishly-sweet fruit drinks and ice-cold hand-towels. A golf-cart buggy, driven by a boy carrying a walkie-talkie and wearing a white uniform and black headband, takes us to our rooms. Communication with him is restricted to globally inescapable Americanisms ("no problem," "have a good day").

The villa's appointments combine modern and traditional with less than complete success. While the tub in the polished marble bathroom, elevated on 1890s-style legs, lacks curtains and even a screen, and the shower and toilet are without doors, the roll of toilet tissue is wrapped in an attractively patterned green, yellow, and black batik. The fan in the bedroom's bamboo dome squeals, and the mosquito coils in iron pots placed by the door, as well as the netting draped over the canopied bed, suggest that the heavily scented insecticides are less than wholly effective. After reading the warning on the label of our prophylactic anti-malaria pills—Lariam, the not-quite-anagram for the fever—we decide to risk the disease rather than side effects that include "blindness and cardiac arrest." Our bedside tables stock the Qu'ran and a Gideon, as well as *Mimpi Manis,* a selection of "Bedtime Stories from Bali," some of them from Miguel Covarrubias's classic book about the island. After a brief thunderstorm, the monsoon rains fall steadily, soothingly, through the night.

5. The sweetness of the morning air is almost tangible, but the sky, a soft wan blue, is paler than in Florida. An offering of rice and areca nuts on small squares of palm leaves was served at sunrise to the sculpture of a mythical animal on the far side of our pool, but a moment later loudly chattering birds had consumed it. Opposite the entrance to our compound, a garden surrounds a statue clothed in what looks like a checkered black and white tablecloth, and shielded from the sun and rain by a matching-pattern fringed (passementerie) double-decker parasol of the kind held over kings and divinities in Buddhist friezes. Workmen are trimming and training the plants on the sides of the narrow streets, which are walled and paved with volcanic paras-stone.

At 9 A.M. a minibus takes us to an arts school an hour's drive in the direction of the sacred mountain Gunung Agung, the "navel of the world." Yawa, our guide, white tunic, red and gold sarong, red turban, explains that the black-and-white garment affixed to the statue signifies the eternal struggle between good and evil spirits, and the victory of neither, as does the alternation of black and white curbstones. So, too, the many sculptured depictions en route of standoffs between demons and their benevolent counterparts indicate that they are evenly paired. The cockfighting for which the island was renowned is said to have originated from the same cause, the dark powers having the aggressive character of fighting cocks, and a taste for rooster blood. Evil spirits are believed to be conjured by unfortunate or inexplicable events, such as an unnatural death, or a suspicion of witchcraft. Appeasing or exorcising them might require the ritual sacrifice of animals, a chthonic curse being reversible only by sacrifices in the cardinal directions, a red bullock to the south, a black goat to the north, a white goose to the east, and a bird with yellow feathers to the west. Bali has been immemorially steeped in, and is still governed by, superstition. Shrines stand at each end of even the smallest bridges spanning the island's numerous streams, some of them sculpted figures of Pedandas (temple priests) and winged faces, some altars with offerings of food or woven flowers. But to us the leering, pop-eyed demons seem more prevalent.

Most women walking on the roadsides carry bulging sacks of rice on their heads, or bundles of rice shoots, stalks of sugar cane and bamboo, water buckets, and tied-together stacks of bricks. Some of these loads are said to weigh as much as ninety pounds, and though to remark on the grace of women so burdened seems callous, they are the most beautiful sight in Bali.

Larger roads are clogged with tour buses and trucks polluting the crystalline air with thick black smoke. Automobiles are greatly outnumbered by motorbikes, whose helmeted drivers rev up loudly while waiting at traffic lights, then zoom around slower traffic, crossing lanes from the British-style left side to do so. Except for the main highway out of Denpasar, the roads, some of them mere asphalted dirt paths, are winding, wide enough for only one car, and lacking in warning signs. Since this is a rice-harvesting season, large numbers of people are laboring in the watery fields, each, including the smallest, with a shrine to the rice goddess. Stores, open shops, and family and village temples line the road most of the way. Yawa says that by "traditional law" no structure is permitted to be taller than the coconut palm.

In the arts school at Batubulan, in the Gianyar Regency, we sit in on dance and gamelan-playing classes. One wall in the first of these consists of a mirror with barre, familiar from ballet rehearsals in the West. A young male teacher in blue T-shirt and black tights instructs a group of twenty male and female students, correcting their postures and their arm, hand, and leg movements, and demonstrating new ones which they imitate. After the class he escorts us to another studio where seventeen female and two male dancers perform part of a court-style *Legong*. Music from a CD interacts with, and is inseparable from, the dance, and it contains the secrets of the performers' sudden changes in direction and position. Two female teachers walk among them, adjusting their swaying, bending, kneeling, their manipulation of the fans held in their right hands, and their leg and rapid right-and-left head movements.

Balinese music resembles European in that it is based on structural melodies roughly comparable to the *cantus firmus* in Renaissance polyphony. But the complexities of the embellishing figuration are indecipherable to untrained ears. The rules of *Ijong* figuration, for example, require that each note of the melody is elaborated by sixteen notes. After four melodic notes have been embellished by sixty-four others, a strong accent in the lowest gong signals a change in the music and a switch in the gamelan players' roles. Sometimes two instruments play secondary figuration at a higher pitch to increase the volume. Notation, when used at all—most of the music has been memorized and transmitted by tradition—is engraved on difficult-to-read lontar palm leaves. No wonder the Western listener is able to discern little more than the difference between the pentatonic and heptatonic modes.

The gamelan class is in session in a room much too small for the decibel level of these clangorous instruments, but we are reluctant to enter for the different reason that the Balinese regard music as divine in origin, and spectators from outside the village, let alone the country, are threats. If an alien should happen to touch one of the instruments, it is desecrated and must be purified, a costly process. Urs Ramseyer says that when the Basel Institute of Ethnography sent someone to learn to play a *salonding,* the smith of a neighboring village spent many months under strict supervision fabricating a profane version of the consecrated instrument. Our presence in the room is not acknowledged, and we do not stay long. The teacher plays the basic melody on a high-pitched instrument with seven metal bars, and his pupils repeat it over and over on lower-pitched ones. The piece they eventually perform would have pleased Messiaen and Philip Glass more than it does us.

We continue to Ubud, a tacky art colony blighted by tourism. The paintings exhibited in the principal street compare unfavorably to the works of the 59th Street sidewalk portraitists. Antonio Blanco, the locally acclaimed "eccentric Spanish artist," lives here in affluence from sales of his pictures of "the beauty of the nude female," as Yawa puts it. The home of Colin McPhee, described in his *House in Bali,* stood near Sayan, a small village to the north—difficult to imagine his Steinway grand in this part of the world—and the residence of Margaret Mead and assorted girlfriends, including McPhee's anthropologist wife, Jane Belo, was farther north still. Until 1975 Ubud was without electricity, a novelty in Bali villages even now.

The suffocatingly hot Bird Park, smaller and more intimate than the one in Singapore, is renowned for its birds of paradise, which flit noiselessly from branch to branch, displaying their forked retrorsed tails, its crowned cranes and scarlet egrets, and its *siund,* a glossy black mynah bird (starling) with yellow trimmings, which exists only here. The *siund* repeats words in its throat like an echo, in the deep, gravelly register of a voicebox. When Yawa pronounces the first four syllables of the National Anthem, it squawks the music after him. It also whistles the opening trumpet call of Strauss's

Zarathustra, though the upper octave is slightly sharp. Hearing this remarkable creature repeat the notes of Yawa's four syllables, I whistle Beethoven's "V for Victory" motive, and after several moments of eyeing me with *méfiance,* it vociferates the music back at me perfectly in tune.

The flora is as exotic and magical as the highly sheened feathered population, and the horticultural grooming is immaculate. The lotus pads in the ponds are bedizened with translucent drops of water, pearl-shaped but glistening like diamonds. The reptile section has one large Komodo dragon and, in a separate, securely walled and rocky habitat, two small ones. An Australian visitor tells us that the prehistoric creatures, which have smooth skin (no scales), like to have their backs stroked, but he warns that the extrusion of the tongue is lightning fast.

At a musical instrument factory in Blabatuh we watch gongsmiths forge tiny bells and the metallic components of gamelans. In the foundry, at the rear of the establishment, one young boy stokes the fire while another presses the bellows. A caster explains the skills required in the fusion of bronze, copper, and tin to obtain the desired tone quality and pitch. Others carve, and lacquer in red and gold, the wood frames and cases for the six or so gamelans that are the yearly yield of this artisanal mode of production. I think of Edgard Varèse among his beloved Chinese gongs, which he struck very softly, and of how much he would have enjoyed this visit.

The chef at our hotel should have heeded Kipling's prediction, since its "East Meets West" cuisine ruins both. Not every European dish is improved by curry, and though we prefer rice *al dente,* the sticky Asian kind is the only one for Nasi Padang (rijsttafel). Fishing is not an occupation of great importance in Bali, and, except for small prawns, the menu offers imports only. We have not seen a boat of any kind in our bay, whose waters are said to be infested with sharks, poisonous sea snakes, and saltwater crocodiles. The Balinese look inland, to their sacred mountains.

6. Badulu. The whereabouts of the cave of Goa Gajah (elephant), described in a fourteenth-century chronicle as a hermitage, was not known until 1923,

but it has become so holy since then that female visitors are required to rent ground-length saris to conceal their legs, and they are not allowed on the premises during menstruation. (How is this enforced?) The cave itself, the three newly excavated baths, and the sanctuary's other venerated properties are at the bottom of a steep ravine reached by several flights of winding, irregular, and rickety steps. A statue of Ganesh resides in the cave, and among the features of a demon carved over the doorway are tusklike fangs and floppy elephant ears. The human inhabitants evidently belonged to a Shivaite lingam cult—three large stone phalluses rise from a common base—but the lair also contains statues of Hariti, the Buddhist goddess of children, with seven of her offspring. The usually reliable *Indonesian Handbook* is well-informed about the spooky cave and its gloomy environs, but what we would like the author to have explained is how "archaeologists derive the date of a monument by reading certain animals in its structure: Three frogs, two crabs, three iguanas, and one eel, for instance, add up to A.D. 1455."

From the most confining space on the island we go to Penelokan, the most open, with its panoramic views of Mount Batur and the crater lake, but the souvenir hawkers operating here are persistent and rapacious, and Yawa warns us that to look long or closely at their baubles is to commit oneself to buy. Penglipuran, on the return, a "model village" touted as "very interesting," is an agglomeration of dark and windowless bamboo huts on stilts, in which the older inhabitants spend their time preparing offerings. On the return ride we see several bare-breasted women, some with head-loads, all of them prelapsarian in their unselfconsciousness.

7. For some reason all the passengers on Garuda Air to Yogyakarta are seated at the back of the plane, as if to keep it from tipping forward. A coincidence: as we fly over the Solo River, a conference of paleontologists in Europe is concluding that the 300,000-year-old Java Man (*Homo erectus*) discovered here in 1891, and the fossilized skulls found not long ago at nearby Ngandong, still existed as recently as 27,000 years ago, thereby overlapping with the earliest known humans in Australia and with the dying out of Neanderthal man in Spain. The human family tree may have had only one trunk but there were more branches than heretofore believed.

At Yogyakarta, Tiss, a tiny middle-aged lady, escorts us to yet another Mitsubishi minibus. Seating herself sideways next to the driver, she addresses the merely two of us through a booming loudspeaker as "ladies and gentlemen." A Ministry of Propaganda lecture follows, complete with statistics of economic, educational, and other growth in the over-populated (eighty millions) island, a spiel she interrupts only to identify ugly new government buildings. One of these silences, however, provides an opportunity for us to change the subject to the pro-democracy movement ruthlessly suppressed in Jakarta by Suharto last July, and the student protesters now on trial there for their lives. But all she will say is that at one time Suharto did much good for the country. Nor will she admit that the current Borneo gold rush will make him and his family, already the wealthiest people in Indonesia, richer still. We contend that Java's recent history is even more brutal than it was during the three-and-a-half centuries of exploitation by the Dutch.

In February 1942 the Japanese invaders retained Sukarno to help govern the country. After Hiroshima, he proclaimed an independent Republic of Indonesia, but the anachronistic Dutch returned, and, with full American support, tried to reimpose their colonial rule. When Sukarno moved the government to Yogyakarta, the Dutch bombed it, and their paratroopers captured and interned him. For the next four years the cities remained under Dutch control, the provinces under that of the new Republic, whose independence the USSR, the Arab states, and Mao's China quickly recognized. Finally, in 1949, the Dutch conceded the futility of their campaign and Sukarno, released, assumed dictatorial powers. He ruined the economy, squandering billions on huge stadiums, erecting Soviet-style statues of himself, and allowing the inflation level to reach 650 percent. In 1965 a coup, generally regarded as having been engineered by the CIA, although U.S. documents relating to it are still classified and inaccessible, replaced him by his general, Suharto, whose "New Order" was equally repressive but economically successful. Suharto's mass murders of Communists were as bloody as the purges of Stalin and Mao, but they qualified him as a candidate for the American support that he is still receiving. As I write, the American government has announced its intention to sell the most sophisticated fighter planes and other weaponry to this enemy of democracy, thus enabling him to bring Timor and other outer islands under tight control. Tiss, a non-stop talker, keeps quiet regarding our observations, but not surprisingly, since the country's laws proscribe all political discussion.

The road to Mayalong and Borobudur is wide, smooth, straight, and flanked by curbed lanes for bicycle and rickshaw traffic. Unlike the Balinese beast of burden, women here carry their loads on their backs. Rice and tapioca fields extend beyond both sides of the road. (Nicolson's Java book expresses distaste for the "glutinous root" and astonishment that "profit could be made from it in the manufacture of an unwanted milk-pudding for English children.") Every few kilometers we are confronted by huge Chinese-style propaganda billboards picturing the new Indonesia, the family unit, the military might (airplanes, tanks), the advance of technology (factories, happy workers), schools (classrooms and smiling children), and the tricolor emblems in which religious harmony is symbolized by Islamic green (90 percent of the population), Hindu and Buddhist red and yellow.

The Borobudur monument is a three-mile walk from the parking lot, but Tiss talks to guards, gates are opened, and a stopping place is found for us near the main entrance. At first sight, the colossal structure seems like an apparition, but an elating one, and we stand for several moments in disbelief.

The great stepped-pyramid, stupa-crowned building—"boro" means "monastery," "budur" is the place-name (mentioned in a manuscript of 1365)—was begun in the last decades of the eighth century by an architect called Gunadharma. Though largely buried by jungle overgrowth, it had been known to the Javanese for more than a millennium when Sir Thomas

Raffles, the interregnum governor during the Napoleonic period, discovered and partly excavated it (1814). After the publication of his *History of Java* four years later, French, English, and Dutch predators and adventurers came, and in 1845 parts of the building were photographed. In the 1880s Paul Gauguin saw photos of some of its 27,000 square feet of stone relief sculptures, and by 1896 all of it had been substantially documented by the camera. Now picture books proliferate and films have been made, notably Brian Brake's *Borobudur: The Cosmic Mountain*—the "Mahameru" that connects heaven and earth.

The restoration, begun in 1975 and completed in the 1980s with UNESCO help and IBM computerized programming, is a feat second only to that of the original construction. Starting on the north side, four of the superimposed rectangular layers (galleries, terraces) were dismantled, a total of 1,600,000 blocks of andesite, the porphyritic rock found in the riverbed between it and the Manoreh mountains to the south. When reassembled, by means of anastylosis, a drainage system, with a hundred spouts and gutters from upper levels directed toward lower ones, was installed behind the walls and under the floors.

The low rhyolite hill on which the original monument was erected ultimately determined its form. The first builders leveled it but covered its uneven surfaces with a clay that failed to prevent sliding from rainwater, and when only a few layers had been finished, the base sank beneath the surface. At this point the original architectural concept was abandoned, the pyramid truncated about halfway to the apex, and a decision made to complete the structure with three concentric circles, also pyramidal, supporting seventy-two bell-shaped and latticed stupas.

Borobudur is not a temple but a monastery school (*vihara*)—some of the relief panels depict Brahmans and monks toting books and instructing pupils—and the terminus of pilgrimages. It may also be thought of as an abode for ancestors and gods, though it has no roof, which explains the absence of arches here and throughout Southeast Asia: they admit large numbers of people. Most of the relief panels, which are read from right to left, and from upper to lower registers, illustrate holy legends. Only the above-ground base, the lowest surface, is wide enough for processions, which would have circumambulated the building, keeping it to their right. The uppermost corridors are passageways for priests, teachers, seers, holy men.

Appearing three centuries later than the first free-standing Hindu stone buildings, in Karnataka, India, Javanese stone structures deviate widely from Indian models, as do Javanese religious traditions, in which Hinduism and Buddhism merge. (One king was posthumously deified as Sivabuddha.) India was the source, nevertheless, and the instructions to the sculptors left above the unfinished reliefs at the base are carved in Sanskrit, the written language of the Indian intellectual world as Latin was of the European. The narrative sculpture of Borobudur pictures the imagined Indianized world of the *Gandavyuba,* a Mahavana sutra and a Sanskrit text originally, now surviving only in Chinese and Tibetan translations. Its subject is the young Sudhana's quest for Enlightenment, which takes place in India, and the last chapter, the *Bhadracari,* tells of his eventual attainment of it, after years of wandering, initiation, instructive encounters with gurus and Bodhisattvas, meditation. Four hundred and sixty of the relief panels illustrate the *Gandavyuba.*

The Buddhism of Borobudur is of the Dhyani (cosmic) meditating variety, meaning that its Buddhas are not enlightened earthly beings, in the tradition of the historical Siddhartha Gautama, but transcendental ones. As represented at Borobudur, the principal episode in the Buddha's life was his decision to descend to earth from a heaven in which he is surrounded by soaring celestial beings and musicians. (During the downward flight his throne is cushioned on clouds, while, to show movement, pennants flutter in the wind and attendants' parasols, status symbols, tilt.) On earth, he enters the womb of his mother, Queen Maya, in the form of a small white elephant with six tusks, an event that she experiences as a dream. Seven days after giving birth, she died and became a celestial being, which did not prevent her from visiting her son again on earth. Siddhartha's father, King Suddhadana, sought to make him a worldly leader, but the Prince's compassion for suffering humans compelled him to choose a different path, which he did under the name of Sakyamuni. At Borobudur, the chronicle of the historical Buddha ends with his first sermon, at Varanasi.

In addition to the relief panels, Borobudur has 504 human-size Buddha statues along the balustrades and inside the latticed stupas on the top storey. Each of them has been carved in the round out of a single block of andesite, and all are seated, right leg crossed over the left in the lotus position. Reputedly they are endowed with distinct individual personalities, but since half have been decapitated by vandals and souvenir hunters, and since the results of a worldwide computer program to match their acephalous bodies with heads have been meager, this has yet to be established. What does distinguish them are their mudra positions, which correspond to the cardinal directions in which they face. Like their Indian counterparts in fifth-century Gupta statuary, lips are bow-shaped, and the *urna* on the forehead, and the *ushnisha,* the knot on the top of the head, are prominent, but faces and limbs are softer and more rounded here than in India. All wear the *civara* robe, which hugs the body tightly but leaves the right shoulder bare. The hair of all consists of small, shrimp-like curls turned clockwise.

None of the rain- and wind-battered sculpture of Borobudur can be compared to such masterpieces as the statue of Prajnaparamita, goddess of transcendental wisdom, shown in the Metropolitan Museum and now returned to the National Museum in Jakarta, also carved from andesite but protected by enshrinement in a temple. Traditionally it has been seen as embodying the moment of transformation of this first queen of Singasari into a goddess, of the mortal into the personification of a sacred idea. At first glance, her sumptuous jewelry and ornamented conical headdress might appear overly rich, her mudra gesture, symbolizing the Turning of the Wheel of the Law, meretricious, but at second, and thereafter, the eloquence and perfection of the image, eyes closed in inner absorption, hold the viewer in thrall.

The Borobudur relief sculptures include mitered kings, mustached and bearded ministers and warriors, dancing girls (the choreography is South

Indian) both celestial (*apsaras*) and terrestrial, "topless" girls brandishing fly-whisks, and flora and fauna—birds, fish, serpents, tortoises, lions, monkeys, gazelles, boars, rabbits, groomed horses, elephants. Some of the most memorable panels are of these last, one of them draped from tail to neck with strings of bells, and another wearing what looks like a Cardinal's broad-brimmed, low-crowned hat. A horse is shown being carried out of a palace to avoid the clopping of its hooves on the floor. Memorable, too, are the hair styles of "humans," as shown in the barbering of the Buddha (a pile of his locks), and in the long tresses coiled on top and wound like turbans around the heads of the deep-forest ascetics.

According to Tiss, 3,000 people climb the five storeys to the stupas each day, but of the multitudes of foreign visitors each year, fewer than 1,000 are from the U.S. This information does not prepare us for the display of enthusiasm for things American in the Javanese we encounter, most of them schoolchildren. Pretty girls and handsome boys crowd around smiling, laughing with us, asking for our autographs and to be photographed with us. One small girl gives a notebook to me in which she has written questions in block-letter English, asking me to write my answers. When I oblige, her classmates applaud and cheer me on at each new line. Many of the boys wear "New York" and "Yankees" T-shirts. One child's shirt incorporates the American flag. Their parents and teachers are equally friendly, kind, polite. Since the galleries are oven-hot in the afternoon sun, and today is the rare one without rain, the step-climbing and descending, in most cases uneven and without the iron-pipe railings that have been installed in a few places, are tiring. Seeing that I do this with some effort, the Javanese wait at the top or bottom of each flight of stairs, leaving the path to me alone. Some people draw my attention to loose stones and gaps in the pavement and even lend me a helping arm or hand.

Tiss is a devout Muslim who rises before dawn to pray, and who prays again at four other times daily. This said, she is impressively knowledgeable about Buddhism and Hinduism and can provide exegeses of a considerable portion of the panels in the lower galleries. (By no means all of them have been identified, partly because of deviations in their Sanskrit, Tibetan, Pali, and Chinese origins.) She is primarily concerned with the theology of the great labyrinth's architectural symbolism, and, but for lack of commonality of language, would like to discuss it with us. The going interpretation of Borobudur in terms of the cosmology of its architecture is that the friezes of the lower three levels represent the Sphere of Desire, in which the human spirit is entangled in fantasies and in bondage to greed. The next highest level represents the Sphere of Form, in which the spirit has been liberated from greed but still cannot transcend the phenomenal world. The highest level, that of the stupas, is the Sphere of Formlessness, in which the liberated spirit has left all earthly considerations behind. Ultimate truth is formlessness, and the supreme essence is emptiness. Here nothing is separate from anything else, and attributes and predicates do not exist. Higher still is immanence, marked here by a Buddha statue of unforgettable majesty.

We leave feeling uplifted, but wanting to know more. Why, when the monument was reconstructed, were the below-the-surface panels not preserved in a museum? What is the basis for Jan Fontein's conclusion (*The Sculpture of Indonesia*) that many of the panels imply the equality of men and women? What, too, of the argument in Louis Frédéric's *Borobudur* (1996), the best of the books, that during the seventy years in which the labyrinth was built "there were no fundamental differences between Hinduism and Mahavana Buddhism"? And what was the significance of music in the culture? Tusita (Heaven) is never without it, and the most common bronze relics found in Central and East Java are ceremonial bells (in contrast to the paucity of arrowheads and weapons); monks wore bells and mendicants jangled metal rings inside the finials of their staves.

Dinner music at the Radisson consists of a suite of Vivaldi concertos—not the *Seasons,* whose programmatic images of winter and summer would make little sense here—gently played by a small string ensemble. Part of the restaurant is a buffet for an Australian tour group, whose two hungriest patrons could be cast as Cinderella's sisters, one might think, except that one of them is in drag, as her bass voice, figure, legs, and ill-fitting wig confirm. But the twosome seem to be putting on a show and to be enjoying it.

8. Tiss takes us to a performance at the Puppet Gallery of a half-hour or so of the nine-hour *Ramayana* epic. An incomprehensible synopsis of the plot in English is provided, but what we see, so far from European marionette theater, is skiagraphy, shadows or silhouettes on a screen—known here as shadow plays—in black and white. The action is unrelentingly violent, and though any one of the blows inflicted by the combating warriors would be mortal, the recipients quickly rebound, good as new. The gamelans in the hidden orchestra are softer than their Balinese counterparts, but as the episode approaches its convulsive climax, the gongs and the two-headed *handang* hand drum, which is exactly the same as those depicted at Borobudur, become deafening. Music apart, the show resembles a "Tom and Jerry" cartoon.

Like Borobudur, the temples of Prambanan swarm with dragonflies. Dedicated to the supreme Hindu trinity, Brahma, Shiva, and Vishnu, the spiky buildings from a distance remind the viewer of Golgotha: the Brahma and Vishnu flanking the Shiva are of the same lower height and distance from it as the crucified thieves in Christian iconography. A fourth, facing Shiva, contains a large replica of Nandi, the god's sacred bull. The path from the entrance to the wide walk-around gallery of the temples leads between souvenir stalls selling several sizes of inflatable Donald Duck, small buzzing beehives, bolts of batik, models of classic automobiles (Pierce-Arrows, Rollses, Duisenbergs), but the ground is flat and the stairs to the building are easy to negotiate.

The stones for the reliefs here are larger, affording greater freedom of composition, than those at Borobudur, where heads, torsos, legs, and feet are on different, often imperfectly aligned blocks; the largest example of the "vase of abundance," one of the most common motifs at Borobudur, spreads over parts of six slabs. The difference in subject matter is polar—the inner-wall scenes illustrate the *Ramayana*—except for sixty-two panels portraying dancing figures and celestial musicians. Animals, trees, monkeys, are more stylized and dynamic, the erotic element more pronounced, than in the sculptures at Borobudur, and whereas most scenes there evoke peace, snarling monsters are more salient here. As Jan Fontein remarks, the "sculptors at Prambanan seem to have been reluctant to skip even a single demon." He also notes that here, as at Borobudur, the ornamentation of the façade does not compete with the architecture but supports it and coordinates with it: "The architects selected the shape and size of their building blocks in anticipation of the decoration that was going to be applied to them."

10. Back to secular S'pore, the fast-track, high-tech meritocracy, the world of Internet, as its spokespeople refer to it.

11. En route to London, we see nothing except the snow- and icebound shores of the Sea of Azov, until suddenly, over the Ukraine, three supersonic fighter planes break through the cloud banks worryingly close to us, as if to check us out. Are we off-course? Borobudur has made me think so.

China

Alva and I had planned to go to China before the Tian-an-men massacre, and were a bit nervous about going even two years after it. But the arrangements for private tours, as distinguished from those for large groups, were impossible to change without forfeiting deposits. A New York musician and impresario, Michael Feldman, who, with his Chinese wife, shepherded musical ensembles there for concert tours two or three times a year, was instrumental in convincing us to go. The trip was the most exciting and rewarding of all those recounted in this book. We flew via Paris and returned there.

November 16, 1992. Hong Kong. Daydreaming, I see myself as a small boy only recently out of the sandbox digging a hole in our backyard as deep as I was tall. My mother said that if I burrowed on I would come out in China, a name I had heard in connection with our pigtailed laundryman, our living-room rug, and our best tableware. I continued to dig for a time, hoping for a glimpse, no matter how distant, "Through caverns measureless to man." Tonight the tunneling ends in Guilin, which is "spelled six different ways but pronounced Kuei-lin" (how is that pronounced?). This is in the Guangxi Zhuang Autonomous Region of the People's Republic, where, according to Zheng Yi's *Red Memorial,* cannibalism, "eating class-enemies," was practiced during the Cultural Revolution—which sounds like Amy Tan folklore but is not.

Shortly before we leave, Gerald Hatherly, Canadian Sinophile and travel agent, delivers tickets, itineraries, charts of the Imperial Dynasties, souvenir packets of chopsticks, and warnings: tap water and raw food are certain death; toilets, if any, are holes in the ground; avoid everything touched by hands and wash your own at every opportunity; reconfirm reservations on each arrival because of overbooking; the penalty for losing the carbon copy of an entry Customs Declaration is a fine of $300 (we had expected him to say "beheading," Chinese history being what it is). "Suzie Wong," his swaggering, cellular-phoning, half-pint assistant, accompanies us to the airport to help with checking-in, money-changing—foreigners and Chinese nationals have different currencies—and paying overweight charges: our six bags are bulging with books. In a camera shop earlier in the day, Ms. Wong helped us to choose a "no frash" model, and the "r" for "l" interchange suddenly "flashed" a mental picture of the Stravinskys here in 1959, a thought that leaves me feeling an emptiness, like the last leaf on the tree.

Our China Southern Airline Boeing 737, blaring American rock music, fills up in five minutes and takes off while passengers are still standing in the aisles. The Customs Declaration is in Chinese only, and the stewardesses are unable to help us with the English answers, but they say it is no longer required anyway. After an ear-crackling descent, we are on the ground before seeing any lights, and the few that frame the landing strip are dispiritingly dim.

[Two days later, another 737, or possibly the same, crashed into a mountain on the approach to Guilin, killing all 141 on board. A minute or so after the pilot had informed the control tower that the plane was at an altitude of 6,000 feet, radar showed it at 1,800 feet. A China Airlines official claimed that the flight recorders, recovered the next day, were too damaged to read, but a Boeing spokesman, charging the "usual Chinese cover-up," protested that even the most damaged ones yield crucial information. Three thousand soldiers were flown to the site, near Baitun village, to prevent relatives of the victims from searching for remains, which infuriated the families because "spirit rites must be performed within 72 hours of death. Wearing white headbands, they scattered paper money for the journey to the next world, and set off firecrackers."]

The interior of the terminal is even darker than the airport. We surrender landing cards and show passports, but the Customs form is not wanted. Spotting our white identity pins, Wan Wei, our guide, a shy college girl with a nervous laugh, packs us into a car and reels off the tectonic history of the Li Valley karst pinnacles we have come to see, their seismic emergence from a tropical ocean hundreds of millions of years ago, and the subsequent erosion and weathering. The narrow and deeply rutted road is without light, like the reflectorless bicycles and foot-drawn farmers' carts competing for passage.

The US-Chinese "joint venture" Sheraton is up-to-date: unenclosed glass capsule elevators, open lobby-side balconies, CNN in every room. Guilin's restaurants—the local specialties are civet cat, owl, scaly pangolin, and flying fruit bat—close early, but room service brings "Australian steaks" (kangaroo?) and Mumms, the first bottle ever popped here, so the polite, eager, good-looking young people who bring it tell us, pooling their English vocabularies. "Are you celebrating?" one of them asks, and he blames the steep cost of doing so on taxes. But they do not know how to open it, and the detonation, ceilingward trajectory of the cork, and bubbly overflow astonishes them. We brush our teeth in Evian water, and go to bed trying to memorize the dates of the Dynasties and the sounds of the Romanized consonants in Pinyin, the official People's Republic orthography: X = the hissing s, Z = ds, gh = the unaspirated j (jug).

Construction noise from a building across the street begins before sunrise (and continues after sunset). On the floor opposite ours, about thirty men, where four or five would be employed in the US, are hammering, mortaring, toting lumber and bricks. A fuse has blown in our room and the engineer who replaces it is a teenage girl wearing what looks like a New York theater usher's uniform. Some of the breakfast ingredients come from far away, New Zealand butter, Swiss fruit jellies, and the bathroom scales, stamped "Not Legal for Trade," were made in Ireland.

Guilin was occupied and destroyed by the Japanese during the war. The name dates only from the Ming (1369); under the first Ch'in Emperor (214 B.C.) it was Guizhou. It suffers now from the choking, blinding pollution of factories, truck and bus exhausts, and street dust constantly recirculated by men and women sweeping with large besoms. The roads are clogged with motorized rickshaws, blue trishaw pedicycle taxis with surrey tops and open sides, countless bicycles, donkey and pedestrian carts over-freighted with bricks, hay, sugar cane, sorghum, taro, firewood. Wan says that the market here is an example of China's mixed-economy policy in that vegetables and fruit are sold at free-market stalls, meat, poultry, and fish at the state-run kind. Individually owned enterprises in China have grown from zilch to fourteen million in little more than a decade.

The pinnacles, mountain tops without the mountains, that rise on the plain on both sides of the road to the Li River, were pushed up from under the sea about two hundred million years ago. Many are conical and sharply pointed—the Tang poet Han Yu (768-824) compared them to "blue jade hairpins"—but the strangest are tall, thin, non-sloping, making unimaginable the geological convulsions that formed them. Some have names: Camel Hill, Elephant Trunk Hill, Yearning-For-Husband's-Return Rock. No paintings survive by the one artist known to have lived here, Mi Fu (1052-1107), but some mountainscapes by Li Gonglin (twelfth century), the greatest master of Northern Sung painting, and Yu Daoing (eleventh century) would seem to be impressions of the Li Valley rather than of the "Five Sacred Mountains," those intermediary realms between heaven and earth.

Souvenir hawkers—"Hello Wannabuy"—wait in ambush by the foot-path to six flat-bottomed three-decker steamboats embarking passengers for the five-hour, 80-kilometer ride to Yangshuo village, where our driver will meet us. In summer, with ten times as many boats, the excursions are the largest source of revenue in the region, designated "autonomous" because of its large ethnic minorities—Han is the Chinese majority—in this case the Thai-related Zhuang and the Yao and Miao mountain people. Most of our 250 or so fellow passengers are well-dressed Japanese, but a tour-group of American senior citizens is also aboard, all of them sporting "high-tech" white sneakers. During a merciful hour or so when these compatriots are eating and watching "folk-dances" below, we have the top deck's front railing to ourselves.

In this dry season the river is shallow, often no deeper than three feet, and our keel scrapes the river bed more than once. Apart from galley garbage, the water is crystalline, reflecting the landscape on the sides, ahead and behind. The rear view is as new as the forward, and we never recognize the formations between which we have just passed. In the narrowest gorges, we try to picture the torrent that roared through them millions of years ago. The pinnacles here are sheer and untapering, and with each meander of the limpid Li the perspectives change, apparitions of peaks behind peaks emerging ghostlike from mist and cloud.

Every arable ell of the lush land at the river's edges grows plumed bamboo, palm, banana and orange trees, while goats browse, and bare-legged men plow, plant, tend pigs, cattle, water buffalo, and fenced-in fish farms. The most arresting occupation to watch is cormorant fishing from slender bamboo rafts with slightly upturned ends like pagoda eaves. The black raptorial birds perch on the balancing shoulder poles of their agile, sure-footed masters, then dive toward their prey. A tether above the neck pouch forces them to disgorge the catch.

Rounding a bend in a labyrinthine passage, the boat emits a hollow hoot that reverberates against the rocks and provokes a quacking of river ducks. As we approach a rice-paddy village, swarms of half-naked children run to the shore hoping for money flung from the boat. The scene reminds me of Isherwood's account in *Journey to a War* of a coin tossed from a steamer to a Shanghai wharf and landing next to a small boy who pretends not to see it, covers it with his toe, and slowly works it into a position from which he can pick it up undetected.

The *retour* road from Yangshua to Guilin, a great improvement on the *aller,* is shaded by willows, oleanders, sycamores, camphor and cassia trees and lined by stalls selling kumquats, grapefruit, pomelos, mangosteens; *"Gui"* means cassia (Osmanthus) and *"lin"* forest. The weird, unearthly pinnacles are less dense and less steep here than by the river, and their lower flanks are terraced, like ziggurats. Many of the village walls closest to the road are covered with slogans in red paint. Wan reads one of them for us, tracing each character in the air with her finger, vertically and horizontally, from which we deduce that sense travels from left to right and depends on linkages of the brush strokes: in China the poet is also the painter. Wan says she can render the idea of the ideogram, but not the words, and that the idea of this one is propaganda: "We must take care of the land."

At night we finish Fairbanks's *China, A New History,* which seems to be sound on scapulimancy, the roles of the *wennen* (literati), the eunuchs, the Legalists, the compradores; and the inveteracy of the social traditions, meaning the unquestioning acceptance of the superiority of parents to children, men to women, rulers to subjects, past to present. He says more about the horrifying thousand-year-old practice of footbinding than the other historians we have read, but throws no light on the male fetish behind it. Whether true or not that the deformation of the feet affected the development of the thighs (it definitely atrophied the calves) and the folds of the vaginal skin, as both Chinese and foreign writers have claimed, the illustrations of women during copulation in such classics as *The Clouds and the Rain* and Chin Ping Mei's novel *The Plum in the Golden Vase,* portray slippered three-inch feet with a normal big toe covered in red cloth. Women were made lifelong invalids to enhance male sexual gratification. One thinks of Montaigne on the superiority of female partners confined to sedentary occupations such as needlework!

Fairbanks does not mention Leibniz's writings on China, though the great philosopher's *Discourse on the Natural Theology of the Chinese* (1716) makes the best case for ecumenical dialogue between Christian and Oriental cultures. Moreover, Fairbanks's account of the doctrine of Kong Fuzzi (Master Kong, Confucius), that educating people is the equivalent of moralizing them, and that "for Confucius, Man, not God, is the center of the universe," is absurdly reductionist. Consider this in the light of Max Weber's comparison between Confucianism and European Puritanism: the belief of the former in a cosmic order and the harmony of heaven and earth versus the latter's faith in a supramundane God; the Confucian supremacy of familial piety and kinship relations versus the subjugation of all human relations to the service of God; and the Confucian attitude to wealth as necessary to dignity and self-perfection versus the Protestant ethic that wealth is the unintended by-product of a virtuous life. Fairbanks even neglects to say that Chinese civilization is characterized by the *absence* of both religious prophecy and a powerful priesthood, Weber's principal tenets.

In providing parallels with the West, Fairbanks offers helpful contexts for non-specialist readers, but in telling us that the Chinese had as many miles of road as their Roman contemporaries, he should have explained the philological methods of Joseph Scaliger's chronology sequence. Nor does he mention such striking examples as the exhibiting of an East African giraffe in Beijing on the same day as the Battle of Agincourt, and the features in common between twelfth-century Chinese and medieval-to-Bosch European depictions of Hell: the scowling, pitchfork-prodding demon torturers, the bludgeons, the cangues, the serpents, the weighing of souls in balances, the infernal machine breathing coils of fire and flame-belching dogs (*cf.* the *Ten Kings Sutra*). Buddhist Hells were portrayed as prisons in which the sinner "did time." Sins could be remitted during a thousand kalpas, at four billion years each.

Fairbanks criticizes Joseph Needham's monumental *Science and Civilization in China* and *The Great Astronomical Clocks of Medieval China* for vaunting Chinese superiority over the pre-Renaissance West in, for starters, astronomy (the epact); decimal metrology; advanced algebra and trigonometry; the invention of movable type and manufacture of paper; the discovery of immunization. (Variolation: in yin-yang tradition, the cotton with the pustule secretion was inserted in one nostril in the male and in the other nostril in the female.) But surely such comparisons help rather than hinder reciprocal East-West comprehension.

We sleep only lightly and sporadically, unable to put the harsh, precarious existences of the river people out of mind. Are medical facilities available to them, and medicines (antibiotics) other than herbs? A single riverside irrigation pump was the only evidence of electric power.

18. An article on the Autonomous Region of Tibet in today's *China Daily,* which prints "only optimistic news," describes the Region's newfound prosperity—up to an annual $81 per capita (what could it have been before?)—and "the improvement of Yak varieties since the peaceful liberation." Liberation from what? Tibetan culture, those 6,500 destroyed monasteries? Tibetans, a minority people in their homeland, refer to the liberation as the Occupation.

The firetruck-red People's Republic flag flaps over the entrance to the airport, together with a banner in English and Chinese proclaiming "Unity-Friendship-Progress." The matching exit banner in Shanghai's Hong Quia airport is more immediately pertinent: "Traffic Safety Brings You Happiness And Joy." This, we soon understand, is a warning that motor traffic in the metropolis of six million urban and seven million suburban residents is the most tangled in the world, bicycle and pedestrian traffic the densest. The streets are small and narrow, except where the walls of the pre-Communist foreign concessions have been demolished. Older and more cramped districts are virtually without traffic lights, and at one gridlocked intersection the drivers of a truck and a car trying to pass each other in opposite directions are able to do so only by removing their outside rearview mirrors. Our guide, Mr. Chee, heavy-set, good-natured, is outwardly calm and patient in even the most claustrophobic situations. He explains that the people who work downtown and live farthest away commute by bus, the others by bicycle, and adds that the new subway system, slow to construct in this city built on fens, will alleviate the overcrowding. Pedestrian overpasses connect the sides of otherwise untraversable main arteries, and tunnels those of the broadest thoroughfare, the Bund. The Yangtze River teems with tankers, trains of linked-together barges, commercial steamers, cruise ships, junks. It is the busiest harbor I have ever seen.

So far, our impression of the city accords with Isherwood's in 1937:

> Seen from the river...the semi-skyscrapers of the Bund present, impressively, the façade of a great city. But it is only a façade. The spirit which dumped them upon this unhealthy mud-bank...has

been too purely and brutally competitive. The biggest animals have pushed their way down to the brink of the water; behind them is a sordid and shabby mob of smaller buildings....

Mr. Chee's English will take some, well, orientation. For one obstacle, he omits crucial consonants. Passing the unique wall with no factory behind it we wonder aloud what this absence might indicate. "Used to be" (not "was"; the Chinese language is tenseless) "fo gol" (a golf course). For another, he does not enumerate sequentially. "How many colleges does Shanghai have?" we ask. "Maybe thirty, fifty, six, eleven." (This seems to reflect the awkwardness of counting in Chinese, in which the 365-day year is "three hundreds, six tens, a five, and one out of four parts of a degree," which, come to think of it, is not so different from *trois cents soixante cinq.*) Well informed about New York for someone who has not been abroad, he is remarkably familiar with Central Park South. After we have seen our rooms at the Hilton, he wishes to know how it compares with Manhattan's Plaza Hotel. "Glitzier," we say, an unfamiliar word that he interprets as a compliment. He repeatedly refers to Shanghai's "new rich" as a consequence of the growth of private enterprises and the foreign business partnerships. But the least tangible of the imports is also the most potent, Mr. Chee's own American-style obsession with progress and faith in the capitalist future. Deeply proud of the New China, he notes—presciently, in the opinion of most economists—that "Today all Chinese want visas for America, but in another generation or two they will not."

Shanghailanders and New Yorkers resemble each other in their chutzpah, hurry, savvy, indifference, but the old quarter here has many more signs in English than our Chinatown. American films and fast-food emporia (Pizza Hut, Kentucky Fried Chicken) are conspicuous, and Chinese-American joint ventures (McDonnell-Douglas, Cherokee, Squibb, IBM, Xerox (which Mr. Chee pronounces as the single-syllable "chocks"), are said to outnumber German and Japanese. Other features common to both cities are the cosmopolitanism, the tenacity of panhandlers, and the fame of the 1930s

Underworld of Cassia Ma, the Nightsoil Queen (nightsoil collection is still a lucrative business), and Big-Eared Du, Du Yue-sheng, the opium trafficker and Chiang Kai-shek henchman. Auden and Isherwood visited Du in 1937 when he was head of the Chinese Red Cross. Isherwood wrote:

> He was tall and thin, with a face that seemed hewn out of stone, a Chinese version of the Sphinx. Peculiarly and inexplicably terrifying were his feet, in their silk socks and smart pointed European boots, emerging from beneath the long silken gown. Perhaps the Sphinx, too, would be even more frightening if it wore a modern top-hat.

Nothing here about ears. Mr. Chee wants to hear more about New York gangsters. Unable to remember any except "Legs" Diamond, I borrow two names from restaurant menus, "Eggs" Benedict and "Chicken" Cacciatore. Thanks to heavy rain this morning and the forecast of a typhoon, we decide to go to Suzhou (Suchow). Since this is not an itinerary option, Chee says that we must pay more. When we immediately agree to the piddling sum he names—a drive of the same distance in Italy would have cost twenty times as much—he is unhappy, realizing that he could have done better. He does not want to go anyway, but is a good sport about it. Our even less enthusiastic driver says that we must obtain a permit to cross into another Province, but we ultimately do not comply. The border concept in Chinese culture, nevertheless, is a subject of ancient and continuing significance (Li Po: "along the border of Heaven"). County vehicles cannot cross the city boundary, and to cross it in the other direction ourselves we must pay a toll; small vehicles must have green licenses, large ones red. The driver takes a fire extinguisher with us "just in case," and we are obliged to leave the car while fueling at one of the only two gasoline stations on the way.

The road in Kiangsu Province is wider and smoother, but the landscape on one side, which includes the Kunsha Economic Development Zone, is unrelievedly industrial: telecom factories, power plants, cranes and building machinery, a cement works with, incongruously in this automated world, coolies loading back-bending bags. We are more interested in the boat life of the Grand Canal, which abuts the other side most of the way, goes on for a thousand miles, and is one of the great engineering feats of antiquity. Shoals of bicycles fill both sides of the road the entire eighty miles. According to Chee, the WC that, for a substantial charge, we patronize near the halfway point is the only modern one in all China.

Suzhou was founded in 514 B.C. after a geomancer of one of the Wu kings had "made favorable astrological tellings." It is a moated and walled city with "eight water and eight land gates," willow-lined cobblestone streets, canals and bridges, balconies with carved-wood lattices, pagodas, and more than a hundred classical gardens. Marco Polo remarked on its great wealth and "incalculable number of people" (it was the most populous city in the world at the time), among them "many philosophers" and "skilled craftsmen." The greatest Ming scroll painters lived in Suzhou, which is also one of the settings of *The Dream of the Red Chamber*. As the inimitable People's Publishing House puts it, "In the great age, poets, artists, and calligraphers emerged hot on the heels of one another."

Sericulture, the art of gorging silkworms on the leaves of the white mulberry (*cf.* the pathology of pâté de foie gras), nurturing them through phases of molting, cocoon spinning, diapause (hibernation), then of unwinding the cocoon to produce raw silk, has been practiced in Suzhou for 3,000 years. It began 4,000 years earlier than that in the northern Province of Liaoning, as Neolithic ornaments found there, carved in the shape of silkworms, attest. According to legend, the Empress Hsi Ling-Shi, retrieving a cocoon that had accidentally fallen into hot water, or tea, noticed that it came out on a thread of silk (*cf.* the accident factor in Charles Lamb's roast pig). Only the nobility were allowed to use silk, one bolt of which (60 cm. in width) could be exchanged for slaves. In the tenth century (Five Dynasties period) the Chinese monopoly had been broken, what with Persia producing an annual 10,000 zooms (5,000 bales) of fiber. About a third of the Silk Road export came from Suzhou, and the city still manufactures a sixth of all Chinese silk.

Chee conducts us through an ill-lighted silk-spinning factory where

1,700 female throwsters soak the cocoons in water, then submerge them for two or three minutes in the boiling water that kills the pupated worm and softens the integument so that the thread can be caught and unraveled by the prongs of a metal churner. Extruded and solidified from liquid silk, this filament is reeled onto overhead bobbins that rewind and dry the fiber. A hundred pounds of mulberry leaf yield fifteen cocoons, but 900 cocoons are required to make one shirt.

The nearest of Suzhou's famed gardens, across a steeply arched pedestrian bridge, is the romantic "Master of the Nets," a copy of which in the Metropolitan Museum in New York conveys nothing of the atmosphere of the original.

> Blue, blue, is the grass about the river
> And the willows have overfilled the close garden.

The return to Shanghai is slow in spite of digital signs at intersections ticking off the seconds until the red light turns green, thereby effecting a faster as well as more orderly and efficient movement of traffic. Bicyclists, appearing briefly in our headlights, accompany us all the way, in spite of the cold, the torrential rains, and strong winds. My indelible memory of the Malthusian nightmare of China will be of them. (But could Malthus's prescription of birth control by infibulation, today's tubal ligation, have succeeded anywhere at any time?)

The Shanghai Museum of Art, renowned for its collection of ancient bronzes, is also a haven of solitude. We encounter only a single attendant on each floor and no visitors, perhaps for the reason that the unheated exhibition rooms are even colder than the outdoors. The presentation is chronological: Neolithic pottery; bronzes (countless wine containers, ritual ewers, lamps, incense burners, mirrors, weapons); scrolls—too many Ching and Manchu chrysanthemums—and a decline in quality after the Suzhou masters; tricolored Tang ceramics (stunning figurines of equestriennes); porcelains; jades; kilometers of calligraphy. Dumpy, pot-bellied jade

Buddhas are on display—the Buddhist flowering came to an end in the ninth century—but much less prominently than in the Musée Guimet and the Metropolitan. The most striking of the Ming scrolls, not reproduced in Shen Zhiyu's catalog of the Museum, depicts the bathing of a white elephant, an allusion to the dream of Buddha's mother before she gave birth. (In a Tang cave mural, still *in situ* in Dunhuang, the sacred white elephant carries Buddhist texts on its back.) The most impressive of the bronzes are musical instruments, behemoth bells and drums from the fourteenth century B.C., ten different sizes of dome-shaped gongs, zhengs, and zhongs from 476 B.C. suspended from a stand. Ancient Chinese armies advanced in response to drum rolls and retreated at the sound of the gong. Apparently the Museum never acquired textiles of the caliber of the embroidered-silk altar valances and sendals from the Dunhuang caves now in the British Museum.

Chee leaves us at noon, and we are shepherded to the airport by Frank, a young English lit major at Shanghai University, remarkably fluent in the language. He complains of having been made to spend a year reading *Paradise Lost*—what an assignment, given the remoteness of the theology and the uselessness of much of the vocabulary!—but expresses enthusiasm for a course on the American novel in which he most liked *Sister Carrie*.

Boarding passes are issued by young, fast, officious, and sharp-elbowed female panjandrums, a new breed, also found at hotel and restaurant reception desks. The departure lounge is a small, airless hecatomb in which hundreds of people have packed themselves so thickly that dead people could not fall. A few early arrivals have found room to squat on their heels against the walls, but everyone else stands facing the unique departure gate. When our turn comes, I try to run interference and we somehow manage to cleave through the mass of bodies, find places on the smelly bus, and lead the charge up the stairs of our Northwest China airplane.

The sky turns vermilion as we near Xi'an (Shee'an, or Ch'ang-an in the aspirate-apostrophe style needed to pronounce the name of the First Emperor Qin Shi Huangdi correctly: "Ch'in"). This ancient capital of China, for a total of 1,100 years, was the terminus of the Silk Road, and was one of the two largest cities (2,000,000) in the world during the Tang Dynasty (618-906), the other being the Baghdad of Harun-ar-Rashid. Yet until 1934 it could be reached only by a six-day trek overland. Forty years later, with the discovery of the buried terracotta legion of the First Emperor, Ch'in, Ch'ang-an became China's greatest source of tourist revenue. Hotels are in construction throughout the city; the airport is brand new, like most of the road between it and the city.

But poorly lighted. Shen, who meets us, resents having to help with the baggage and is ungracious in every way, not to say adversarial, openly regarding us as "haves," himself as a "have-not"; we regret the loss of our affable erstwhile escorts. Instead of volunteering information, he asks impertinent questions about us. When we ask if he is a native of Ch'ang-an, the answer is that the blessed event occurred in Shanghai, but that like all Chinese he prefers to be near his parents, who live here. At first the highway, illuminated by autumnal corn-stalk fires in fields to the sides, is divided and newly paved, then, ooops, becomes a narrow dirt lane, dark except for tree trunks painted white, with a long defile of scarcely moving farmers' wagons ahead. The air is chappingly dry and on the fitfully-paved main artery of the city, thick with dust. In spite of the wintry night and traces of yesterday's snow, people are eating *al fresco* on benches by open-fire cooking stalls, or in open-fronted restaurants festooned with white or colored lights.

In the Golden Flower, a Swedish-managed hotel, room lights are controlled by inserting a magnetic card in a slot on an *inside* wall which, therefore, has to be groped for in the dark. The plaques in the bathrooms warning that "Tap Water Is Not Potable" are made of brass, indicating that the situation is not soon expected to improve. We retreat to our rooms for yet another struggle with Australian steaks, but the Beychevelle is served by a well-trained young sommelier who bows after each pouring. The local wine is the thick yellow Osmanthus, and the local delicacies are sliced pig tripe, duck gizzard, white fungus and mutton dumpling soup, served in copper chafing dishes.

Trucks in Ch'ang-an are greatly outnumbered by human- and donkey-drawn carts carrying bean noodles, panniers of plucked chickens, live piglets, lumps of coal, tanks of nightsoil. Remembering that the basis of ancient atomic theory was the transmission of minute particles of odorous substances by olfaction, we buy surgical masks; except for a few cyclists wearing them, no one here seems to notice the pollution. Isherwood observed in 1937 that in Ch'ang-an rickshaws, the upholstery, flower-embroidered blue or white hoodcovers, contained typhus lice.

The Neolithic village at Banpo, in the vast loessic terrace of the Yellow River, is the most comprehensive presentation of a 7,000-year-old agricultural settlement in the world. The architecture of its forty-five mud houses is thought to indicate an evolution from round to rectangular, analogous to that in the painted ceramics from representational (running deer, open-mouthed fish, scenes of animal husbandry) to abstract. The separation between dwellings and drainage ditches suggests a comparatively high degree of social organization, as does the evidence of cooking by steam: the center of each of the slightly sunken floors is a fire pit. Some anthropologists believe that Banpo society may have been matriarchal, since more funerary objects were interred with women than with men in the 250 graves so far discovered.

In nearby Lintong the first view of the excavated "First Emperor's Terracotta Legion" is a *bouleversant* experience, no matter how familiar from photographs, books, and films. Unlike Mycenae, Troy, Tutankhamen, the discovery, in 1974, by farmers sinking a well, was totally unexpected, and the contents correspond to nothing else in art or archeology. The figures can only be portraits of living men whose faces, whether with Shaanxi characteristics (broad cheeks and thick lips) or Sechuan (round faces), look as they did 2,200 years ago. At first sight the life-size (5'11") ceramic soldiers, standing and kneeling in ranks and columns, might be dead people perfectly preserved. The degree of realism is eerie, and if the painted colors of the uniforms at the time of burial had not faded—green robes and red tunics, lavender collars and cuffs, dark blue trousers, black shoes with red laces—

we would be afraid to look at them. This is a unique glimpse into the reality of a remote past, not a reconstructed diorama, but a living scene that leaves little to be filled in by the imagination.

The Emperor's belief that his mausoleum and passage to the next world could be protected by an afterlife bodyguard of clay soldiers is unimaginable, like the history of his mass murder of the living models, the three or four makers of each statue, as well as of everyone else with knowledge of the tomb, a slaughter estimated in the hundreds of thousands. Nothing in that nightmare of cruelty, the flip side of the history of China's high civilization, matches the deeds of Ch'in Shi Huangdi, the first Emperor (reigned 221-210 B.C.), who conquered, unified, and enslaved the country, constructed canals and frontier fortifications, and standardized written script, currency (introducing the circular coin with a square hole in the center), weights and measures, even musical pitch. But his magnum opus was his tomb, which became, perhaps more reluctantly, the tomb as well of his barren wives, who were buried alive with him, together with the retainers who continued to serve his posthumous meals, since present needs were expected to continue in the afterlife. Out of respect for this "greatest of the past rulers of China," as the People's Republic officially designates him, the mausoleum itself, eight miles in circumference at the base, beside the slopes of Black Horse Mountain, has never been opened.

Virtually all knowledge of Ch'in and his mausoleum comes from a single source, the *Records of Shiji* by Sima Qian, Grand Historian of the Han Dynasty from 107 B.C.[1] Sima Qian died in 90 B.C., after suffering imprisonment and castration by order of the emperor Han Wudi, possibly for the reason that the *Shiji*'s unfavorable account of Ch'in was suspected of being a veiled criticism of himself. Since Sima Qian wrote more than a century after Ch'in's death, and in a totally different—a Confucian—ideological climate, the *Shiji*'s reliability has been questioned. But its description of the mausoleum's appointments is too original to be dismissed as fiction. The ceiling

1. English version by Richard Dawson, Oxford.

represented the sky, in which the moon and stars were made of pearls, the seas and rivers of mercury, ducks and geese of silver, silkworms of gold. The floor was a three-dimensional topographical map in stone of Ch'in's empire. (Quantitative cartography was highly developed in China centuries before the West.) Poisoned-arrow booby-traps were aimed at possible intruders and set to shoot automatically.

Chinese archeologists emphasize that the ceramic men and horses (pricked-up ears, flared nostrils, open mouths, and unheard neighs) are the creations of branded and castrated convicts and slaves, but the tortured anonymous sculptors—carvers is the only correct sense of that word—deserve to be recognized as artists. They used molds, of course, and to some extent the more than 7,000 effigies, hollow torsos joined to solid legs, hands and heads made separately and luted on, are clones. The art historians Wan-Go Weng and Yang Boda tell us that the cylindrical torsos and tubular arms and legs are too rigid, but doesn't stiffness befit soldiers, particularly guards? The figures in toto are animated and, within their constricting military formations, varied in posture and gesture. Every face has a different expression, and each head is incised with a slightly different hairdo, even though the hair of all is pulled up to the top right of the head and knotted in a chignon. Mustaches and beards are different, and, like the armor, the clothing, and the patterns of the soles of kneeling archers' footgear, cut in low relief. If it can be said that Greco-Roman sculpture is primarily concerned with anatomy and the expression of character and feeling through pose and implied muscular movement, then the psychological quality of the terracotta figures is implicit and internalized.

By no means all the artifacts on exhibit were known before the excavations. The buried weapons were real, not made of pottery, and the wooden parts have decomposed: scabbards, bows (made of quince and tangerine wood), and war chariots (the Emperor's quadranga-limousine excepted; its components, including the umbrella-shaped canopy, were made of bronze, silver, and 3,462 bits of gold). All that remains of the crossbows and repeating crossbows, which could shoot ten bolts in fifteen seconds, are the bronze triggers, pawls, cams, and the rhino-horn ivory that fortified resilience. Iron, heavy and impeding maneuverability, was not used for breastplates, brassards, epaulieres, and other armor, but rhino leather. Snaffles were made of iron, arrowheads of bronze mixed with lethal amounts of lead and equipped with flight-control feathering measured by high-precision calipers. Chinese metallurgists were familiar with the properties of nickel, zinc, bismuth, and silicon. And they were far ahead of the West in alloying technology, having discovered that a 21 percent tin content in a sword increased the hardness to a degree comparable to our tempered carbon steel. In the discovery of chrome plating, they were two millennia ahead.

Copies of the Ch'in soldiers are inescapable in Ch'ang-an. They guard the entrances of buildings, march in souvenir shops and sidewalk displays, and have invaded the lobby of the Golden Flower where they look macabre. The gesture of a Ch'in general touching right thumb and index finger indicates a resourceful mind.

Tourists do not flock in great numbers to the stunning Tang tomb frescoes in the new Shaanxi History Museum. Only a dozen or so of the paintings, discovered since 1952 in some twenty-five tombs, are on exhibit, but we had obtained permission in Hong Kong to see others in the basement storage rooms. In this luminescent and climate-controlled vault, where we shed our shoes in exchange for blue elastic rubbers, the frescoes are attached to electrically powered panels that slide out on rails from a side wall. Some of the paintings are almost perfectly preserved, some are fragmented, but all are fresh in color. The subject matter is secular, genre painting of a kind that does not appear in Europe until the miniaturists of the Books of Hours, in contrast to which the Tang figures are life-size or larger, and their movements and poses have been eloquently choreographed. Here are scenes of music-making, dancing, picnicking, polo-playing, hunting (in one mural forty huntsmen on galloping mounts are followed by camels carrying supplies), and vignettes of family life in which the maidservants bringing trays of fruit or wielding fans have the same high-domed and bun hairstyles as their mistresses. In several pictures women wear men's clothes—turban hats, long red robes, soft shoes—to show that they possess, in the curator's words, "the male virtues of energy and vigor."

Depicting the reception of an envoy from Byzantium, the artist invidiously endows the guest with grotesque features—a bulbous, W.C. Fields nose, thick lips, popping eyes, bald pate—and coarse and poorly pigmented clothes, as against the refined faces and rich orpiment robes of his hosts. One of the most striking portraits is of a dwarf, rouged and with comically plucked brows for the clownish amusement of the court. Eunuchs are invariably shown as sycophantic and ugly—flabby faces, stuck-up noses, toothy smiles. But the good life as seen in the pictures is belied by the brutality recorded in the captions: "At age seventeen the seventh daughter of the Emperor Zhongzong was poisoned by her grandmother"; "at age thirty-one the sixth son of the Emperor was driven to suicide"; "at nineteen the Crown Prince was flogged to death by order of his grandmother who suspected that he had made a critical remark about her."

The Shaanxi Museum's stone library, within the bastion of the old city, is ill-lighted, and not all the characters in the oldest texts of Confucius, 650,000 of them engraved in 837 on 114 dolmen-shaped gray and black steles, are visible. This hardly matters to us, for whom they are calligraphy only, but neither are they literature or philosophy for most Chinese people; the educated say that they can read the characters but do not understand the grammar and meaning. A tombstone here dated 874 is inscribed in both Chinese and Persian Pahlavi, and a Nestorian stele records, in Chinese and Syriac, the establishment of a chapel in 781.

The performance of the so-called "Tang Period Music and Dance" that we attend in the early evening is mind-numbing. The musical ensemble on stage at the beginning is indeed set up like an orchestra in one of the tomb frescoes, and its instruments are modern versions of similar lutes, flutes, gambas, gongs, drums. But the music itself is Chinese-flavored Hollywood kitsch and the soprano sounds like a corncrake.

23. On the way to the airport for Beijing we visit one of the Yangling excavation sites of the imperial tomb complex of the Han emperor Jing Di (second century B.C.). During the recent construction of an access road to the airport, twenty-four satellite tombs were discovered—not altogether surprisingly, one would think, in view of the innumerable tumuli in the area, and the high probability that almost any ground near Xi'an is archeologically auriferous. We follow an unmarked dirt road to the middle of nowhere, then trudge single-file on a muddy footpath between rice paddies, jumping irrigation ditches and stumbling down a steep hill to a village in which vacant-faced old people sit in front of rudimentary dwellings, and a pregnant sow sleeps on a compost heap.

An archeologist appears and conducts us to a hut stacked with partly broken and not-yet-cleaned objects, to which his young female assistant brings suitcases packed with doll-like, twenty-inch-tall totemic pottery figures, some with traces of silk clothes and paint. The anatomy is stylized, slender bodies and straight-together, Pharaonic-style legs, male genitalia disproportionately large, but the beatifically smiling faces are differentiated and exquisitely carved. The accompanying artifacts have been made to scale: tiny bronze arrowheads, belt buckles, halberds, stirrups (which the Ch'in army did not have), a toothed-saw, several sizes of bronze measuring cups, pottery animals, lacquerwares. The curator says that some of the soldiers are female, the first so far excavated in China. A "tumbling E" Snellen chart, the large E turned in all directions used to test the eyesight of non-alphabet peoples, hangs on one of the walls, but why here?

The Great Wall, looping up and down like a roller-coaster on the ridges of the Yen Shan Mountains, is in view twenty minutes before we land at Beijing. Yu Lily, a debonair young woman of about thirty with a remarkable resemblance to the film actress Gong Li, fetches us and explains that the Chinese athletes on posters in the airport area are training for the future Beijing Olympics after the beginning of what the Chinese think of as their chiliad. A new airport road is being built in preparation for this event, she adds, and when I say that this seems an excellent idea, the one we are on being the worst ever, she laughs, a welcome change after Shen. She does not repeat her guide-talk mechanically or adjust her responses to what she thinks we think. Nor does she avoid politics. When we ask about the Emperor Akihito's recent visit, she says, "We don't know anything about it. The censorship is tight—my correspondence with my husband, who is studying mechanical engineering in England, is censored—but in any case we don't like the Japanese Emperor." When the subject switches to the Ch'in Emperor's massacres, she says, "Just like Mao"—the first time the great scourge has been mentioned to us in his native land.

Three Rolls-Royces are parked in the courtyard of the Palace Hotel, which seems to have as many escalators to its two basement levels of smart stores as Bloomingdale's. Our room is a duplex with bathrooms on both floors, and the hotel's "Roma Restaurant" (actually Padovan), with quiet guitar and mandolin duo, is an agreeable surprise.

The Mu-Tain-Yu segment of the Great Wall is said to be more panoramic and less thronged than the Pa-ta-ling of the Nixon photos. Bordered by walnut trees, poplars, and persimmons, and blocked at one point by a herd of black goats, the road is in better repair than our Nissan, which breaks down, refuses to be jump-started, and resumes only after numerous calls between the driver and a Beijing garage mechanic. A museum-piece sedan chair, the conveyance of an earlier era, is displayed at the beginning of the footpath from the parking lot to the cable car, but unless carried sideways, the incline of the last thousand or so feet is so steep that it would be at a sixty-degree tilt most of the way. The building materials must have been hoisted by winches. The climb from the cable car to the top of the wall, an altitude of 6,000 feet, leaves my ears popping, heart pounding, and breath, physically as well as metaphorically, taken. The width and other dimensions of the wall are even greater, the vistas even grander than anticipated. Visitors are confronted at the entrance by a bronze plaque in German commemorating the Henkel (Düsseldorf) sponsorship of the reconstruction of this part of the wall, but because of the extreme cold, we are today's only visitors—the first time in her experience as a guide, Lily says, that she has been "alone" here.

Segments of the wall appear behind mountains, and again disappear, and no stretch is flat. The Mongolian side is terraced almost to the summit, and a farmer, donkey tied to a pine tree, is working there in spite of snow patches and shivering, icy winds. The steps to the brick watchtowers and crenellations, which date from the late Ming period, are paved with single but uneven blocks of stone, easy to climb, but, for me anyway, perilous to descend. So, too, the cable car, open like the Wright brothers' airplane, bothers me more going down than up, for which reason I look backward— not a new thing in my case—rather than toward the colorful quilts of cultivated land stretching in the distance below.

Back in the Nissan, we ask Lily if she has heard of Fang Lizhi's *Bringing Down the Great Wall.* "Not the book," she tells us, adding that during Fang's sanctuary in the US Embassy, Beijingers wondered why "a mere professor" was regarded as so great a threat to the government. "Tian-an-men was an economic disaster. It killed the tourist industry, and it was certainly not a political success for us, in the sense that neighborhood surveillance and informing were stepped up. Those activities are still prevalent." At this we would like to broach the subject of China's civil rights record but, afraid of muffing it, tell her instead that we were shocked by a story in the *China Daily* two days ago about the execution of a man convicted of what sounds like a case of petty fraud. ("China has a Minister of Punishment but no Minister of Justice," Malraux observes in his Peking diary, and he might have added that it also has a divinity, the Queen of Jade Mountain, human in appearance but with leopard's tail and tiger's teeth, who administers "the five punishments.") "Corruption is increasing," Lily responds, obviously not sharing our feeling, "and older people want a new strong man. This is why pictures of Mao are reappearing." (English editions of Mao's high-camp *Thoughts* were on sale everywhere in Ch'ang-an.) "You see them in buses as talismans against accidents, meaning that he has become a god."

When the subject turns to literature, we learn that she has not heard of Jung Chang's *Wild Swans,* or similar books by other Chinese refugees. She knows *The Wen Family's Lawsuit* but has not seen *Qiu Ju,* the film based on it, in which the system is made to seem ridiculous, though its officials are shown as understanding and reasonable. She has not read any foreign author on twentieth-century China, not Malraux, who has enjoyed hero status here since his 1933 novel, *La Condition humaine;* or Pierre Loti, who has a footnote in Chinese history, having seen the sisters who inspired the Boxer Rebellion; or Claudel, who, quoth Auden, wrote "well," and never better than in the *Ode to Peking,* in which city, as French Ambassador, he learned to do calligraphic ideograms.

In any case, it seems to us that Kafka understood China more profoundly than any foreign writer who actually visited it. His brilliant extrapolation in the story "The Great Wall" disposes of the conscripted labor theory, and with it the legends of the bodies of dead laborers being used as landfill, by imagining the construction in the thoughts and feelings of those whose lives were dominated by it. He envisages "a mobilization of the people's energies for the stupendous new work: who with the first stone which they sank in the ground felt themselves a part of the wall. Every fellow-countryman was a brother for whom one was building a wall of protection." Still more remarkable, Kafka understood that the wall had to have been raised piecemeal:

> gangs of twenty workers were formed who had to accomplish a length, say, of five hundred yards of wall, while a similar gang built another stretch of the same length to meet the first. After the junction had been made the construction of the wall was not carried on from the point where this thousand yards ended; instead, the two groups of workers were transferred to begin building again in quite different neighborhoods. Naturally in this way many gaps were left... it is said that there are gaps which have never been filled in at all, an assertion which is probably one of the many legends to which the building of the wall gave rise, and which cannot be verified by any single man... on account of the extent of the structure.

This is not significantly different from Arthur Waldron's conclusion in *The*

Great Wall of China: From History to Myth: "The defenses were not continuous." As for verification by a single man, the first on-foot survey of the entire extent of the wall was unofficial and did not take place until 1984. Even the latest Beijing atlas does not map the wall correctly. The most accurate survey, albeit confused with a road in one segment, is the one provided by US Army satellite photos.

Kafka's genius assumes the persona of a Chinese child

> at a time when masonry had been proclaimed the most important branch of knowledge throughout the whole area of China that was to be walled round: I can still remember...standing in our teacher's garden and being ordered to build a sort of wall out of pebbles; and then the teacher, girding up his robe, ran full tilt against the wall, of course knocking it down, and scolded us so terribly for the shoddiness of our work that we ran weeping in all directions to our parents.

24. The snow leopard in the Beijing Zoo, padding the perimeter of his cage to keep in shape for parole, has translucent yellow-gray eyes, an off-white, brindled—rosetted—camouflaging coat, and a long tail. Though the giant pandas are asleep, their long, dangerous-looking claws twitch, and even the smallest of the species does not look at all cuddly. The bears perform for food, standing on their hind legs, backs against the spectators' side of their pit, heads up, mouths open.

The Summer Palace is a multiple-building memorial to the ruthless behavior and bad taste of the Dowager Empress Cixi. The guards in some of the rooms are made-up, period-costumed girls who, the single center stilt under their Manchu-style clogs forcing them to stand like statues, seem to be part of the decor, and the discovery that they breathe and blink jolts us. The most curious exhibits are the Empress's collection of player-pianos and her 1898 Mercedes Benz, which briefly amused the capricious and cruel woman, but then offended her because the chauffeur's seat was in front of hers. Her

Garden of Joy and Harmony is familiar from Bertolucci's film *The Last Emperor*. When Cixi came here to fish, one or two of her 384 eunuchs would slip into the water and impale a catch on her hook.

Like Shanghai, Beijing has a "Number One Shopping Store" on a "Number One Shopping Street." Lily purchased her Italian-style shoes here; they are stamped in English "Made in Italy," but, she says, were made in China all the same. She enlightens us on the advertisements for moxibustion, meaning massage, rather than the burning of mugwort on the surface of the body, introduced in the third century B.C. and depicted in a well-known tenth-century painting by Li Tang.

After a late Thanksgiving turkey dinner in the "Roma," we read Malraux's diary as de Gaulle's envoy to Beijing before the Cultural Revolution; during it, he wrote, "peasant women prayed to be reborn as dogs, to be less miserable." Even at this earlier time, Mao walked stiffly, "as if he were not bending his knees, like the Commendatore…a legendary figure from some imperial grave." When Mao is quoted—"The Chinese woman does not yet exist…but she is beginning to want to exist"—the Existentialist sentiment is surely apocryphal, as are many of Malraux's conversations with the powerful (Nehru) and famous (Picasso)—the writer sought to give the impression that he was in China when writing *La Condition humaine,* but had not been nearer to it than the Khmer country. So, too, the comment: "Three hundred years of European energy are now on the wane; the Chinese era is dawning," sounds more like Malraux than Mao.

25. A photograph of Peter Ustinov, to advertise his recorded headset lecture, overlooks the foreigners' entrance to the Forbidden City, through which some 35,000,000 foreign tourists will pass this year. The gates, palaces, courtyards, and halls—Hall of Great Harmony, Hall of Central Harmony, Hall of Preserving Harmony—are gargantuan, the guides correspondingly oratorical, and the Pompeiian-red walls and yellow-green tile roofs too freshly lacquered. After a while the picture of decadent imperial domesticity, the primping court ladies, the decorative motif of snarling, slithering dragons, the Ping, Pen, Pan, and Pu vases, suffocates. Unlike ourselves, Chinese tourists, including soldiers with the red shoulder tabs of the People's Army, are spellbound by every detail, as if nostalgic for another god-emperor. The appealing Beijing is the rapidly disappearing one, the old city of courtyard houses and the communities of lanes, the Wangfuying shopping street, the labyrinthine Eastern Peace market. The high-rises are dwarfing the historic temples and palaces, and the bulldozer is destroying the narrow streets and low, taupe-colored houses with voluted roofs. High, brightly colored walls were forbidden to everyone except the Emperor.

A visit from Yu Feng, the young conductor of the China Youth Symphony Orchestra which will soon give the Beijing premiere of *The Rite of Spring.* I encourage him to offer a program of Chinoiserie: an excerpt from Vivaldi's Chinese opera *Teuzzone,* Weber's *Turandot* Overture, the Chinese dances from *Nutcracker, Parade,* and the *Song of the Nightingale.*

Tonight's program at the Beijing Opera includes a pantomime of a fisherman rowing a woman across a lake to a rendezvous. Her movements are feline, and her vocal art could be described as mewing. The second opera is part of the epic *White Snake,* the same part described by Stephen Spender, but with different episodes. Subtitles in incomprehensible Chinglish are flashed on a side board from time to time, but without Lily we would not know that the plot is about a woman who comes down from a mountain and marries a scholar who is then informed by a monk that she is really a transformed snake. Her husband inebriates her, closes her bed curtains around her, reopens them later, sees a snake, and kills himself, after which the widow searches for herbs that will bring him back to life. What we see, however, is a succession of duels, an acrobatic circus of cartwheel-turning and juggling in which a woman in white defeats several men, both individually and corporately.

26. The last day. A morning visit to Tian-an-men. The enormous photograph of Mao over the Gate of Heavenly Peace is a replica of the one that on May 23, 1989 was pummeled with eggshells filled with ink and yellow paint.

As this emulsion drooled down the icon's nose and over the famous wart, police appeared, arrested the three culprits, from Mao's native Hunan Province, and the violent crackdown began.

Because of a shemozzle in the airport even worse than the one in Shanghai, our departure could not be less romantic. After two hours in front of a ticket-counter fighting to keep our places in line—the Chinese do not respect queues—word is passed back that the computer is down; but the delay is never explained officially. Farewell to "Combula, seat of Cathian Can."

Appendix

November 1996. London. The most mysterious of the "Mysteries of Ancient China" in the British Museum's exhibition is a startling, larger-than-life bronze statue found a decade ago in a sacrificial burial pit at Sanxingdui (Sechuan Province), together with bronzes in the shape of human heads, jades, and a large pile of elephant tusks. Nothing is known about the peoples who lived in this area at the time—the later second millennium B.C.—nor is it known whether the figure represented a deity, ancestor, shaman, sacerdotalist, or enactor of some other, unimaginable role. To compound the enigma, most of the contents of the Sanxingdui pits were deliberately broken and burned. The contemporary Shang peoples of Anyang had developed writing by *c.* 1350 B.C., but no examples of it mention the Sanxingdui, and contact between the two cultures has been assumed only because bronze, jade, and gold were used by both. Moreover, the Shang did not make large images, nor did the Shaanxi, who traded with Sechuanese peoples through passes in the Quinling mountains.

What can be said is that this atavistic sculpture, towering on the pedestal found attached to it, is obviously the product of a highly sophisticated culture with a long history. Its hypnotizing feature is a pair of exaggeratedly large hands, each coiled into a complete circumference and clearly intended to hold something massive. The curved angle between the high, uplifted right hand and the lowered left hand suggests that the object might have been an elephant tusk. In proportion to the height of the figure, the body is long and narrow—in fact streamlined; one thinks of Brancusi—the head disproportionately large, as are the eyes for the mask-like face. The line of the mouth and thin lips is straight and jaw-to-jaw, and the huge ears protrude perpendicularly. The expression is frighteningly austere.

January 27, 1997. London. Today's newspapers announce the rediscovery in the Public Records Office of Ben Jonson's masque, *The Key Keeper,* a "royal entertainment in praise of trade," written for the opening of Inigo Jones's New Exchange on the Strand, at a site now occupied by an American fast-food establishment. The text reveals the amazing extent of commerce between China and "Britain," James the First's name for the country that united England and Scotland under him. On April 11, 1609, the King, Queen, and court attended the inaugural celebration, which began with "loud cornets" and ended with "soft music." The cast is confined to two characters, the master of a shop and his young boy assistant. The latter enters with a cry and a description of commodities that include

> China chains, China bracelets, China scarves, China fans, China girdles, China knives, China boxes, China cabinets, caskets, umbrellas, sundials, hourglasses, looking glasses, burning glasses, concave glasses, triangular glasses, convex glasses, crystal glasses, waxen pictures, Estrich eggs, Birds of Paradise, Mustacals, China dogs and China cats, flowers of silk, mosaic fish, purslane dishes, China toothpicks, falchions, vizards, spectacles.

The master interrupts him to proclaim the superiority of the New Exchange to the "divers China houses about the town," and, indeed, "throughout Europe." He exhibits a porcelain dish "translucent as amber and subtler than crystal."

Stateside

Las Vegas, New York

Las Vegas

I was invited to lecture and conduct a concert in this city of sin in October 1983 and, to my surprise, obtained the best performance I have ever heard of Mozart's Gran Partita. I found the student audience of the University of Nevada among the most discriminating and appreciative I had ever encountered.

Slot machines fill the wall space of the air terminal between the ramps of our arriving plane and a monitory at the entrance to the escalator: "No bare feet, no pets." Trouble with discalced Carmelites? Do many passengers fly barefoot nowadays and bring their favorite birds and beasts aboard unbagged? At ten-second intervals during the automated walk to the carousel, alternating soprano, tenor, and bass voices loudspeak the line: "Hi, my name is… Welcome to paradise. Meanwhile, stand to the right, pass to the left."

At midnight, in one of five queues backed up from the reception counter of the Tropicana Hotel, a young female behind me whispers to an older male companion: "I'm not really a hooker." Too tired to carry my heavy, book-filled bags, I ask for a bellhop. A small girl appears, lifts them as if they were empty, and, having classified me as "beyond it" in all senses, calls me "honey" en route. The walls of the fake rococo bedroom are covered with copies of risqué eighteenth-century engravings.

18. After my lecture at the University of Nevada, I go as a railbird (spectator) to the hotel casino, a combination purgatory (no clock, no windows, and no differences between night and day), bordello (ceiling mirrors), and Nibelung underworld (the smithy-like jangle of the slot machines). For a moment I feel self-conscious in my suit and tie, but no eye strays from the blue baize of the baccarat, blackjack, craps, poker, and roulette tables. Most of the players are elderly, several are in wheelchairs, some ambulate by means of frame walkers, and in the case of a blind man pumping a one-armed bandit, white cane and seeing-eye dog. No one seems to be having a good time, and some may well be staking pension and Social Security checks. Everybody, young and old, female and male, is in tight jeans. Most women sport high heels and bleached beehive hairdos; most men wear boots, shirts with plastic name tags, and Stetsons.

Why do I watch? Partly because the perfect aim of the dealers sliding cards across the tables to the bettors is riveting, and partly for the sorry spectacle of the losers unsuccessfully feigning indifference: a young cowpoke kisses the dice before tossing them, wins three times, then goes broke. Was his goad the mystique of a "winning streak"? Hasn't he heard of *"Un coup de dés…"?*

The Strip—Glitter Gulch, the Horseshoe, the Golden Nugget—advertises "$100 slot machines, played with silver chips," and the ghastly *double-entendre,* "hottest slots in town." The smaller casinos are adjoined by pawnshops, bail-bond brokers, and chapels for "Immediate Weddings" that sell "licenses, rings, flowers, all you need under one roof." The "in" thing here is to have your automobile fixed to tilt forward and backward by hydraulic suspension. The movements are galvanic, the front or rear of a car being only an inch from the pavement at one moment and three feet in the air at the next. Many cars in the slower-moving lanes look like bucking broncos.

For enlightenment on the concept of play, since gambling seems like hard labor, I read A. Alvarez's *The Biggest Game in Town.* His subjects are the professionals and the immortals, and one of his descriptions of a defeated player borrows a comparison from Nietzsche: "Timid, ashamed, awkward, like a tiger whose leap has failed." One wonders just how timid and ashamed of themselves tigers can get.

New York

My perspectives concerning the city in which I have lived longer than any other are nevertheless those of a traveler, whose home base since the late 1980s has been South Florida.

May 3, 1989. A late-evening walk, fighting off panhandlers and credit-card whores, dodging a religious fanatic, braving the gauntlets of West Africans selling cut-price watches, avoiding scavengers overturning refuse bins, nearly run *into* by joggers, rollerblade skaters, helmeted bicyclists, and run *over* by behemoth limos. The 59th Street sidewalk between Sixth and Fifth Avenues, piled high with black plastic garbage bags and narrowed by scaffoldings of under-construction buildings, is virtually impassable, the Con Ed drilling, wailing of ambulances, ululations of police cars, are deafening, and the bus exhausts, wafts of pot, horse manure, and, by the wall on the Park side, micturition, suffocate. The luckiest of the derelict population bed down for the night in coffin-like boxes placed in the entranceways of Fifth Avenue stores, and a whole encampment occupies the doorsteps of St. Thomas's. At night, midtown Manhattan is a doss house.

August 14. Sweltering heat; the city is a sudatorium. We drive to Marlboro and the "Ship Lantern," about 60 miles upstate on 9W. A few miles from there and a short distance off the road is the oldest existing Jewish residence in North America, the 1714 home of Luis Moses Gomez, who received the land parcel, as did some of my ancestors for what is now Portchester, by a grant from Queen Anne. Gomez and his son Daniel were fur traders, and the house-museum exhibits their menorah and a grandfather clock purchased by a descendant.

June 12, 1990. The "Literary Walk" at the south end of the Central Park Mall is very short, what with only four statues, Burns, Scott, Shakespeare, Fitz-Greene Halleck (!). Where are the great New Yorkers, Whitman, Melville, James, Edith Wharton? To go from these four blackened bronzes, and the no less unburnished "Dante" at 65th and Broadway, to Grand Army Plaza and Saint-Gaudens's freshly regilded equestrian of William Tecumseh Sherman led on foot by "Victory," is to be momentarily blinded. The General's new coat of gold supposedly replicates the statue's glitter when installed in 1903, but the Midas touch would have been more appropriate then, when the surroundings were cleaner, brighter, and comparatively homogeneous architecturally. But why does New York, of all cities, honor an anti-abolitionist? The shiny, not to say gaudy, Sherman ensemble looks toward the south side of 59th Street and Karl Bitter's newly patinated Pomona bent over her fruit bowl. Her pedestal-fountain is again cascading, but the pool beneath, no deeper than a horse trough, is for knee-deep wading only, which contradicts F. Scott Fitzgerald's claim to have been diving in it.

Gulf Stream

Gulf Stream, where we live, is the closest to the actual current, 200 yards off-shore, of any place on the Florida Gold Coast. On a rare rainy and chill winter day, wisps of steam rise from the ocean.

The area was inhabited by the Abaniki Indians in the thirteenth century, but did not attain recognition on maps until 1923, with the creation of a golf club by the architect Addison Mizner. He had been building Renaissance castles and Venetian palaces for the super rich in Palm Beach, on the hunch that these antiquities would substitute for the impressive family histories they lacked. His Gulf Stream edifice, a quarter of a mile up the road, is plain, contemporary, without crenellations and turrets, the pink stone not garish, the landscaping proportionate and tasteful.

The town of Gulf Stream, halfway between Palm Beach and Fort Lauderdale, is very small. Its few houses, both oceanside and Indian River side, are set back and out of earshot from the road. Except for an occasional patrolling helicopter, and the roll, or in storms the heave, of the waves, our house is noiseless, ideal for reading and writing, but also for daydreaming, and boat- and bird-watching: the pelicans that flap and glide scanning the water, the herons that drink from our Jacuzzi (a locution I have heretofore associated only with Emile Zola), the racing wind-surfers cutting the waves like blades, and on windless days kayaks, ketches, and, farther out, tall, rainbow-striped, or orange and blue spinnakers. But the most distracting sight is of the shapelier naiads whose bikini thongs, referred to hereabouts as anal floss, disappear between the intergluteal folds and expose as much tush as the Rokeby Venus. In late afternoon we watch the changing forms of sea clouds, and after that the eastern sky turning vespertinal violet, as it reflects the setting sun.

One morning during a Cuban exodus we awoke to find three wrecked boats on our shore, a flimsy white hull, an overturned scow covered with barnacles, and a rusted iron tub with an iron bedstead frame mounted on empty oil barrels, which, together with blocks of Styrofoam, had kept it afloat. We wondered how these unwieldy makeshift conveyances could have crossed the more than 450 miles of perilous open sea. The eerie and only signs of life were a sodden straw hat and jacket, and a plastic water container in the barrel-borne boat. We hoped that the Coast Guard did not apprehend the refugees and send them to Guantanamo, the fate of twenty-eight who landed a few miles from here recently, but the logo daubed in orange paint on the front of each craft indicated that they had been caught up with some-where. Conversely, the inner-tube life-preservers and articles of clothing that littered the beach farther north, and the trampled shrubbery at the edge of the sand, suggested that people had reached the shore. We agreed to give food and refuge to any of them who, unlike ourselves, managed to outwit our electrical security system, but decided that one of us must stand by the telephone with the police number in hand in case our guests were armed or violent.

In recent months, the illegal immigrants landing on the southeast coast have included drug-traffickers. They cross the Florida Straits in large vessels and at Bimini in the Bahamas are transferred to speedboats that blend with the normal Florida boat activity. We hear of law-enforcement personnel interrogating people on the beaches because of suspicious behavior. During the 1998 Christmas holidays, eighty two were apprehended, some carrying cocaine, when human cargo smugglers dropped them off at eight places between Key West and Palm Beach. Three months later forty people drowned when two boats capsized in rough water near Nassau.

A stretch of coast not far south of here used to be annually invaded by nesting herds of sea-turtles. They would emerge from the surf on moonlit nights in mid-May, lumber up the beach to Government-protected areas of sward-covered sand, bury their egg clutches, then put out to sea again. But they come no more.

Today's shrinking Everglades area is becoming too small for an estimated fresh-water alligator population of a million and a half, which accounts for the increasingly frequent apparitions of these dragons in golf-course and condo pools, parking lots and, on the prowl for savorous pets, private lawns. The cousin-species salt-water crocodile, currently crawling its way back from near extinction blamed on the luggage industry, is also turning up on Key Biscayne golf courses and on Key Largo. Approximately the same size as the alligator (8-9 feet), it has larger teeth, reddish eyes, and a thin, more tapered snout. It also moves faster on land and glides more gracefully in water. The mother buries her eggs in berms or river-bank mud, as her ancestors have been doing for 200 million years, drifts nearby, waiting for hatching time, then instinctively climbs ashore, listens with a keen auricular sense for movements and cries from under the soil, helps to dig the little ones out, and prepares the nest.

In a land of hurricanes, we chose to sit out our first challenge, watching storefront windows in nearby Delray being taped and battened with plywood, and, in the canals, boats loosened from their moorings tossing in the rough water. We were on the mainland there when the winds began to gust to a 9 or 10 on the Beaufort Scale, and, fearing to be stranded by an electrical outage, crossed the drawbridge on George Bush Road back to our house, where we watched television scenes of residents in low-lying areas being evacuated to schools, animals being transferred from a zoo to another on higher ground, and women in the ninth month in ambulances on the way to maternity hospitals: the sudden drop in barometric pressure can induce the onset of labor. For us, the worst of the experience was in the anticipation, the whining wind through rattling metal shutters, the police and fire-truck sirens, the crackle of downed electrical wires, and the fall and bump of outside objects, including pantiles from our roof and coconuts from the clusters on our masculinely well-endowed palm trees.

The demography of Southern Florida is bewildering. Beginning in the Fifties with refugees from Castro's Cuba, hordes of immigrants from South America and the Caribbean vied with flocks of "snowbirds" from Canada and the northern United States to settle on every available plot of land. More settled in Miami (the Seminole word for "sweet river") than anywhere else, and the city soon became both bilingual and over-populated. The main approach to it from the north is on a 12-lane speedway where accidents paralyze traffic for hours and maneuvering to the exits is tricky and treacherous. At one place five twisting concrete overpasses vault the road, a confusing prospect that helps explain why two nearby hospitals are called "Trauma Centers." (The alternative Florida Turnpike is less hectic, but the back-up at the toll-booths can extend to ten miles; some commuters are spending a quarter of their lives in automobiles.) At inner-city intersections, the driver must wait out three or four traffic-light changes on streets that are not numbered sequentially, and are interspersed with oddly onymous Seminole ones such as "Osceola" and "Okeechobee" ("Big Water"). The drive west from "Little Havana," through a limbo of empty or used-car lots, tatty strip-malls—bars blaring rock or calypso music, run-down bodegas, used-bike shops, side-by-side Jewish and Catholic mortuaries—is dangerous in that to seek help from pedestrians is to risk robbery or even the abbreviation of life.

Retirement communities, developed for all strata of the middle class, have become a prominent feature of every part of Florida, as have, less conspicuously, "Hemlock Societies." The former tend to self-segregate, one regrets to admit, into gentile (John Knox Village) and Jewish (Century Villages), the largest of the latter boasting a population of 32,000. The owners must be at least fifty-five years of age, though most are considerably older. Visits by grandchildren are restricted because the very old and frail, ambulating with canes and walkers, fear being run into by them. After the age of seventy-five, single women outnumber men three to one. The widows advertise in magazines for dates with widowers, preferably younger, saying that they want an "LTR" (long-term relationship), while realistically hoping only for male companionship.

Afro-Americans of all ages still suffer from racial discrimination in Florida, and live at the lowest level, working in menial jobs. Employment agencies for domestic help provide Colombians instead. The small grandson of our Peruvian part-time housekeeper, Tomasa, refuses to attend his kindergarten because the other children taunt him as "black." (She tells him to say he is cinnamon.) In a society dependent on restaurants, and with more of them perhaps than any other place in the world, black waiters are rarely seen.

Music, literature, and the arts will no doubt thrive in Florida, but it cannot honestly be said that they do at present. Frederick Delius and Ernst von Dohnányi are the only composers of any consequence to have lived here. Recently Ellen Taaffe Zwilich, Florida-born and -educated, has become prominent. The site of Delius's burned-down plantation house at Solano Grove can still be visited (in a dense forest in which I have seen the supposedly extinct budgerigar) and his opera on the theme of the love-death of the navigator Solano and an Indian girl, the waters of the fountain of youth turning out to be poisonous, is occasionally staged, and excerpts from it, *Florida Suite,* performed in concert. The ruins are close to the St. Johns River, a few miles west of Harriet Beecher Stowe's home in Mandarin. This is where D.H. Lawrence, Bertrand Russell, Philip Heseltine (alias Peter Warlock), Dikran Kouzoumdjian (Michael Arlen, future author of *The Green Hat*), and the young Aldous Huxley planned to establish their pantisocracy during World War I. One regrets that this lunacy did not come to fruition, if only for the book that would have resulted.

In the performing arts, Miami is best known for the Coconut Grove Playhouse (which gave the first American performance, in 1955, of *Waiting for Godot),* Edward Villela's Miami Ballet, and the New World Symphony under telegenic Michael Tilson Thomas. (The London Symphony Orchestra summers briefly in Daytona Beach.) The Florida Grand Opera appears in Fort Lauderdale, Miami, and Palm Beach in alternation, importing singers from the Metropolitan in New York for a short season of largely popular works.

Florida inspired at least three of America's finest painters, George McInnes, whose landscapes of the north central state are too little known, Winslow Homer, and Martin Johnson Heade, the latter two celebrated for their seascapes, *cum* thunderstorms in Heade's case. Frederick Remington worked for a time in Tampa. The top treasures of the museums are in Sarasota's Ringling collection: Piero di Cosimo's *spalliera, The Building of the*

Double Palace, Poussin's *The Holy Family and St. John,* a Gentile Bellini, and three pictures by the two masters from Metz, known in Naples, where they worked, as "Monsù Desiderio." Of contemporaries, the late Duane Hanson made the biggest splash with his polyester and fiberglass beach mannequins, a morgue of the fake living, flesh made of silicon rubber and plastic poured into molds, limbs soldered to airbrushed, painted (suntanned) bodies.

Zora Neale Hurston may have been the most gifted native-born Florida writer, but this cult figure in Harlem and Greenwich Village is little appreciated here. Of visiting writers, Stephen Crane was active in Jacksonville during the build-up for the invasion of Cuba in the Spanish-American War, and his magnum opus, "The Open Boat," was experienced, as well as written, there. A few years after his death, his one-time friend Henry James published *The American Scene,* but the book is negative about Florida ("you may in fact live there with an idea, if you are content that your idea should consist of grapefruit and oranges"), and limited territorially. He did not brave the country below Palm Beach, though the Florida East Coast Railway had been completed to Miami in 1896, and he does not mention Tallahassee and the ante-bellum Old South to the north. But I should have remarked in the first place that literature got off to a bad start here in Pensacola, where, in the 1760s, James Macpherson wrote his "Ossian" forgeries, that favorite book of Napoleon and Goethe.

Since then, Key West has been the sometime speakeasy of "Hem," Wallace Stevens, and Capote Williams. Robert Frost bought a property near Miami and was a Florida regular. The poet Laura Riding, Robert Graves's jilted one-time companion, spent forty-four years laboring on her, and her husband S.B. Jackson's, *Rational Meaning* in the mid-East Coast town of Wabasso. But the liveliest writing about the state is in Norman Mailer's racy accounts, in *Fire on the Moon,* of the redneck invasion of Cape Canaveral in July 1969, and, in *St. George and the Godfather,* of the 1972 Miami convention. Nixon looked like an "undertaker's assistant," he says, and trying to breathe in Miami Beach in the summer was "not unlike making love to a 300-pound woman who has decided to get on top."

The most comprehensive history of Florida, from the early Pleistocene to the late 1940s, may be Marjory Stoneman Douglas's *The Everglades: River of Grass.* It was largely responsible for the designation, a half-century ago, of the Everglades as a National Wildlife Preserve. The writing has not dated, either stylistically or in environmentalist philosophy, and the book is still in print. Douglas, a spunky lady who died in 1998 aged 108, and whose father owned the *Miami Herald,* is particularly enlightening on the Indian populations, and their main language groups, Muskogee and Hitchiti. She tells the story of the archaic (A.D. 900) Timucuans, who were eventually Christianized by the Spaniards, and imaginatively reconstructs the conditions of human existence in the swamps eight centuries ago, when women wore skirts made of tree moss and men a breechclout of plaited palmetto strips and raccoon tails behind. Their dwellings were simple elevated platforms roofed and thatched with palmetto. They survived mosquitoes and sandflies with smudge fires and by smearing their bodies with fish oils, however they dealt with snakes, alligators, and wildcats. To judge by the evolution in their burial practices from the discarding of bodies in nearby refuse heaps in earlier centuries to the construction of vast, distant mounds in later ones, death seems to have become increasingly important to them.

Small Seminole villages can still be visited in reservations. On the way to them one might glimpse snowy egrets, osprey, scarlet tanagers, and, now rarely seen in the wild, a flock of flamingoes. The Indians sell wampum beads and trinkets at roadside stands.

"J'ai heurté, vous savez, d'incroyable Florîdes," the truculent teenage *poète maudit* wrote, but what did he imagine by the words?

Index